DARKBEAT

DARKBEAT

JAMES SOLO

IGUANA

Editors: Greg Ioannou, Lisa Sparks
Book Design: Greg Ioannou, Ainslie Keith
Cover Design: Lisa Cowey
Author Photo: Richard Pierre

Library and Archives Canada Cataloguing in Publication

Solo, James
    Darkbeat / James Solo.

Issued also in electronic formats.
ISBN 978-0-9878267-1-8

    I. Title.

PS8615.I355D37 2011   C813'.6   C2011-907113-4

This is the original print edition of *DarkBeat*.

DARKBEAT

Fiend behind the fiend behind the fiend behind the
Fiend. Mastodon with mastery, monster with an ache
At the tooth of the ego, the dead drunk judge:
Wheresoever Thou art our agony will find Thee
Enthroned on the darkest altar of our heartbreak
Perfect. Beast, brute, bastard. O dog my God!

— George Barker
Sacred Elegy V

Prologue

Cuba, 1953

"But why can't I come, father?"

"I told you before that you are too young. So do as I ask and stay with your mother tonight."

There was an all-too-familiar sternness to his voice that stopped Ricardo from pursuing the matter any further. The older man went out the front door and walked briskly along the stone path to the lane, disappearing into the darkness a few moments later, the sound of his footsteps lost too amid the chatter of crickets.

The boy went into the study where his mother sat at a large dark-stained desk writing a letter. Her hair was pulled up into a bun the color of charcoal, a sharp contrast to the silvery satin dressing gown she wore. He smelled the perfumed talc she used on her body every evening.

"Goodnight. I am going to read in bed."

"What — so early?" she asked, putting down her fountain pen and motioning her son to her side, draping an arm around his narrow shoulders and hugging him. "I hope you are not angry with your father."

"No."

"Well, you are disappointed; it is written all over your face. I know how you must feel…twelve years old, constantly told to act like an adult but treated like a child. Still, your father was only doing what he thinks is best for you."

His shoes clattered on the tile floor in the hall as he went to the bedroom wing, stopping along the way to bid goodnight to their housekeeper and cook. It had been the servants who told Ricardo in the first place about their mysterious new neighbors. Gossip had been rife after they first arrived in Santa Clara from Havana six months earlier, moving in to the finest property in the city, a rambling estate with mature gardens and a pastel-blue mansion — right next to Ricardo's house.

He closed the door behind him tightly and flopped onto the bed. Nearly all of the loose talk focused on the neighbors' daughter, Anna, a young woman of nineteen who was gravely ill. Ricardo could picture her now, the long dark brown hair framing a perfectly oval face with wide curious eyes and a mouth right off a porcelain doll. At least that's how he remembered her from the glimpses he'd caught a few months before, when her condition wasn't so severe — before the incident, which was still vivid in his mind. One blistering hot day, he had been with other boys playing in the city square when he caught sight of her walking, accompanied by two servants. Suddenly she began to growl like a wild dog and spin around, as if a madness had overtaken her, lashing out with her hands and spitting when one of the women with her tried to help. His friends began to mock her and laugh, the way boys do. Soon everyone in the square had stopped what they were doing and moved in closer for a look. It took the strength of both servants to finally subdue Anna, holding her down as she struggled and kicked up a cloud of dust, until quite abruptly she seemed to fall unconscious even though her body still quivered.

That was the last time Ricardo had seen her. But he'd heard all of the stories. About how there was to have been an arranged marriage. But at the last minute she refused to wed the man, who was from an equally wealthy Havana family. Supposedly her father sold his business interests, and they moved inland to Santa Clara to escape the anger of the groom-to-be. After only a few weeks in the new city, Anna began to act strangely, with the symptoms growing steadily worse. Back to Havana they went for a series of medical tests; but the doctors drew a blank. As the rages and convulsions increased, a Catholic priest was summoned. Yet no amount of prayer made the slightest difference in her deteriorating condition.

Ricardo stuffed pillows under the covers, slapping them into shape, just as he'd seen done in a western that was playing at the cinema. Then he turned out the lights and tiptoed over to one of the bedroom windows. Opening the louvers, he squeezed his hand between the shutters and felt around for the loosened screw, which he undid. Once the other screw across from it was undone, he was able to pull the bottom of the louvers out from the wall enough to permit his body to sandwich through. Dozens of red and pink hibiscus blooms cushioned his headfirst descent. Bouncing to his feet in an instant, he deftly pulled the louvers back in place and closed the shutters again — as he always did when sneaking out of the house.

It took only a few seconds to race across the gardens and out to the lane. All the while, his mind was on Anna. He'd heard many things: that she was possessed by spirits; that her boyfriend practiced black magic and sent them to her; that the police had been called in. Ricardo didn't know if any of this were true but he knew for certain what would transpire tonight. Along with some other neighbors, his father had been asked to help Anna by attending a ritual. Her parents had found a santero — a special kind of priest. Now he would try to cure her.

The imposing three-storey home was set well back from the lane and almost hidden by trees and shrubbery. All the lights were out except in one room at the side of the house, where the flicker of candles was evident through partially closed louvers. Ricardo ran in that direction, glancing furtively to the left and right to make sure no one was watching him. Near the window, he slowed down and then lowered to a crouch when —

— Piercing cries broke the stillness, startling him so much he fell onto his face in the scrubby grass. But it was just three birds, disturbed from their sleep, making their displeasure known as they flew out of a tree beside him.

On hands and knees he inched his way until the blue stucco wall loomed over him. Slowly he got up and flattened himself against the wall, edging over to the window, leaning slightly sideways to peer in with one eye. Half a dozen candles provided the only light. Furniture had been pushed aside. A white-haired man with thick eyeglasses stood solemnly at one side of the room, dressed in a dark flowing robe. In front of him sitting in a chair was Anna. Ricardo gasped. He couldn't believe the sight of her, more like an apparition than a human being, pale as the ivory nightgown she wore, eyes sunken and black, hollowed-out cheeks, lifeless stringy hair. If she hadn't stirred, Ricardo would have thought her dead.

He saw his father too, standing near the front among a crowd of familiar faces, both residents and their servants. They were all facing Anna and the santero about ten feet away. As the boy craned his neck to get a better view, he noticed a man and woman sitting on the floor at the other side of the room, each with drums in front of them. After a nod from the priest, they picked up their sticks and began to beat very lightly, almost inaudibly. Then the santero started to chant, gesturing with his hands for all those present to accompany him. "Cast out the vile darkness," he said, over and over, as more voices joined in until everyone repeated those five words in unison. As the drums got louder, so did the chanting.

Ricardo could see the santero preparing something at a small table, but the distance between them was too great to make out any detail, just that the old man was mixing things in a decrepit-looking wooden bowl, his lips moving to the chant while he did so. Now it was becoming downright noisy, the drums and voices gaining in intensity with each passing minute. In spite of this, Anna's scream could be heard over the din. The santero motioned to everyone to continue, to pay no attention to her. In an earsplitting torrent, words began to flow from her mouth, blasphemies and every foul expression in the Cuban language. Suddenly she slid out of the chair onto her knees, shaking her fists above her head and shouting. Louder and louder the crowd kept chanting, augmented by the booming, echoing drums. Grasping the neck of her gown with both hands, Anna ripped it open, exposing her breasts, which heaved with her labored breathing and shouting. Her mother stepped forward, about to go to her, when the santero shook his head and waved her back. "Three inside me! Three inside me!" screamed Anna. "They are dead, and they're inside me!" Convulsing now, she tore at the rest of the gown, splitting it down the front and baring the rest of her body.

At the window, Ricardo was trembling almost as much as she was. In the midst of his fear and confusion at what was unfolding before him, something strange was happening too. It had occurred a few times recently, when he'd been shinnying up trees or a pole on the swing set: a fluttery tingle between his legs, a feeling he'd never experienced before, one that confounded him and of which he told no one. Of all places, it spread over him here, as his eyes were transfixed by Anna's nakedness, and his heartbeat quickened. He had not seen a woman uncovered before, except for little black-and-white photographs in an art book, of nudes by Chagall, Modigliani, Gaugin, Toulouse-Lautrec and other masters of modern painting. Despite the horror Anna was enduring, he couldn't turn his eyes away — and felt a wave of guilt for not doing so. Instead, he drank in her thrashing body, the breasts, belly and darkness between the legs. As suddenly as the feeling came, it went, just as it did when he was climbing. And like before he was left out of breath, with a brief fatigue. Only this time there was a difference: a stickiness in his pants. He had no idea what it might be. Nor did he want to find out, because inside the window there was another frightening image.

The santero was behaving queerly, his head staring upward and just the whites of his eyes showing, no pupils. His hands were immersed in the bowl on the table. Just then Anna's voice changed in mid-sentence; it was deep, hissing, like an animal's — and no longer in Spanish. They were definitely words but in another language. Ricardo froze at the sound of it. So did everyone in the crowd. Their voices trailed off. Even the drums were silenced by it.

All of a sudden she was thrown back, like she'd been hit, her head coming into hard contact with the ceramic floor. She slid backward, as if pushed by an invisible force. Ricardo couldn't see anymore after that because his father and her parents rushed in, and the others followed, gathering around her — all except the santero, who wavered for a moment before his knees crumpled and he fell to the floor, taking the wooden bowl with him.

Chapter One

Canada, 1988

"This sucks." Chuck Bolan's words were mingled with a trail of blue smoke as he tiredly exhaled both his cigarette and his conversation.

"Well, what about me?" said his partner, Rita Barrett. "It's my first time, and I don't want anything to go wrong."

"Thanks for the encouragement," replied Bolan sarcastically. "Nothing's ever gone wrong at the farm before, so why should it be any different today–except that you're along for the ride?"

Barrett ignored his jibe. About a quarter-mile ahead was a black Plymouth squatting on the side of the highway. It was an unmarked squad car. "I wonder how long Tibbles and LaPointe have been here?" she asked.

"Pull over soon," Bolan barked, "and give them a couple of hundred yards between us." The car slowed onto the muddy shoulder and came to a halt.

"So, I presume we sit here and wait now."

"You got it, sister." Bolan turned his head and gazed out the side window at puddles forming in the short grass beside the highway, with silvery circular patterns that the wind made on them, thinking about how quickly summer had turned into a cool, wet September.

Hardly a word was spoken during the next twenty minutes. Rita's eyes were fixed on the rearview mirror.

Bolan stubbed his cigarette and leaned back, thoughts beginning to distort and melt together, his head rolling on his shoulders, as heavy as a cannonball, until it finally came to rest on the edge of the seat, jammed between the window and shoulder-belt holder. His thoughts jumbled as sleep crept over him, memories receding into a dream.

A few moments later, the drone of the Dodge's motor and constant swish-swish of windshield wipers invaded his dream, as his eyes opened halfway and he dangled on that thin edge between consciousness and sleep, fighting a heroic battle of the nods. He straightened in the seat, moving his neck around to limber it up and ease the stiffness that had set in from flopping back and forth as he dozed.

"Were you sleeping?" Barrett asked, eyes glancing off the rearview mirror for a second.

"Nope, not really," mumbled Bolan. "Well, sort of, I guess. I was just thinking."

"About what?"

"All the assholes we have to put up with."

"I can see we're not going to have much of a conversation this morning, are we?"

Bolan grunted and reached awkwardly into his jacket pocket. Cars always seemed cramped to someone six-foot-three and two hundred forty pounds. He pulled out a pack of Marlboros, sliding one into his mouth and passing another to Rita. His thick hand dwarfed the disposable lighter that he held out unsteadily, its flame jiggling in front of her face. She glanced over at him.

"You out partyin' last night or something?" she asked, her eyes glued to the rearview mirror again.

"Right. A party of one." Bolan slouched down into the seat more and looked away, out the side window.

Barrett didn't intend to let her partner off the hook so easily. Being teamed up with Bolan for the past year had taught this easygoing woman a lot about his moods and body language. Words like "equal opportunity" had never been part of his vocabulary — until now anyway. Since coming from Jamaica, she'd worked extremely hard and distinguished herself, right from her days as a motorcycle cop, and was so proud — at thirty-two — to be the first black woman on the force who made the rank of detective. What a struggle at first to be paired with the Chuck Bolan, who openly scoffed at racial issues and women's issues and political issues — just about any issues. But she fought for and earned his respect, grudgingly as it was served up, and now they actually had a strong and productive working relationship.

"Listen," she went on, "you've been hittin' it pretty hard — too hard for your own good, man. I've been watchin'. I can see what's goin' on. Something's eating at you, Chuck. I know it for sure because I see it every day."

"Rita, let me tell you something. There's nothing wrong with me that I can't take care of myself." Bolan's voice had an irritated lilt, as though he'd been through this before, maybe with his wife.

"Don't bullshit me!" Barrett was louder now. "Maybe you can take care of it yourself, but I don't notice any improvement. It's gettin' worse not better. You understand, man? That's why you've got to get some counseling."

"Just what I need…a partner who thinks she's a shrink."

"That's it. Patronize me for trying to help. And build a big wall up around yourself. Well, I'll tell you something: it's not just me who notices. I hear about it from others too — especially about your drinking."

"I'm fine, okay? So let's knock it off. A few things are bugging me, that's all." Bolan listened to his own words and thought about the previous week, with its one-two punch — the Police Association election and promotion exams for detective-sergeant. His friends had been sure he would win the vice-presidency of the association, especially after all the work he'd done over the years. But it wasn't to be; he got squeezed by eleven votes, and a younger cop — a sergeant in the suburbs — came out on top. The day after, nursing a terrible hangover, he tried the tests for promotion — and failed them for the third and last time. So a detective he would remain, as he had been for the past seven years. His career would be permanently in neutral. The thought had been irritating him for days, a slow burn like a smoldering ember. "Those exams really piss me off," he said, spitting out the words and cigarette smoke. "Not only do they expect you to work day and night on your goddamned job, but they want you to memorize books too. It isn't fair, especially for somebody like me who was never good at school. But I'm a good cop."

Rita was nodding. "No question, man. You, me, the association, everybody thinks the system sucks, but they're not going to change it. So quit letting the thing eat at you. You know you're a good man. So think positively and try not to get so down."

"Yeah, right," said Bolan, his voice almost drowned by the rush of damp air as he opened the window and tossed out the last of his cigarette. "You give them your guts and the best years of your life. You put up with society's rejects every day — and it's still not good enough. If you work in the association, good luck because they'll think you're a fuckin' labor leader and pass you over for every promotion. So what do you do? Tell me, what do you do? Really. Do you quit and wait for your pension to kick in? Sometimes it gets to me, Rita. You and I have known three guys who couldn't hack it and killed themselves. Let's face it, the force is a meatgrinder." There was silence for a minute as the pouring rain loudly splattered the car like a million tiny bullets. He shook his head and gave an exasperated smile. "And now we have to spend a shitty Sunday morning at the farm."

Bolan did not want to go to the farm. It was about thirty-five minutes east of downtown, straight along the six-lane highway. A speculator owned the rundown, two-hundred acre spread and was waiting for the voracious appetite of the city's urban sprawl to consume everything nearby. Even now, housing subdivisions were creeping closer, so the land's value had probably quadrupled in the past decade, the same length of time that the police had been using it — without permission, of course. What a gem it was, and so handy, at an overpass just off the main highway, with a narrow dirt drive full of potholes that threaded its way to the dilapitated Victorian house. The best part was that it couldn't be seen from the highway or the sideroad, as though it had been made to order —

which is why the farm got so much use. A few senior police on the Toronto force knew about it, as did the Ontario Provincial Police outside the city. Nobody would admit to that though. The farm solved a lot of problems, especially when lax immigration laws and cross-border crime from the United States were taken for granted. Virtually anybody could cross the line into Canada — which was a sore point with many police like Bolan who saw imported criminals back on Toronto streets a day after they'd been sent back down south. The farm was an alternative.

Working with a network of U.S. police and informants, it wasn't difficult to keep tabs on crack dealers, hold-up men or, in this case, gunrunners. If they were just punks without organized-crime connections, most of them left a noticeable trail of stupid mistakes on their way north. Often they had guns or drugs — or both — stashed in compartments under their car or in the trunk, which were obvious places that would be searched at once. State police in New York, not wanting the bother of lengthy trials or bail jumping if they arrested the felons, would monitor their location carefully and watch them cross the border, where the provincial police would take over. Approaching the outskirts of Toronto their car would be pulled over for a routine search by two unmarked cruisers. After finding something suspicious the city detectives would fake it, pretending to take their captives in — but instead, drive to the farm, beat them senseless and send them back on a return journey. No deportation. No trials. No trouble. And everyone kept their mouths shut about it, playing dumb so some inquiring newspaper reporter or upwardly mobile politician wouldn't catch on.

Bolan had received his "wake-up" call about eight in the morning from the desk sergeant at Fifty-Two Division, who told him that two suspects — repeaters from New York who had been to the farm before — were about a hundred miles away now. They were known to deal in high-tech weapons, the kinds you couldn't possibly get in Canada because of stricter gun controls. The U.S. police had been tracking them on their drive northward, keeping the Canadian authorities aware of every step of the journey, knowing just how it would end. There was no rise and shine for Bolan though, who stumbled out of bed feeling as dry as prairie sand and with a head pulsating like it was three times its size — thanks to a couple of dozen beer the night before. He immediately called another detective, Dave Tibbles, and let him know the plan. Then he stared at the telephone for a few moments, hesitating but in the end deciding not to go back on his word. "Stupid broad," he mumbled to himself out loud. Then he dialed Rita Barrett's number.

She had asked to go along, to see for herself what happened out at the farm. Until now she'd always been excluded, which hadn't bothered her at first. In fact, the year before when she'd just been promoted to detective, Rita spoke out against this kind of illegal treatment of suspects, claiming it disgusted her. She equated it with other kinds of excessive force, such as the shooting of an inordinate number of blacks compared to whites. But as she'd become more seasoned in her job, the farm started to seem like the exclusive domain of a "boys' club," and no place for a woman — even if she had proven herself to be as tough a cop as any male. Whenever she'd asked for her turn on farm duty, there were red faces and stupid excuses, big men awkwardly scuffling about trying to tell her in a nice way that this was no place for the likes of Rita Barrett. But she had persisted until Bolan agreed to take her, figuring that verbal abuse from his fellow officers was a lesser evil than having to put up with Rita hounding him on the job every day.

Now in the car, he straightened up in his seat and lit another Marlboro, not even bothering to offer one to Rita, since he knew it was too soon for her. "They should be along pretty soon," he said.

She nodded and looked over at him for a second. "So what exactly is the situation when we get there?" There was a measure of apprehension in her voice.

"Nothing too complicated. These amateurs never put up a fight, especially when they're outnumbered four to two. We'll slap them around a little. Rough 'em up and scare the shit out of them, so they won't bother coming back again. Maybe send a signal that they need new jobs — instead of arming our criminals up here."

"But I heard these two had the treatment last spring. Seems strange. Does that happen often?" Barrett didn't take her eyes off the mirror for even an instant.

Bolan took a couple of drags on his cigarette before answering. "Nah, I don't think so. Maybe the guys who gave them the treatment last time were too soft. Could be these scumbags are too stupid to learn their lesson."

"Sounds kind of odd to me. Especially since some of these guys run guns to customers with mob connections and legit businesses. We don't even know who we're tangling with here."

"Listen, I don't like this shit any better than you do–even though I've been out to the farm about seven or eight times. It doesn't get any easier. So quit asking questions and–"

"–Look behind us," she interrupted. "There's a Maxima that fits the description. License plate looks right too. Must be them."

***

It was routine. In fact, Detective Bolan found himself yawning a few times, his mind in low gear thinking about recent hot summer weekends in the backyard with a cold beer, the bottle sweating in the sun, chaise lounge tilted way back, and him stretched out soaking up the warmth. He stood there daydreaming as Tibbles checked the driver's identification, began to snoop inside the vehicle and uncovered a stash of three dozen automatic pistols and several AK-47s — all illegal in Canada — in a compartment under the false floor of the Nissan. Once in a while Bolan gave the two punks a threatening look so they wouldn't try anything. Both were slight of build and quite young, perhaps in their mid-twenties. One of them, a black man, wore a baseball cap backward and had on more gold than King Tut, most of it around his neck in chains of various thicknesses. The other had unkempt-looking fair hair, a nose ring and an array of tattoos covering both of his arms, which were exposed, since he wore only a T-shirt and jeans despite the cool wet weather. Neither of them said a word throughout the search or when they were roughly pushed into Tibbles' squad car by Jean LaPointe, a burly French Canadian whose two hundred and twenty pounds spilled out of a five-foot-ten-inch frame. Bolan drove their Nissan to the farm, with Rita Barrett following up the rear in the Dodge.

Fifteen minutes later, as he carefully snaked his bulk out of the car to avoid banging his head, everything appeared to be going smoothly — to the point of boredom. He looked up at the ribbon of a driveway, potholes overflowing with rain and stubbly weeds knee-high everywhere, sticking up out of the mud. Funny, he mused, how godforsaken it looked today, but on a sunny afternoon with the air smelling fresh and the sound of the birds singing, it was entirely different, almost a pleasant experience, in spite of the dirty business that always awaited them.

"Charles, wait up." It was obviously Rita, since no one else ever had the nerve to call him that, even jokingly. She was a hundred feet behind him, trudging briskly but meticulously avoiding puddles.

"What the hell are you doing way back there?" He stared incredulously at their car, which was parked farther back on the grass beside the driveway. "Shit, you could've pulled up closer than that."

"No way, man. It's far too messy — I might get stuck in all this muck."

"For Christ's sake, hurry up then," yelled Bolan, annoyed because he was soaked by now, his clothes like a blotter, the driving downpour streaming at an angle into his eyes. "The last thing I want is to go back with a goddamned cold." He wheeled around quickly to get the rain out of his eyes and stood there momentarily waiting, hands deep in his pockets — which were already soggy inside. He stared at the old farmhouse ahead, with its steep V-shaped roof, stiff

Victorian brickwork around each window and elaborate pillars that held up the veranda. It seemed so out of place, standing proudly like an upper-crust matron from the last century, hanging on stubbornly as the rot crept in and massive concrete high rises edged ever nearer.

"Chuck!"

Rita's scream startled him. Then he saw it, up ahead, Tibbles bobbing up and down in the backseat of the squad car like he was on a trampoline, struggling with one of the punks. At that instant LaPointe was being hammered from behind as he rushed to get in the rear door. Rita was already at her partner's side, gun drawn, when Bolan broke into a run, splashing and tripping on the muddy road. He was going for a record forty-yard dash before there was any real trouble. But the sounds of men fighting and rain pouring and feet pounding had drowned out the engine drone, putting it somewhere in the back of Bolan's head, away from clear thinking, until it turned into a deafening roar like a bear — and by then it was too late. He turned around just when it hit, heaving him onto the hood for a half-second and then tossing him down. He bounced to a halt at the side of the car. At the moment of impact his first thought had been of Rita, who'd been hit too…from behind. That notion spurred him as he started to rise but —

— A slam as someone kicked the door open into his face while he was on his hands and knees, crushing his nose and driving his chin up, with a force that threw him flat onto his back. And as everything dissolved into tears and blood and mud and rain, his bleary eyes managed to focus for just an instant on the black sportscar — a Porsche 911 convertible, he knew — with a long-haired man at the wheel and a woman beside him who were fast becoming a blur as they sped backward past the parked Nissan, grinding the underside of the expensive automobile into the ragged crevices on the dirt driveway. He squinted to read numbers on the licence plate, but darkness was overriding his last vestige of consciousness.

***

Rita Barrett, completely caked with mud and her curly black hair full of grass and burrs, was kneeling over him, a hand under his head. "Oh Chuck, please, Chuck. Are you there, Chuck?"

Bolan nodded feebly and raised his head slightly, wiping blood away from his eyes and nose despite the searing jets of pain with each touch. "Son of a bitch," he mumbled, tongue skimming over two sensitive spots where teeth had been chipped in half.

"Thank God," she panted, sounding out of breath. "You're alive."

He stared into her face. "Are you all right?"

She nodded. "I was lucky. It knocked me for a loop but pushed me sideways into the bushes over there. I think I was only out for a few seconds."

"What about me?" His voice still sounded groggy.

"You look like hell, and I think you've been under for a couple of minutes. But you were lying so still, it scared the life out of me."

Bolan tried to sit up, grunting in pain with the slightest move. "What about — "

" — Both of them look bad, maybe Tibbles worse than LaPointe. They've been pistol-whipped, I think. Lots of blood. But they're conscious...only they can' hardly move ."

"Oh shit. Did you get on the radio?"

"Uh-uh. You know what would happen if any reporters were monitoring us right now for a story. We're out here all beat up. I didn't know what to do."

"Yeah, of course...it's my fault, I should've told you. We've got a radio code worked out, disguised so nobody'll know it's an APB." He pushed himself up to a wobbly standing position and took a few breaths, while Barrett grabbed his arm to steady him. "I better get descriptions out on those pricks' cars before they're too far away or they decide to ditch them."

"Okay, but let's try to hurry." Worry was painted all over Rita's face. "We've got to get the other guys in their cruiser so I can take them to hospital. What about you — can you drive?"

Bolan managed a tight-lipped smile. "Yeah, no sweat. Let's go."

***

The two of them were seated on the couch in a spacious seventh-floor office. Chuck Bolan stared with a vacant expression at a wildlife painting on the opposite wall, hands crossed neatly in his lap. Every once in a while he glanced to his side at Rita, who fidgeted in her seat and cleared her throat nervously, like a school kid in the principal's office for the first time. A waft of men's cologne drifted his way, sweet yet peppery, and probably expensive, he thought.

"You had horseshoes up your asses, that's all I can say." William McMichael was flabbergasted, searching for the right words a police chief should be saying at a moment like this. To Bolan, his voice always had the paternal ring of a minister, even when he was upset. This ability to sound as though he hadn't lost his cool was probably one reason why he'd made it to the top on the force ahead of eight thousand others–and could afford a designer scent. "I'm aware that it goes on; everybody knows it goes on. We look the other way to make it easier for you...but this kind of business cannot be condoned–and won't be tolerated–if there are any more mistakes. You know we're fighting a battle right now. Public relations is working time-and-a-half because of all the media coverage. Excessive force, they're screaming. Trigger happy. Racist for shooting more blacks than whites. Not enough visible minorities in the ranks. You name it — and we're supposedly guilty of it. A lot of people in this city hate our guts, including some of the politicians. You don't know how close you all came to creating a real scandal for us."

The chief's tired-looking, slightly beady eyes scrutinized the bandages on Bolan's nose and chin, and then settled on Barrett's bruised features. Not a word was spoken. McMichael scratched the top of his head, through the thin grey hair that still remained, swept over from a part that began near his ear. The stern gaze remained on his pink face for another minute or so.

Bolan could empathize with his superior. It wasn't easy being the chief of police anymore — not that it had ever been fun and games. But now more than ever the demands placed on the city's law-enforcement body were far outpacing its ability to deliver. So budget cutbacks meant fewer officers on duty at events and patrolling the streets. Yet the city's population was growing in leaps and bounds, mainly with immigrants and refugees from Third World countries — which created a whole new set of problems. There were gang wars with the Vietnamese in Chinatown. A few coke dealers with Jamaican origins were armed to the teeth and not afraid to put their lives on the line. The murder rate was almost double what it had been the previous year. Weapons were continually turning up in school lockers. Every day thousands of people visited food banks because they didn't have enough to eat — something virtually unheard of just a few years before. The gap between the "haves" and "have-nots" was ever widening. Another thing too: the kind of violence that plagues large U.S. cities had spread northward like a disease. And to make McMichael's job even more challenging was political correctness, where an almost immediate solution was demanded to change the face of a predominately white, male police force.

The chief walked over to his old-fashioned oak desk and picked up a paper, studying it for a moment, and then focused his attention back on the two detectives. "Anyway," he said, "we can be thankful that nobody was seriously hurt in this incident. I have the medical report here on Tibbles and LaPointe. How are they doing?"

Bolan smiled to himself, painfully, as muscles in his face stretched scabs and bandages. Thousands on the force, he thought, and McMichael makes a point of calling two guys by name. What belief in a leadership role. "They'll be back on the job within two weeks," he mumbled through a swollen mouth. "Most of their injuries were skin deep, even though they looked pretty bad at the time." Instantly he flashed back to the crimson-stained back seat of Tibbles' squad car after they'd arrived at the hospital — the two men moaning through their teeth, trying to wipe away blood from gashes to their heads, necks and shoulders. The two doctors and head nurse had been rather nonplussed about it, having seen this sort of thing before, and demanded to know what had happened. After being told, they agreed to be quiet unless asked point-blank, in which case they wouldn't lie. This had relieved Bolan immensely, even more than the painkillers they'd fed him, along with the tape and gauze they'd laid over his broken nose and lacerated chin. The purple egg on his forehead and black eyes would clear up by themselves, he'd been informed, as if he — a twenty-five-year veteran of other people's bad intent — didn't know.

"You're sure there haven't been any inquiries at the hospital?" asked McMichael cautiously, licking his dry, chapped lips, and leaving human interest aside for the moment.

Rita spoke for the first time in twenty minutes. "Nothing, sir. I checked Monday morning and this morning too. No reporters, nobody except next-of-kin wanting to visit the guys."

"Fine, fine. I think we got out of this one by a hair. But remember what I said: there can't be a next time. If there is, and I have that lesbian activist on the Police Commission and some of those pinko city politicians nipping my ass, there's going to be hell to pay. So spread the word. I don't care what you do in your jobs but anybody caught out of limits doing something like this will end up in court, not in my office. Do I make myself clear?"

Bolan and Barrett nodded.

McMichael strode over to the window, glancing down at the traffic in the street for a few seconds as the two detectives rose. He joined them as they padded quietly across the plush brown carpet and past the coffee table to the door, which the chief held open, nodding a goodbye to each of them.

Outside the office, Bolan's feet clacked on the tile floor in the hall, echoing down the narrow corridor where various highly placed policemen worked at desks in private offices sized according to rank. "That one doctor — y'know, the old broad," he said to Rita, "she gave me so many prescriptions I couldn't believe it. I was telling her how things have been kind of tough at work lately, and she wrote me out something for tranquilizers for the next three months. And a year's worth of Prozac. Then she told me to take these painkillers until a specialist has a look at my nose. Christ, I was having trouble concentrating on what the chief was saying in there." He felt an odd combination of being both depressed and lightheaded at once.

"Well, you better do as the doctor says," advised Rita, who had an old-fashioned reverence for medical people, that clinging belief about them always being right because they have the power to write prescriptions. She pressed the elevator button and turned around, raising her arms and stretching as she did so, loosening up after her confinement in the chief's office — a new and unpleasant experience for her. She had the wet armpits to prove it.

"Ah, I'm going to my own doctor," said Bolan. "Before I keep gobbling pills, I want to make sure they're right for me. Anyway, they might not mix too good with beer." He chuckled, expecting a rise out of his partner.

Barrett didn't disappoint him. She looked up with a steely gaze. "The last thing you need right now is beer." Her words were cut short by the arrival of the elevator, which was almost full.

"What kind of party pooper are you anyway?" Bolan smiled and it hurt. He held the doors for Rita and followed her, squeezing in among the crowd.

She smiled and spoke in a low voice, her large dark eyes twinkling. "You know, Chuck, we should get one thing straight: working with you is not at all like a party."

On the main floor they walked through the atrium of the modern headquarters building and outside, where sun streamed down and the glare off sidewalks and pavement forced them to squint. It was one of those hot clear September days that makes people feel a little less mournful of summer's passing.

Rita sighed and looked over at Bolan. "So, do you think those shitheads made it back to the States?" she asked.

"Nope."

"Neither do I."

"With an APB out on them, the easiest place for those bastards to get lost would be here in the city."

"They would definitely be caught back at the border or in some quiet little town."

"Yeah," chimed in Bolan, "especially with a black Porsche…if they're still driving it. That's not a good choice of a stolen car if you want to be inconspicuous."

"Right. I'm sure there's only forty or fifty of them in Toronto, let alone the countryside."

"They were planning to unload those guns with a regular customer — and they were ready for us. Why else would they have their friends following them in another car?"

Rita nodded as the light changed to green and they started across the busy intersection. Smoke from a street vendor's gas grill assaulted her nostrils with the smell of greasy hot dogs. "That's what I've been thinking too. They probably stole new plates, and they're driving around here somewhere downtown, trying to make a deal."

"Those pukes are probably close by," said Bolan, walking at a brisk clip on the sidewalk and dodging slower pedestrians. Someone's boombox nearby blasted out Faith, an overplayed song by George Michael. "If we could find them, we might learn more about who's behind them." He approached the expired meter where his own car — an Oldsmobile — was parked and mumbled an obscenity as he pulled a yellow parking tag from under the windshield.

Inside the car, Rita pulled out a cigarette and offered one to him. "You know what I'd like?" she asked, flicking a disposable lighter. "To find out exactly what those people are up to before they do it — and then nail them in the act."

Bolan fired the engine and moved out onto the street, making an illegal U-turn. "You know what I'd like?" he echoed, his chipped teeth showing as he smiled, a jack-o'-lantern grin. "To have those two who ran us down with the sports car. Just five minutes with them, that's all I'd need."

Chapter Two

"Hey, are you coming?" Her words rang out from downstairs and invaded his thoughts.

"I'll be down soon," he yelled, a slight edge to his voice. "I'm still working."

"I just don't want to be late," she said, not so loud this time.

Adrian Lee was sitting back in a deeply cushioned wing chair, feet propped up on his desk, notebook in hand, staring into row after row of leather-bound volumes that filled the shelves of his and Jennifer's library. Sometimes he was still in awe, contemplating his life and playing that mental game of children, imagining until now it had all been a dream–and when he awoke it would be over. Often this was how he started writing lyrics, by thinking ingenuous thoughts to clear the slate and start fresh. His notebook, with tattered, ripping pages, carried almost seventeen years worth of inspiration: little sayings, bits of slang, brief descriptions of things that had impressed or affected him. Sooner or later these fleeting and seemingly inconsequential morsels of life found their way into songs.

He grabbed the small black remote control from his desk, aimed it at the stereo on one of the bookshelves and started the cassette rolling again. The room came alive with the sounds of Denny Yorke's bass and Cam Goodman's guitar, doing a basic rhythm "bed" for a new song, mistakes and all. The melodies were always composed first by the other two band members. Denny's distinctive nasal voice hummed along to where the verses and chorus would be — once Adrian had written them. He'd already completed two songs during the past week, with fifteen still to come. After that, the three musicians would rehearse the material for a couple of weeks before heading into the recording studio, this time in Switzerland. There, the fundamental tracks would be laid down first, the guts of each song. Then, through the miracle of audio technology, he could record many of his drum parts separately to get them just right, as Cam would for the guitar leads. There would be plenty of overdubs with Denny's handiwork on synthesizers. Last would come Denny singing on separate tracks, often with his voice overdubbed twice or three times, especially on the chorus to flesh out the sound and give it a fullness that singing alone simply couldn't match. From all the songs that had been recorded, eleven or twelve would be selected for the new release.

Of course, those tracks had to be mixed and mastered, so a studio had been booked in New York a few weeks after the initial recording in Switzerland. During this lull their producer, Terry Kendall, might come up with ideas to build on the music even more: extra keyboard parts, string sections, choirs, special effects. He'd try to sell the others in the band on these concepts; most often they would agree because over the years his knack for fattening their sound had never failed.

Then the eighteenth Tangent album would be in the can.

This is where it started though, in Adrian's library as he kept replaying the same melody over and over and over, trying to find a "hook," some catchy phrase upon which to build the rest of the song.

He flicked the remote gun again, silencing the music. Sliding out of the chair, he padded around the library for a few moments, feet sinking into the rich wool of an antique Persian carpet. There wasn't enough pressure on him yet to write quickly. He always produced his best lyrics as the deadline loomed perilously close, when Cam, Denny and their manager, Reg Howarth, would telephone anxiously every second day to see how it was going. A month still remained before that would happen though, so Adrian could afford to procrastinate, like the proverbial kid who ended up cramming for final exams the night before.

Into the eighties, his writing had really matured, was actually transformed into poetry at times, with intricate rhyming schemes and subtle innuendo. From his notebook and fertile imagination emerged songs that avoided clichés and dealt sensitively with their subject matter: torture in police states, being elderly and unwanted, the plight of aboriginal peoples — even the demise of the Cold War. His interests and flights of fancy began to show up in the music too; after touring Australia he flew to Java for a week and wrote of what he'd seen there. Marathon running and cross-country skiing occupied much of his spare time for a few years, so they too had been worked into songs.

But it wasn't only his lyrics that had seasoned. Time and continual practice had nurtured his already considerable prowess on a set of drums, to the point where he was a "musician's" musician, on the advisory board for *Modern Drummer Magazine* and quoted often in others like *Musician*. Those were the publications that mattered to Adrian Lee — and to all good musicians. He was often infuriated by the mainstream media's treatment of Tangent, still regarding it as a heavy metal band, something light years away from the kind of music they played today. *People Magazine* had proclaimed their last recording as dinosaur rock. A review in *Playboy* five years earlier still made Adrian seethe: stating that Tangent's songs were for "valley girls" — probably a more apt description for the magazine's ridiculous Playmates. Then there was *Rolling Stone* — down on Tangent from the start — along with numerous other bands that confused their record reviewers by using more than four chords and a four-four beat.

So Adrian and his two partners eschewed the high-profile life where possible and quietly went about making records, seventeen in all that had sold over thirty million copies. And more than fifteen years later they could still sell out two consecutive shows at Madison Square Gardens in New York and receive the Golden Ticket Award for filling more than a hundred thousand seats during visits there on past tours. And despite the frequent blasts from critics, Tangent never felt the need to play "corporate" rock, to compromise their sound for more popularity. This pleased Adrian the most because, unlike other stars who had become parodies of themselves and continued to play the same kinds of songs over and over, Tangent had never stopped expanding and improving their musicianship. Songs had stronger melodies now. And with voice training, Denny's singing was continually improving, a broader range and better enunciation. Each recording went in a new direction without any deliberate thoughts of which songs might be hits. Yet with barely any airplay on commercial radio, their records were hits. Many of their older fans still bought them; each album attracted a new age group too. Now when Tangent played, most of the concert-goers were about half the age of the musicians. Adrian liked that part too, relating to people from so many eras, being able to literally strike a chord in them through words and music. He was also proud of the fact that a whole new wave of young drummers had been influenced by his style.

Occasionally he wondered how long it would last. Tangent had peaked in 1982. And for the past six years their music hadn't conformed to the lightweight British techno-pop that had caught the public's ear. What passed for metal now were American bands with poodle-haired musicians in eyeliner and overdone leather, whose singers sounded as though they'd been castrated at puberty. But there were bright signs too: rumblings out of Seattle with bands like Soundgarden, Screaming Trees and Mudhoney, playing grunge rock, combining new energy with heavy sounds from the seventies. A return to basic, straight-ahead music. Time for the next wave. Adrian wasn't sure how long he could keep up the pace anymore. The last tour had been almost nine months long, with one hundred and fifty concerts around the world. Now just a month later, here he was putting lyrics to melodies that Cam and Denny had composed together on the road. Then the whole cycle of rehearsing, recording, shooting videos and touring would begin again.

Adrian sighed and ran a hand through his long blondish brown hair. It was still thick; although styles came and went, he'd always worn it long, swept back and behind his ears down to his shoulders. Sometimes he was concerned that as more lines around his eyes matured his face, the long hair would seem silly. But Jennifer frequently reassured him that he looked just fine. Attempting to appear as young as the audience was a necessity in his business, especially now with all the emphasis on video. He was in better shape than most of his youthful fans, what with working out and physically attacking eleven drums and fifteen cymbals almost nightly for months at a time. Even the effects of a slowing metabolism hadn't altered his physique much over the years; his weight still hovered around a hundred and seventy pounds, which looked quite trim spread over five feet eleven inches.

Adrian came out of his thoughts and found himself staring vacantly out the window to the street below. The door opened behind him.

"How's it going in here now?" Jennifer glanced first at his empty chair and then to where he stood. "I didn't hear the tape going on and off as much," she said, cracking a little smile, "so I thought I'd see what you were up to."

"Just daydreaming a bit."

"I know, there's lots of time for daydreaming now. But next month you'll be scrambling like a madman." She eased up to him and put her arm around his slender waist.

"So why should I change now?" asked Adrian, grinning as he placed his hands on her shoulders and leaned forward to lightly nuzzle her cheek. Jennifer's cool grey eyes met his — she was only an inch or so shorter than he was — and she pressed her lips onto his for a lingering kiss. He ran his fingers through her long fine blonde hair. "Anyway, I'd rather daydream than have nightmares. Do you remember last night?"

"A little. I was half-asleep when you were describing it to me."

"Since I got back from the tour…like clockwork. Every night about the same time, scaring me shitless."

"You know, it might be better if you didn't concentrate so much on those dreams of yours. Lighten up a little. Don't be afraid of them."

"Easy for you to say."

"Just don't dwell on them so much."

"Yeah, maybe," he said, starting to force his mouth on hers.

Jennifer pushed him back a little. "Well, it seems like you're ready to call it quits for today."

"Yeah," Adrian replied. He tried to squeeze his hands down the front of her jeans. "But maybe I could start something else before we leave."

Gently guiding his hands to her waist, Jennifer gestured toward the antique railroad clock on the wall between two bookshelves. "Our reservation's for twelve. Why don't we skip dessert and have playtime later this afternoon?"

Adrian's grip on her relaxed, and he patted her behind. "Okay, deal." He turned off the cassette player and straightened the papers on his desk. "God, it's great to be home, to stay in one place for a while. You've been there. You know what's it like."

Jennifer sighed and began to head out the door. "Yes, I've been there — about five or six short visits on a year-long tour."

"Come on, you could be on the road with us the whole time if you wanted."

"You know I couldn't be away that long."

"Sure you could."

"What about CANFAR?"

Adrian shook his head. Canadians For AIDS Research. Jennifer had been involved since the organization's inception in the mid-eighties, organizing fundraisers, lobbying various levels of government, signing up new volunteers. "They could live without you," he muttered, almost inaudibly.

"Listen, it's important to me," said Jennifer, visibly stiffening.

"And that's more important than being around your husband while he's touring?"

"You know there's a lot more to it than that."

"I don't think there is."

"Let's not go through this, Adrian, and put an edge on our day together. My volunteer work means a hell of a lot to me — something that doesn't seem to click in your brain. I gave up my chance at a career. And in case you've forgotten, I quit university and didn't go on for my Master's...just to be with you."

Adrian bristled, his arm recoiling from her side like a snake. "That wasn't my point. After all these years, it must be obvious just how we work our balls off playing music for the entire world. It's not a game, not now, after you've done it so many times: the travel, disorientation, trying to get up for it each night, to be the best you can be. Playing the same crowd-pleasing songs that you've played thousands of times — and trying to make them seem fresh. To give everybody an awesome show for their money. To leave them with something they'll never forget."

"Oh no, this 'dude with a mission' stuff again. Gimme a break. Let's not inflate being a musician into some kind of altruistic calling. You're not curing cancer or making the world a kinder place. I realize how talented you are and how hard you work. But you're paid like royalty, hundreds of thousands of dollars per show. You fly first-class, stay in the best hotels on the planet, have dozens of flacks to do your bidding. Think about it. You even put your karate teacher on the payroll and took him along."

"So what! He keeps me healthy and occupied, so I don't sit around vacuuming powder up my nose or partying all the time. Anyway, Cam brings his hair stylist on tours, so why can't I indulge a little?"

Jennifer drew a breath. "It's different with Cam," she said, walking downstairs in front of him. "He needs to have his hair weave adjusted. It's important to the act."

"This conversation is getting ridiculous. Cam's hair weave is important, and my karate isn't? It's important he cover up his balding head and pretend to be the eternal teenager?"

"Don't you ever mention Cam's insecurities about getting old! At least he's got a family. He's never avoided having children. The same with Denny — he and Danielle have three beautiful kids. They're really a family, not just two people like us living together in a dream world where we can have whatever we want. And I've got news for you, Adrian: you're not Peter Pan."

"You're full of shit."

Jennifer bristled. "And you're pushing forty."

He was silent now. Then he practically bounded off the bottom stair and quickly moved down the hall into the living room, settling into an easychair. She walked in after and took a seat on the sofa opposite him, crossing her long jean-clad legs.

"Listen," he began, "we'll start a family eventually. Now just isn't the right time yet."

"That's what you always say. The same lame line. I'm thirty-four now, Adrian. We've known each other for fifteen years. I want to have a baby. You've left me without a career or a family." Tears started to well up in her eyes.

"But I want to be around for my child — not touring, not the absent dad. My father was a salesman, and I didn't see a lot of him when I was young. That's a mistake I don't want to make."

"Well, Denny and Cam's kids haven't seemed to suffer. I think you're losing touch more and more."

"What's that supposed to mean?" he asked brusquely.

"You're becoming cut off from the real world. You pretend to write about it in your songs but I don't think you'd know it if it hit you on the head."

There was a short silence. "Okay, okay, that's enough. Let's not spoil our day together." Adrian got up, sidled over to her chair and half-sat on the arm, looking down on her. "It's natural for us to be like this," he said soothingly. "After we're apart for months, it takes time to knit us back together again, to feel the closeness we both need."

She grabbed his hand and held it to her cheek, which was moist now from the tears. "I don't want us to be like this either. But you're becoming so…so driven and obsessive. It's not enough for you to be one in a million, a talented and successful musician. But then you've got to be the best at everything else in your life — karate, body-building, reading, car collecting…who knows what's next? I just want the real Adrian Lee, the one I knew when I was nineteen. You've changed so much since then."

"Have I really?" he asked, almost in a whisper.

Chapter Three

Ten minutes after the APB, when Chuck Bolan and Rita Barrett arrived on the scene, there were already more than one hundred police milling about like ants on a hill. That was usually the case whenever anything dramatic happened — a hostage-taking incident or armed robbery — because it provided an exciting, much-needed break in the boring routine of many cops who were writing tickets or leisurely patrolling their beats. It was a chance to get involved, to feed undernourished egos, to experience in real life what was always portrayed on television.

As Bolan pushed past the crowd of reporters, photographers and curious onlookers, he studied the area cordoned off by squad cars with flashing lights. On each side of the building and behind it were larger structures, high-rise apartments and office complexes. So there was virtually no escape. Now there were so many police, he thought, it was turning into a carnival. Members of the Emergency Task Force stood around in bulletproof vests, uniformed cops directed traffic away from Church Street and plainclothes officers strutted about looking as self-important as their TV heroes.

"Chuck." It was the duty inspector, Steve Edmund, the man in charge of the chaos. With a nod of his head, he beckoned Bolan and Barrett over to where he was conferring with four other policemen. With his all-American good looks — trim blonde hair, chiseled jaw and the body of a linebacker — Edmund stood out in any crowd.

Rita nudged Bolan as they walked over. "Just watch yourself, Chuck," she cautioned. "You're a mess today, and you know it."

Her partner bristled at the advice. "Get off my back," he said in a low voice while he flashed his badge at a uniformed officer to let him pass.

The two of them had been arguing earlier that morning just before the call on the police radio. Rita wanted him to go home because it was increasingly evident that he wasn't himself. The night before he'd been drinking heavily; then he'd been so hung over that he'd taken an extra tranquilizer along with aspirins, followed up with his painkiller, which was prescribed for every four hours. Rita could tell that Bolan was having trouble concentrating on what she was saying, even her idle threat of being reassigned to work with someone else.

Bolan felt like he was in a bubble watching and listening to everything going on around him but not really being a part of it — almost dream-like. And through the bubble he saw the fine features and blue eyes of Duty Inspector

Edmund giving him a once-over, paying special attention to the bandage and scabs.

"I've seen stiffs that look better than you, Chuck," he said dryly. "Christ, they certainly did some job on that nose of yours — not that it was any prize to begin with."

"So what's the word?" asked Bolan.

"Horrible. Looks like we've had an officer shot. And it seems like your boys — from the description anyway — are holed up in there."

Rita gasped. "Who got shot?"

"Angela Debari — works out of your division."

"Is she dead?"

"Don't know yet. Looks bad though."

All Rita could think about was the young, dark-haired woman she'd bumped into once or twice at the station, who had just returned to work after six months of maternity leave. "How did this happen?"

"Constable Tingley here" — Edmund turned to a ghost-faced young man in uniform — "and Angela were doing a check of the garage on their beat. Two guys were selling weapons to a third, right out of the trunk of a car." Edmund turned away momentarily to bark orders at some plainclothes officers. "Look, I've got a lot of work to do. Tingley, you fill them in." He nodded to the rookie and then walked over to where two detective-sergeants were discussing something.

Ian Tingley was having a tough time, his fresh face full of anguish as he told the story. "The attendant in the garage called us over while we were on foot patrol," he explained, fighting back tears. "Said there was something funny. Two cars had gone up and nobody had walked down the stairs to the street. So I radioed the station and told them we were heading up to have a look. We walked up the stairs. Angie was going on about her baby, Kyla, and how she missed being away from her at work." There was a long pause as the young constable took a deep breath.

"Yeah..." said Bolan impatiently. "What happened next?"

"Nobody on the second floor. So we climbed to the third. We'd just stepped out of the stairwell when–three guys up ahead. I yelled to them. One of them fired at us. Lots of shots. Angela went down...without even a word and then —
"

Bolan cut him short. " — And the description matches those pukes who took us for a ride last Sunday?"

"That's what the inspector says."

"Okay, thanks. I know it's rotten for you, kid. Take care of yourself." Bolan stumbled away abruptly and stopped a serious-looking detective-sergeant who was walking by.

Rita eyed her partner nervously for a second, and then she thanked the young policeman for his help, putting her arm around the shocked rookie's shoulders and hugging him for a moment.

"We've got four rifles behind the garage in the alley," the detective-sergeant was telling Bolan, pointing out the locations with a crooked forefinger. "And a couple of uniformed men too, to make sure no bystanders wander by."

Bolan nodded. "Looks like they're really hemmed in then." His words slurred a little but only Rita noticed.

"For sure," continued the detective-sergeant. He was a squat man, quite stocky, with a shiny bald head and bushy eyebrows. "They can't even move to the stairs to come down or they'll be in full view at the front of the building. At the rear, as I said, there's no exit and no way down — unless they feel like jumping."

"Any people in there with them?" asked Barrett.

"Nope. Garage attendant says the three of them were the only ones inside at the time. Constable Tingley didn't see anyone else when he was up there either. Everybody parks here in the morning before work. Not many around at eleven."

Rita glanced up at the building. "They must be scared shitless in there."

"Yeah. This thing should go without a hitch — as long as the scumbag who did the shooting isn't a total psychotic."

"We were working on this case," said Bolan. "How about letting us cover from the rear with the others there? They might need some help."

The detective-sergeant thought for a second, scratching the top of his smooth hairless dome, and then pointed to the police van. "You'll find a couple of vests in there. You" — he gestured to Bolan — "take charge until I come around behind."

Rita Barrett cringed but decided not to say anything. The September sun warmed her back, making her wish she were somewhere else, maybe on a beach near her hometown in Jamaica, but not here, not now. It had to happen on a Friday, she thought, with Bolan half out of his mind, walking around dazed.

***

"Rita, lookit, over there."

"What?"

Bolan gestured with his head. He was staring at a painter's van in the deserted alley behind the parking garage. A constable stood beside it. "See that truck?"

"Yes. So what?"

"It's got ladders on it — extension ladders. We could grab one and go up. We've got cover here, lots of it. These guys could splatter a pear on the third floor, no problem." He glanced over at an Emergency Task Force marksman squatting behind some garbage cans, peering through the telescopic sights of his poised rifle.

"You are out of your mind, Chuck. You didn't get orders to pull a stunt like that."

Her dark eyes were fixed on him, glaring.

"Loosen up, will ya'? I could flush them out without firing a shot. If I went up there" — he pointed to a corner of the building — "then they couldn't even see me on account of that concrete beam. Anyway, look at all the cars parked up there. Too many obstructions for them. I'd be in the clear. Besides, we're in charge here, remember?" He hustled across the alley, moving clumsily at times in his bulletproof vest, until he met the uniformed officer. Together they began lifting paint-splattered ladders off the beige Ford van. Bolan caught the attention of two marksmen and signaled with his hands, showing them that he intended to go up and needed cover.

Rita's stomach fluttered and head spun as she watched her partner talking to one of the riflemen. She could sense they were excited by the plan, like boys playing some war game. They focused their weapons on different areas of the garage's third floor. One saving grace, she thought, was that Bolan seemed calm, more in control of himself, as though a shot of adrenaline had cleared his head of prescription drugs.

The aluminum ladder rattled as it was raised on the wall but there was so much noise coming from the other side of the building, Bolan was sure no one could hear it on the third floor.

"Chuck, listen to me — it doesn't even reach all the way." Rita looked worried.

"Don't sweat it. We're only short by a couple of feet, and I'm a big boy." He smiled at her, and then over at the constable in uniform, who beamed back, thrilled about participating in this escapade.

"Okay, go then. Just don't do something stupid up there. And as soon as you're at the top, I'll start climbing. You'll have to pull me at the end."

Bolan started, fast at first, but more slowly as he got higher, the bulky vest rubbing against his arms and the steps of the ladder, creating a scraping sound that annoyed him. Concentrate, he thought. Concentrate. Got to think clearly. Oh shit, my gun! How do I get my gun out? He stopped at the second floor, his bandaged nose pressed against the chipped and peeling white paint on the rough concrete blocks, hugging the ladder with his chest and one arm, feeling around with his free hand inside the vest for his .38 Police Special. Finally his thick fingers circled the knurled metal grip and he slid the gun out, looking down for an instant and waving it to let his partner know what he'd been doing. He resumed the climb, each step causing the ladder to wiggle back and forth under his bulk. It shook right down to the bottom where Rita and the uniformed cop held on.

Then he was at the end of the ladder, his hands on the top rung, and there were still a few feet to go before he could grab the third-floor railing and hop over. Only one thing to do: he'd have to climb to the last rung, with nowhere to put his arms except flat against the wall until he touched that railing. He'd never climbed a ladder to the end without having at least some of it to hold onto. Fear was starting to sweep over him — that, plus the effects of tranquilizers and painkillers. His stomach felt upset all of a sudden. He got the jitters and began to sway slightly. Get it together, he told himself. You're almost there. You took the gamble — so make it pay off. But standing there thirty feet up seemed so unreal now; this situation couldn't really be happening to him. He swallowed hard, forcing down some taste of vomit that had mixed with his saliva. It was now or never. Make the move, or go back down. No, he couldn't go back down and face everyone. So he took a deep breath and ran up the last four steps, palms of his hands gliding up the wall, and he didn't even think about what he was doing, as though he were somewhere else, mind blank. His fingers felt the iron with its rusty scales, and he knew that he was there, clasping the railing, .38 dangling by the trigger, hanging by a forefinger so he could use the rest of his hand.

Yanking himself up with powerful arms until the rail was at his abdomen, he leaned forward, letting his weight carry him face-first onto the hood of a big Lincoln Town Car that was parked there. He lay motionless, his feet still hanging over the wall, and turned his head, looking to the right and left as he put the pistol into a ready position. It was damp and smelly, the way parking garages get from moisture, dripped oil and stale exhaust in the concrete. Moving as silently as possible Bolan slid across the car and climbed off, crouching beside it for protection. A beam obstructed his view, so he edged nearer to it and looked out. The garage seemed huge, with eight rows of parked vehicles between him and the front of the building. There was no sign of the three men. After examining every inch close by, he moved forward and to his left, half kneeling and half walking, heading toward the center of the garage and closer to the stairs and exit. He stopped briefly to remove his shoes, which clattered on the floor.

By the time he'd reached the fourth aisle he caught sight of them — all with their backs to him — about ninety feet away. He dropped flat onto his stomach and slithered like a snake, peering at them from underneath the cars, inching closer. He could hear one crying, a short skinny youth with a buzz cut and patchy beard, obviously the one who'd been buying the guns.

"Hey, man, what have ya' done?" he sobbed, sitting on the cold dank floor with his head buried in his arms and a rifle at his feet. "They're gonna kill us, man."

"Shut up, you little cocksucker!" The voice had an obvious American drawl, and as Bolan squinted from under a car he could make out the features — the hatchet face, untidy fair hair, gold ring through the right nostril and tattoos covering his arms — of the man who'd hammered LaPointe from behind five days before at the farm. There was a Glock 9 mm semi-automatic pistol clenched tightly in his right hand.

"We're gonna die, man. We're gonna die."

"Shut up, I said — or I'll fuckin' kill ya'."

"He's right, Max." It was the other American, the black one with the baseball cap and gold chains. "We don't stand no chance. You don't kill no cop and get away with it. There's no way out. Give up before they blow our asses to pieces."

Bolan had an excellent vantage point now, staring squarely into their backs. He stopped moving, got up on his knees, resting his pistol across the hood of a Chrysler K-car to steady it, and at the same time as he cocked the trigger his voice rang out, "Freeze!"

It took just a fraction of a second, because the one with the tattoos turned about an inch when the shot thundered throughout the garage at an earsplitting level, slamming him forward off his feet, ripping into his shoulder blade and splattering blood onto his companions. Their hands were high in the air, faces painted with horror and disbelief. Max, moaning in agony, tried to push himself up off his stomach — when a second shot exploded, this one catching him squarely in the temple and ending his life instantly. Bolan got up and walked toward them, glancing at Angela Debari's crumpled body lying in a burgundy puddle about thirty feet away. For a moment there was no sound.

Suddenly that changed; dozens of pounding footsteps echoed in the stairwell and the door was kicked open as six members of the Emergency Task Force burst in with vests, masks, shotguns and tear-gas canisters. They almost fell over each trying to avoid stepping on the young woman's body. Bolan watched their jolted faces as they removed the masks. "Better get an ambulance crew and stretchers right away!" he yelled to them. One of the policemen pulled out a walkie-talkie. Bolan strode over to the other American, towering above him even without his shoes on. The man quivered, fearful eyes like saucers. For a few seconds the detective toyed with the gold chains around his neck, jangling them with a hand big enough to palm a cannonball and tugging at them lightly. Then in a flash he drove his other hand between the man's legs and squeezed like a steel vice. Screams bounced off the concrete walls.

"The other two," roared Bolan, "the ones in the black Porsche. Where are they?" He loosened the grip slightly. "Talk now, you puke, or I'll crush your balls. I'm not fooling either — I'll crush 'em for good." The man cried out again spasmodically as the clench tightened.

"Hold it," yelled the youth with the scraggly beard, who'd been sobbing before. "You mean that guy and his chick? They left about five minutes before the cops came."

"In the black Porsche?"

"Yeah."

"Where were they going?" Bolan stared into the American's eyes.

"Ramada Inn," gasped the black man, almost in a whisper, his face pinched with pain. Tears were rolling down his cheeks. "Hey, man, we didn't shoot that cop."

"It wasn't us — it was him," piped up the bearded one, pointing to Max's inert body.

Bolan let go.

"Stop it right there."

Duty Inspector Edmund was standing at the stairs flanked by an army of policemen. His voice was cold and firm. "You did a fine job, Chuck, but don't go and blow it by acting like this. Half the reporters and photographers in the city are here right now...and I don't want them to find you manhandling prisoners. What's the matter with you anyway?"

"I'm sorry, sir. I kind of forgot myself there, after seeing what they did to one of our people."

Rita came running in puffing. "Where were you?" she asked between breaths. "When I got to the top of the ladder I couldn't reach the railing. There was no way. You've got almost a foot on me. I waited and waited but you weren't there. I had to climb down."

"I got caught up in the heat of the moment, I guess."

She watched as officers handcuffed the two prisoners, and looked down at the paramedics checking for vital signs on the sprawling body of Max. "Looks to me like you didn't need help."

"Hey, there's more to be done. As soon as I get my shoes, we've got to head for the Ramada Inn. Maybe we can wrap all this up and get those two scumbags who ran us over."

Rita glanced down at one of the medics. "What about the police officer over there?" she asked, gesturing with her eyes in the direction of the body that was being carried out on a stretcher.

"No way," nodded the white-coated, bespectacled man. "She was probably dead within minutes of the bullet's impact."

"My God," Rita gasped, her mind flashing to the six-month-old who would never remember her mother.

Then she turned her attention to Bolan. His facial expression seemed rather peculiar to her, and it wasn't because of the broken teeth and bandages. His eyes were glazed over. And his words were coming out funny. Others might not notice it, especially now with dozens of police, ambulance drivers and media people milling about noisily. But Rita noticed — and it bothered her.

Chapter Four

"Adrian, stop speeding. You've gotten enough tickets to last a lifetime–even though you're only in the city three or four months a year." Jennifer had to yell to be heard when the top was down, and didn't particularly like it, especially when she had to compete with a Metallica CD on a blasting stereo as well.

"I'm not speeding."

"Bullshit. I can see the speedometer from here," she said, smiling at her husband's fib. She felt better now that they'd made up but still had a deeply rooted fear about the steady erosion in their marriage over the issue of children.

"Aren't you glad I brought this baby," Adrian asked, his face beaming. "It's probably one of the last times we'll go topless this season."

"Speak for yourself. I may go topless now and then…if you don't mind."

"Hey, I can always handle that. You can go bottomless while you're at it." He geared down and tore into a corner, the car's big wide tires squealing and the engine whining as he did so. Taking his hand off the black leather gearshift, he placed it on Jennifer's knee and slid it up her thigh. She grabbed his wrist and pulled it up to her mouth, nuzzling his hand against her lips, kissing it gently.

As they neared the city's core, a different set of sights, sounds and smells took over. Car exhaust from the congested traffic became more noticeable; streetcars rattled by loudly; and the giant bank towers loomed ahead, sunlight bursting off their metal and glass surfaces. The gold exterior of the Royal Bank Plaza reflected so much light at this time of day that it was painful to look up at.

Stopped for a traffic signal, Adrian turned to Jennifer while she intently watched a young but decayed-looking derelict stumble across the intersection, obviously drunk, in old running shoes two sizes too big and filthy mismatched clothes. "Funny," she said, "how you can't tell their ages when they get like that. And no matter how much richer our society is getting and how many social ser-vices we have, the gap seems to widen — and there will always be people like them."

"It's their lives to do with as they choose," Adrian said, feeling no guilt whatsoever for his hard words. He stared at the man's ruddy, alcohol-ravaged face, trying to imagine him as a little boy full of hope and innocence. Someone who fell between the cracks and was lacking in the fortitude and discipline to set things right. What a contrast he presented compared to other pedestrians — businessmen in their stylish double-breasted suits with shoulder padding like football players, fancy silk ties and multicolored suspenders over crisp white shirts.

"Hey, light's changed."

"Yeah, okay," he said, ramming the car into gear and racing forward — only to slow it a few yards later. "Looks like we don't turn here." A police car with flashing roof lights blocked the entrance to a side street; its uniformed driver leaned against the passenger side with his arms crossed. Adrian veered to the right and kept going straight. "I'll park up ahead," he yelled over the engine's roar, "and we can walk to the restaurant."

Jennifer swung her head around, trying to find out why there was so much commotion and so many police cars. "I wonder what's going on," she said.

Suddenly there was a piercing screech from behind, the sound of tires howling. Instinctively, Adrian's eyes darted to the rearview mirror. "Morons," he mumbled under his breath.

"They're really flying," said Jennifer, craning her neck to get a good look behind and clutching her hair to keep it off her face. "You better move into the right lane and give them lots of room."

Adrian glanced at his mirror again, watching the blue Dodge gain on them, swerving wildly around other cars, its engine screaming like it was flat out. He signaled and moved into the next lane, slowing slightly at the same time. "Maybe these guys are cops too — or else they're nuts," he said.

Then the car was beside them, veering, cutting them off, squeezing them toward the sidewalk. "What the — " yelled Adrian, heart racing, braking as hard as he could when his vehicle hit the curb, hopping over it and grazing a parking meter. The shrill scream of the Dodge's tires skidding to a halt drowned out all other sounds. Jennifer's mouth was wide open but no sounds were coming out.

"Hold it!" shouted a woman with a pistol perched over the roof of her car. Instantly a man — a very heavyset man — burst out of the passenger side and ran toward Adrian.

"Get back here, Chuck," the woman with the gun cried out. "Chuck!"

"Shit," screeched Adrian. "What the fuck do you — " Bolan's huge hands circled the musician's shoulders like bear paws, tugging him straight up and out of the convertible, lifting him as though he were a paperweight, smashing Adrian's face with a fist and elbow, kneeing him in the ribs, slamming his body back and forth into the Porsche's door and windshield.

"Son of a bitch. You fucking scum." Bolan spat out the words unemotionally as he punched and kicked.

Tears filled his eyes and excruciating pain shot through his mouth but Adrian Lee was still conscious, just barely, able to feel Jennifer's arms clawing at his waist as she screamed hysterically. But then everything started getting dark and he felt himself doubling over, his head bouncing with each of Bolan's blows, his midsection and groin burning from the kicks and, somewhere up above faintly he heard a woman's hoarse voice. "Stop!" she was crying out. "Stop it, Chuck!" And just before he blacked out, Adrian looked up as his hunched body, swayed and was on the verge of collapse, and he saw the dark-skinned woman with the gun dragging the goliath by his neck, yanking him backward, trying to pull him off balance, struggling frantically with him.

Chapter Five

The sounds never stop, not even at night. When the sun's last light is gone and the birds' steady chatter ceases, tree frogs and crickets start to zing and chirp, and in the hills wild dogs howl as they scavenge. But later this particular evening, while the moon blazed down from almost straight overhead and bathed the tops of mango and palm trees in harsh white light, the noises of nature would be drowned — by drums.

Their throbbing would be almost a din at first. Gradually it would increase in intensity though, saturating the town that hugged the mountainside. The pounding would fill little wooden homes with thatched roofs, wake young children and cause oxen and chickens and sheep to stir uneasily. Through the valleys of pineapple groves standing stoutly in rows like an army, the beat would resonate and farmers would watch, staring solemnly out of paneless windows.

In a large flat-roofed house that sat on a steep incline overlooking the town, about sixty of them assembled as they had the night before and the one before that. The men were dressed in short-sleeved shirts and light cotton slacks, while the women had on faded dresses and well-worn sandals. Whispering and shuffling about, they got as comfortable as possible on the damp concrete floor, squeezed in elbow to elbow, all facing the rear of the cement-block dwelling, where there was considerably more room. In that spot the old santero worked, spreading long full banana leaves around a crude wooden altar, laying rattles and a bell nearby. In pairs he lifted four drums from a corner and placed them close to the people, never looking up for even a moment, grimly concentrating only on his duty. He wasn't a tall man — in fact, his body verged on frailty — but the sweeping robe he wore gave him presence and stature.

A few stragglers were late to arrive, walking their bicycles up the hill and sputtering along in forty-year-old cars. Near the building they spoke in hushed tones, exchanging greetings, remarking on the weather and joking around. Before entering they removed their jackets and shawls and took a long breath of the chilly air, which was laced with the scent of salt and blossoms. Although a breeze from the ocean whipped up the hill, inside the house it was sweltering, and the faces in the crowd — three-quarters of them black and the rest Latin looking — were glistening with sweat under the solitary yellow light bulb. Many pairs of eyes were shut tightly in prayer, while lips moved inaudibly. A bottle of old dark rum was passed around and swigged straight.

With exceptional care the santero unwrapped a cloth with mud-colored stains all over it and took out the sacred stones — none bigger than a silver dollar — which he then placed on a shelf near the bottom of the altar, closing a curtain over them. Standing up he meticulously arranged some fresh green herbs and resguardo — beads and other protective charms — on top of the shrine. His brown eyes glanced up, and seeing his signal a man and a woman waded through the crowd and knelt behind the drums, clutching a foot-long stick in each hand. Another man and woman came forward also and picked up the rattles and bell.

In his black robe the santero looked like a stick of ebony, body straight and still, bald head shining in the heat. He raised his hands in front of him and started chanting the words of an oricha — muttering at first, then slowly building in intensity — and the deep hollow sound of the drums began, muted but surging, each wave louder than the last, more penetrating. And soon everywhere in the room voices joined in, repeating a single phrase over and over. Heads swayed in time to the drums' tempo. For almost an hour the charge on the atmosphere grew stronger and the noise increasingly frantic, until the people were yelling and clapping hands along to the pounding of the tom-toms.

The old priest's body quivered as he led the crowd, and sweat poured off his head and neck, dripping onto his robe, which was already soaked across the back and under the arms. His eyes were wide, the whites bugging out, as his head jerked spasmodically — almost drugged-looking. Suddenly he brought his arms down.

There was an immediate calm.

This so far had been just foreplay. The saints still had to be fed, thus setting the stage for the climax. It was almost perfectly still again, with only the gentle rhythmic beat of the drums. The santero worked deftly, mixing his special herbs in a bowl full of water that had been placed on the altar. He pulled the lid off a tall clay cylinder and scooped out some wrinkled brown leaves and dried blood, dropping them into the bowl. To this he added the beads and charms. And then, after sliding a sleek double-edged knife out from beneath his robe, he submerged it and his hands in the bowl, moving at a deliberate, sluggish pace — as if to heighten the dramatics. A minute later he took out the dagger and herbal concoction, his eyes fixed on the task, never looking away for even an instant. When he'd finished, the bowl was removed and a black box was put on the floor beside him.

All the people sat transfixed, staring at him through wide eyes, their bodies motionless except for the deep breaths they took — a result of their frantic activity during the chant. The nostrils on the broad nose of the priest flared as a flurry of words left his mouth, overriding the light tapping of the drums. Then he began to chant again, another oricha this time, repeating the words over and over as the beat grew louder. His breathing quickly became heavy and his eyeballs began to bulge as they had before. He continued chanting while he leaned over and opened the black wooden box and withdrew a newly born kid that quivered in these strange surroundings. Then he stood up straight. Curly white fur protruded from his dark arm as he cradled the goat with fingers gripped firmly around its collar bone. There was a look of dread in the animal's round black eyes, almost as though it knew what would happen next. With a jerk he sliced the kid's throat and worked the gleaming blade in slowly and deeply right to the hilt as the animal screamed and gurgled. He pulled the knife out part way and then turned it so the kid's head flopped back, allowing a stream of blood to pour down over the stones, as if from a hose, dripping off the altar and onto the banana leaves. It was caliente, as the blood had to be, so that the powerful invisible fluid of the stones would be strongest. At the sight of blood the priest inhaled and exhaled more rapidly. His eyes turned upward until only the whites were visible. Over the course of a minute his upper body seemed to grow, the chest expanding, giving him added dimension. Then the entire congregation joined in the chanting — the santero leading — and some of the people stood on their feet now, moving their bodies to the drums' loudening pulse. And everything started all over again, only more intense than before — stomping, pounding, crying out — and more feverishly the people released whatever trapped emotions lay in the depth of their souls.

Down the hillside the thunder could be heard in town because the noise was reaching an earsplitting level, growing and growing, pulsating for miles in all directions. Non-believers peered out their windows, looking up the hill, irritated by the commotion as they had been the two previous nights. Children who were yanked from the depths of sleep felt an eerie chill but didn't understand why.

In the house everyone stood now, their clothes drenched in sweat, dancing, singing and jumping to the steady beat. A few fell over, breathing heavily, their wide-open eyes blank, speaking in strange tongues, possessed by something — a saint maybe — but this was good; the more it happened, the stronger the fluid and power of the stones. It meant that the saints were well fed and satisfied. Wilder and wilder the drummers played in unison, sticks flailing the tom-toms from high above their heads; faster and faster the congregation moved, screaming deliriously, swept up in a hypnotic tide, oblivious to what was happening outside. The cement walls seemed to vibrate with the rhythm.

And just a few yards away even the clanking of the old jeep was lost in the sounds of the ritual. The four men in green fatigues were unarmed, and one of them — a sergeant with a young face and slick black hair — led the way from the road to the house, wincing at the sounds that assaulted his ears. Perhaps he was wincing at the job he had to do too. He didn't like to interrupt the Santeria ceremonies. Maybe there was something to them, he thought. But why should they be illegal for the sake of a few animals? It was none of the government's business whether people carried on these religious practices. They'd been doing it for hundreds of years. But his orders were orders and the laws were laws, so he had no choice.

The soldiers were hardly noticed in the clamor, shoving past hot gyrating bodies, dodging swinging outstretched arms, until one of the drummers caught sight of them and abruptly stopped playing. The others followed suit. Still the sound and pandemonium of the crowd continued, their minds now drugged by the ritual, reactions dull and bodies shaking and twitching uncontrollably. Slowly though they took notice and quietened two and three at a time until there was silence. "Para afuere!" shouted the soldiers. "Para afuere!" And the people began to rush for the narrow door, pushing and stumbling over each other, fear evident in their eyes. The sergeant stepped up to the shrine, glancing at the blood-smeared altar and dead animal. "Tine permiso?" he asked. But the santero, looking smaller and weaker now, just bowed his head — he had no permits. The sergeant sighed and looked down at the floor, scuffing his feet a little. "Quedan usted arrestados," he said, lightly grabbing the old man's arm and guiding him to the door.

Outside, the people scattered, some bounding down the hill on foot, others coasting on their bicycles and a few loading their cars with passengers. The soldiers sat in the jeep smoking strong-smelling, unfiltered cigarettes and laughing out loud at their own jokes. They paid little attention to the townspeople rushing down the hill. They lowered their voices slightly when the sergeant approached. He stopped a few feet from the jeep as the old man in the black robe stood up on his toes to whisper something in the sergeant's ear. There was a pause for at least a minute. Then the sergeant did something unexpected: he let his prisoner go, making a big show about letting him off with just a warning this time. He spoke sternly and occasionally wagged a finger in the priest's face. The other soldiers turned to each other and then looked back at their sergeant. The old man turned around and started walking back toward the cement house, his robe sweeping the ground with each step. His facial expression hadn't changed at all during the entire episode, not registering even the slightest twinge of emotion. The sergeant waited a moment, watching the man, and then hopped into the jeep, ordering the driver to leave. His men just stared at him, their faces questioning, but none had the nerve to disobey him or even ask about his behavior. They drove off down the hill into the night.

The sergeant wouldn't show it but he was afraid. If he'd taken the santero in, he knew he would be dead within a month as the old man had warned, struck down by the power of the stones.

***

Ricardo Sosa stood there with the rest of the resort staff, his fifth Monte Cristo of the day clenched firmly between his teeth — no rationing of cigars for him. His eyes were partly closed to avoid the bright noonday light, and his hand waved slowly at all of the people on the two departing luxury buses. Sosa's stare was vacant because he was thinking of other things, not about the fifty people whose sunburned faces peered through the windows of the bus at him. Their week in paradise had come to an end, a week of overeating and drinking, of broiling on the powdery beach sand, of dancing to Afro-Cuban rhythms at night. Now they would be off to the airport in Havana, and after three or four hours of queuing to have their luggage checked, passports stamped and "funny" money exchanged they would be so numbed by exhaustion that the thought of cloudy, frigid weather and the grind of their upper-mddle-class careers wouldn't be as disheartening.

Sosa stopped waving momentarily to relight his cigar. His squinting eyes focused on the kitchen help, bartenders, beach boys and cleaning women of La Sorpresa smiling as they bade farewell to the touristos. It had been his idea as manager to have the employees out in full force twice a week to greet and say goodbye to each group, adding a personal dimension to the resort and helping to ensure that at least some of the Canadians would return for a second visit. As the Spanish-built buses started moving up the hill away from La Sorpresa, the crowd of workers dispersed, heading back to the kitchen and beach to prepare for the next group of money-spending tourists who would arrive in six hours, looking just as tired and disoriented as the last group had. Sweat would be pouring off their ivory skin because they hadn't acclimatized yet. Many of them would be in foul moods after too many drinks on the jet, a seemingly endless stop through customs and agonizingly slow bus trip sixty kilometres to the opulence and seclusion of La Sorpresa. Each week, from September until April — just before the rainy season began — it was the same thing.

But now the tourism industry was more vital than ever to the country's well-being; Canadians alone spent more than seventy-five million dollars a year here. There were few other industries anyway, and without the financial cushion and dirt-cheap oil that Russia had provided for over twenty-five years, Cuba was rocked by the shock waves of a disintegrating Cold War — skimpy food rations, precious little fuel for vehicles, not enough medicine in the hospitals and a beaten people. Even though public protests were forbidden, Sosa had noticed a marked increase in grumbling and complaining, not to mention a growing number of citizens who braved dangerous seas on flimsy rafts in a bid to escape to Florida. Increasingly more of them hadn't even been born at the time of the revolution, let alone fought in it. So what did communism really mean to them? It was a crumbling relic now, something to blame for all of the economic hardships and rationing. It wasn't like the old days anymore, before the tourists came and when American radio and television signals were blacked out, making it much easier to spread the gospel according to Fidel Castro. In a dramatically changed world, the United States had ceased to be an ominous, forever threatening enemy, despite anything their bearded aging leader said to the contrary. In fact, nearly all Cubans longed for the American lifestyle, the consumer goods, the freedom to do and say what you pleased — and most of all, full satisfying meals.

Despite the fact that Sosa had lived in the United States when he first went to university and later — after the revolution — moved to Paris for anthropology and medicine, he'd never had the urge to leave his homeland since. He loved Cuba, with its wild, scrubby interior, long stretches of sandy beaches and steep rocky hills that sloped near the shorelines. To him the island's people — with a combined ancestry from Spain and Africa — were one of a kind, spirited and passionate, unbridled in their emotions and harboring few pretensions. Of course, much of this was due to the fact that most citizens led relatively simple lives in this poor country. Unfortunately, much of that spirit and passion had been drained from the population due to the hardships of the past couple of years.

Sosa watched the buses grow smaller in the distance, chuckling to himself at the behavior of tourists — not just those who visited Cuba, but anywhere on earth, and no matter how well off they might be. There was always a group mentality, a herding instinct of sorts. Maybe it was what happens to people on vacation, when they really let loose, with an overbearing lack of restraint and sometimes downright rudeness. Certainly he'd become an expert on the subject, thanks to managing this resort.

True to its name, La Sorpresa actually was a surprise, an attempt by the tourism ministry to create an expensive high-class establishment, catering to the very kinds of people the revolution had overthrown. The resort itself was a lavishly renovated estate that had once belonged to the scions of a turn-of-the-century U.S. robber baron. It had been built in the 1920s on two hundred acres of rural land and oceanfront. Now the main buildings and guest houses had been converted into spacious hotel suites and villas. For the Cubans, working there meant being part of a privileged class too: supplementing meagre rations with leftovers from tourists' buffets; sneaking drinks from the bars; and wearing clean clothes every day.

When the buses were no longer in view and their engines just a faint drone, Ricardo Sosa started walking up the hill to the dining room. He had time for one or two cervezas before heading to his cabana for an afternoon and evening of reading and studying. The wind was noisy for this time in the morning, whistling around the hills that rose steeply half a mile from beach. In fact, it was difficult to hear the chatter of the birds because of the wind, a sign that a rainstorm was on its way. Something Sosa didn't want. Tourists were even harder to handle if the weather were less than perfect on their arrival.

Treading uphill always made him puff lately, a sign he decided to ignore, knowing full well that at forty-seven years he was sliding out of shape. His belly was beginning to creep over the wide black belt he wore with khaki slacks. He didn't give it more than passing notice. His bushy moustache and thick slicked hair were still the color of tar, and though he wasn't a tall man — only nudging five foot seven — there was definitely a strong sense of machismo in him, as there was in most of his countrymen too.

Surrounded by palm trees and lush flowering bushes, the dining room and bar were in a spectacular old building with louvered walls to let air in when it was very hot. Right now the slats were shut to prevent the stiff breeze from blowing linen napkins and tablecloths at each elegant place setting. The well-stocked bar was situated near the entrance. Like most of the resort, it had been renovated to resemble the period in which it had been built. Lots of chrome, red leather and other Deco-inspired touches. Sosa stepped up and ordered his beer, slapping down a few pesos at the same time, and removing the half-smoked cigar that always protruded under his moustache. Employees received no discount on drinks at La Sorpresa, although Sosa turned a blind eye to the pilfering as long as it didn't get out of hand. He took a big mouthful and swallowed it quickly to quench his thirst and then set down the glass, glancing over a few seats away to where three soldiers were enjoying a leisurely cerveza and talking loudly. They often dropped by while on duty in the area — only when the tourists had departed though. Sosa smiled and nodded at them but kept his distance, not wishing to get involved in their conversation. Still, he couldn't help but overhear the booming voices.

"Yes, I am aware of that," one of them said. "His father was a good fighter in Angola, and this is why he became a sergeant. But now he has the heart of a chicken." All three laughed uproariously at this.

"Afraid of an old man," commented another soldier, small and wiry with a long scar down his cheek. "How can it be? Martinez must believe in these silly rituals, eh? He must be as crazy as the old man." More laughter.

"Maybe then I should be a sergeant," the first one yelled, "since I have no fear of grandfathers." They all exploded over that remark.

Abruptly the talking stopped. Sosa felt the light warm touch of a hand on his shoulder. He turned on his bar stool and looked up into the smiling face of Maria Cuevas. She was a student at the University of Havana who'd taken a year off studies to work in the tourism ministry, and had spent the past two months at La Sorpresa. Obviously the soldiers had seen her before because they were calling out her name.

"Ricardo, is there anything I should be doing now?" she asked, fingers moving slowly on his shoulder.

"No," he answered, trying his best to ignore her flirt. "Tonight I will give you the passports and documents of the new tourists. Until then your time is your own."

Smiling, she glided past him and sat down with the soldiers. Sosa followed her with his eyes, studying her youthful features, remembering what he'd been like at that age–and even younger. He'd taken a sudden leave from university in the United States and rushed back home to join his brother in the revolutionary ranks. They'd been part of the ragged rebel troops that Castro had led down from the Sierra Maestra hills and paraded victoriously through mob-filled streets in 1959; even though Sosa and his family had worked hard for this triumph, along with the rest of the communists, there had been a twinge of uncertainty in him, of wondering what would lie ahead. Now, looking at Maria, he felt the same way and was reminded of his own daughter, twenty years old, who was starting medicine at the university. He wondered what would become of her in a Cuba that was fracturing at the seams, a Cuba whose future seemed more unstable than it had at any time since the revolution. Castro, who had been the solution then, was now the problem.

Sosa sighed deeply, still watching Maria intently. Was his daughter like her, sleeping around casually with men she hardly knew? The thought bothered him; even though trained as a psychiatrist, he couldn't analyze his own feelings objectively and smooth them over with calculated rationale, the way he used to with patients.

On one hand there was the fact that he hadn't been a good father, what with getting divorced five years earlier and working far away from his daughter and two sons. Then too there was the lust he had felt — and still did feel — for Maria. She was so confident and aggressive, different from any woman he'd ever grown up with. Despite her age, being fresh out of school and into a job at the resort, she exuded fierce independence — just as his daughter did. It excited him. And there would be men just like him excited by his own daughter. He decided not to think about his daughter anymore right now.

Maria was chatting with the soldiers, coy one instant with a tight-lipped smile and demure way of moving, then saucy and provoking the next, laughing out loud with them — and at them. She wasn't beautiful, thought Sosa, not in a finely featured way, because there was a lack of definition to her cheeks, and her nose was flat and nondescript. Her light brown hair had no particular style; it was just there, hanging down almost to her shoulders or blowing loosely in the ocean breeze. Sometimes her untanned skin seemed almost pasty, but that didn't matter either, because there was something very sensual about Maria — a simmering passion bubbling within her, ready to spill over — and any male near her could be scalded by it.

Ricardo Sosa gazed at her white shoulders and neck, which were exposed by the light blue dress she wore. He remembered the boat ride he'd taken her on a few weeks before, when he'd been giving her lessons in English. They'd come ashore at a deserted stretch of beach and pulled in the little sailing dinghy. She'd been wearing the same dress and hoisted it up around her thighs as she climbed out of the boat into the shallow foamy water. The sun bearing down from directly overhead glanced off the almost calm sea in the sheltered bay, turning it into a mirror. They'd run across the sand to a spot under some mango trees, taking refuge from the penetrating rays.

While he tried to keep his mind on teaching her new words, desperately he wanted her — and he could see that she knew it. She'd been aware of his longing, just as she'd probably been aware of dozens of other men who responded to her in such a way. While they were sitting there, he found himself mumbling half in English and half in Spanish, much of it utter nonsense. She was giggling at his silly jokes and moving closer to him.

At first her confidence ate away at his old-fashioned manliness, and he found himself just the slightest bit nervous. He was afraid she would notice. But even if she had, Maria didn't let on. She kept her green eyes glued to his, waiting for him to begin another word in English. Occasionally he felt her arm brush against him, or her leg up against his.

After about half an hour she put her forefinger over his lips and leaned forward until her pouting mouth was just about an inch away. "That's enough English for today," she whispered. "Right now I prefer body language." Then she removed her finger.

There was no nervousness left in him now. Sosa reached behind her head and pulled her mouth onto his own. Immediately her tongue darted inside and pressed up against his. After that he felt himself kissing her forehead, her nose, her chin, her ears and her neck. Sighs were turning to moans.

He'd had trouble with the shoulder straps on the dress, and she just smiled as he struggled with the buttons, which at that moment seemed too big for the holes. When he finally peeled the dress down, her heavy breasts spilled into his hands, large round nipples looking faint pink against the pale skin. He squeezed gently, tugging at the tips a little, and then studied them for a few seconds as their color flushed and they began to stiffen. His breathing was excited and labored now. Sosa yanked at her dress, tugging it below her waist, taking her panties with it. She had wide billowy hips and in between them a tummy that was flat and taut now but would probably balloon a little as she grew older, although not in an unpleasant way. He leaned down farther and pulled the clothes right off her ankles so she was completely naked. His eyes fixed for an instant between her legs at the soft thick tufts of brown that spread from her mound onto her thighs and almost completely hid the uneven pink folds. It was evident from Maria's fair skin and lack of a bikini cut that she spent little, if any, time in a bathing suit. Unlike many of the young women who grew up in this climate, she was definitely no beach bunny.

When Sosa glanced up, he saw a broad grin spread across her face. Then she reached out, grabbing a handful of hair, and roughly pulled him up to her. She laughed out loud, and her hand found him under his slacks, as hard as iron. Her grip was wrench-like — almost too strong and verging on real pain — while she undid his pants with the other hand. Panting, he didn't want to wait any longer, and rolled over onto her, both hands now pressing down on her shoulders. But she prodded his pudgy brown belly with her finger. "Wait," she said firmly, "I want you to take off all of your clothes first. This is for me too."

"Are you protected?" he asked, breathless, dragging his jersey over his head.

She laughed mockingly and shook her head as if in disbelief. "Of course I am. Do you think I'd let you get this far if I wasn't?" Then she giggled as he leaned forward to kiss her, stray hairs from his bushy moustache tickling the bottom of her nose.

When he'd finished removing his black socks, Sosa sat there just slightly edgy and uncomfortable in his nakedness, enough to soften his arousal. Maria had reached down by her feet to the dress and appeared to be feeling around for something in it. She turned back to him and leaned over, her hands on his thighs, rubbing them lightly. Desire started to rush back through him.

"Hmmm," she cooed, "stand up for me."

He didn't know what to make of this; no one had ever made love with him this way before, ordering him around. Sosa was at a loss how to react. So he pushed himself up off the sand, standing over her, hardness ebbing away again.

She ran her fingertips around his hips and onto his backside, and then moved her face closer to him, nuzzling and kissing. He instinctively placed both hands on her head, feeling the softness of her hair. Maria's hands moved around to the front; she cupped his balls ever so gently, and her tongue began to flick in and out along his quickly stiffening shaft, making its way to the reddish brown head. One hand slid to its base while she licked and engulfed him with her mouth. His eyes were closed, legs unsteady and his hips pumped in rhythm with her movements.

Then a different feeling brought him back to earth. Sosa glanced down to find her unrolling a condom as she kissed him right over the latex that was already on. He could feel the sun burning his back and the warm sand underfoot. "I thought you meant the pill when you said you were protected," he mumbled.

"So, what does it matter? It's even safer."

"No, no, it's fine, just fine. I was not expecting it, that's all."

He knelt down and took her by the arms, pushing her onto her back in the tree's precious little shade. He kissed her over and over, exploring the inside of her mouth, and slid his hand below her belly and through the thick matted hair that felt like a nest. Her lips had already parted, damp and inviting. Up and down his fingers caressed, from her center of pleasure to the ever-widening entrance. His nose picked up her musky scent against the backdrop of salty sea air.

"Should I go in now?" he gasped, his hips grinding on hers.

Under him, Maria started to giggle. "At this point, you must know I'm ready. Permission is granted, sir." She saluted him military style. Her laughter became more boisterous, causing his body to shake with hers.

The sound of her laughing, with its overly emphasized "ha ha," brought Ricardo Sosa out of his recollection. Noticing that he was partially aroused, he crossed his legs and motioned the bartender to fetch him another cerveza. His cigar had gone out, and he fumbled around reaching into his back pocket for a light. All the while he regarded the young woman, defiant and exuberant, commanding the soldiers' attention just the way she had his, the way she had Carlos the assistant manager's, and Jorge, one of the waiters, and Miguel the lifeguard before that. She'd meant it when she said it was for her too.

But now the mood had changed. They were talking seriously. Sosa could hear Maria's voice above the others.

"Yes, your sergeant was right to let the santero be," she said.

"What!" exclaimed one of the soldiers, who had the scar down his cheek. "You mean that you believe in Santeria?"

"Of course. In Jovellanos, where I grew up, I saw the power of it."

"Then you're as crazy as Sergeant Martinez."

Maria shook her head at him. "I would rather be crazy than stupid."

One of the other soldiers, a tall man with a pock-marked face, scowled at her. "Is this what they teach you in university, woman?"

"No," she replied icily. "They teach me to think, which is more than I can say for any of you. Soldiers have their brains between their legs."

The men shuffled uneasily in their seats before the tall one spoke again. "That's no way for a woman to talk."

"You mean that's not the way your wife would talk. Well, I'm not your wife — thank the Lord." Maria glared at them until they muttered something about leaving and got up from their chairs. Then she wandered over and sat at the bar beside Sosa. The bartender, who'd been enjoying the show, now lowered his head and went about washing glasses, minding his own business.

"It's no use to argue with people who just don't understand you…and never will," said Sosa, putting down his almost empty glass. "No matter what you say or how well you phrase it, they will never change their minds."

Maria exhaled loudly in an exasperated way. "I realize this."

"Well…if you want, you can come back to my cabana and learn some more English. Or you can argue with me if you wish. I think I understand you." He smiled.

Maria looked him in the eye. "I know what you really mean, Ricardo. You're as bad as they are — only smarter."

Chapter Six

First there was a beach: turquoise sea and sugar-white sand. Then palm trees, lush vegetation and a sweeping hillside. Up a steep incline covered with gnarled brush. Big buzzards flying overhead. Then inside a building. The light was piercing, a stomach-churning yellow. And everywhere were people, rows of them, their dark faces covered in sweat and eyes closed. Only their lips moved, just barely, whispering words inaudibly. Perspiration dripped from their shirts and dresses — God, it seemed hot — yet they didn't seem bothered by it. A gentle tapping was gradually becoming a thumping, and as it grew louder their bodies started to move, back and forth, back and forth. And that light was so harsh and bright, so yellow it was nauseating. It shone on the swaying bodies, casting a jaundiced glow over them all as they moved back and forth. Then there was a face up close, an infant, screaming, shrieking, his features contorted in upset, eyes forced shut by the intensity of his rage. Closer and closer until there was only his mouth, wide open, a gaping hole and the darkness within. Everything was black, but the thumping continued.

Adrian Lee's eyes opened slowly. His mind was still racing with the dream, and he shook his head to bring himself around. At his side sat Jennifer, clasping what little of Adrian's fingers protruded through the cast on his right arm.

"God, that dream again," he said as fragments of it bounced in and out of his consciousness. "So vivid. Remember?"

Jennifer nodded. "Sort of. I remember you woke me up a couple of days ago. Describing a dream is like trying to read the comics to someone. It's never as good for the person getting it secondhand."

"Well, if you were the one dreaming, you wouldn't forget it."

"Okay, okay, enough about your nightmare. How are you feeling anyway?"

"What do you think? I feel like shit." Adrian motioned to the end of the bed. "Can you please raise this thing?"

Jennifer jumped from her chair and pulled the crank out at the foot of the bed, turning it counter-clockwise to raise her husband's back to an upright position.

"Thanks," he mumbled, wincing as he moved because of the pain from half a dozen cracked ribs. He'd shaken off the dream now but was feeling peevish. "I can't believe how many people have been here." Words spilled out like there was cotton in his mouth because of the swelling. "A day-and-a-half in hospital and my room's like the subway after work."

"You're lucky you have so many friends."

"Friends, my ass. Most of them are just hangers-on and people from work worried we won't get the record out on time, or that our tour might have to be postponed." He flashed back a few hours to when Susan Monaco, the rep from their record company, sat with him and tried to appear concerned about his misfortune but continually asked questions like how long it would be before he could play drums again.

Jennifer shook her head. "I think I'd rather visit with Scrooge just before Christmas. He'd be a lot more fun than you are."

Adrian managed a half-smile, then turned to her. "Sorry. I'll try to keep it under control. So…anything new about what happened?"

"No, nothing more than I've already told you. The police say one of their detectives mistook us for some criminals driving the same kind of car. They were part of that police killing — the woman who got shot."

"What about me?"

"No news since this morning…so I guess nothing has changed. You'll be out of here tomorrow. The broken ribs will heal slowly on their own. Your arm will have to be checked every couple of weeks — and the cast can't come off for about a month. The good thing is there are no internal injuries. And all those bruises and cuts will go away in a few days. Certainly not the end of the world."

"Did you call the lawyer?"

"I did that last night. He said he'll pop over tomorrow after you're home. I also talked to the dentist yesterday. He's squeezing you in three times next week — Tuesday at ten, Thursday at one and Friday at eleven — to have those teeth capped."

Adrian ran his tongue over the aching spots in his mouth where teeth had broken or chipped and were now literally as sensitive as an exposed nerve. Others were still loose. Even his tongue was in bad shape, having been stitched up because he'd bitten it so many times while being punched. "This whole thing is fucking unbelievable," he said.

"Look on the bright side for a change. You're left-handed, so it was lucky you're right wrist happened to be broken. See? Could've been worse."

"It makes no difference," snapped the musician, tight-lipped as he mumbled, bitterness oozing out of him like poison from a sore. "You can't hit a snare drum with a cast on your arm. Wrist action is the most important part of playing. It'll take me weeks and weeks to get back into shape." His face muscles quivered as the thought sunk in.

There was another silence, this one more awkward than the last as Adrian began to get sullen. Pretty soon a nurse would drop by to feed him another pill to ease the pain, and his mind would get fuzzy enough to forget about the whole thing for a little while. "I just don't know what's going to happen with the songs. I'm not even near finishing those lyrics. And how am I going to concentrate after all that's happened?"

"Adrian, try to stop dwelling on it. There's nothing you can do, except go with the flow. A month from now, you'll be in great shape again. Everybody has setbacks…and they work around them."

"Yeah, but they don't have setbacks like this."

"No, of course not. Millions of people don't starve slowly, die of cancer, get shot, beaten to death, run over, bombed, raped and tortured."

"What about the media coverage?" asked Adrian, changing the subject.

"There's lots."

"Ah, fuck," moaned Adrian, "I suspected as much. The nurses have been screening calls. But they said it's not just the newspapers and TV here. This thing's blown up into an international story. CNN has been pestering for an exclusive interview. So have the tabloid TV shows. *Time*, *People* and *Us* have all been bugging the hell out of me. Even those assholes at *Rolling Stone* want a scoop — and they've never had a good word to say about Tangent in fifteen years."

Jennifer nodded her head. "I don't think that's the point. It's because of who you are. Thousands of people overdose, but there's only a fuss if it's Jim Morrison or Jimi Hendrix or John Bonham. The media doesn't care about Joe Average…and neither does the public. You know that."

"Of course I know that," Adrian barked. "They don't have to look like a wimp in the eyes of the world, the way I do now."

"What do you mean?"

"Because I froze. I choked. I bit it. I wussed out. I did everything but shit my pants. Me, with a brown belt in karate. Me, who stays in killer shape. And it takes a woman to pull the guy off me."

Jennifer noticeably stiffened and let go of Adrian's fingers. "I don't believe what I'm hearing," she gasped. "You're actually worried people won't think you're man enough — or something equally stupid."

"I should've reacted. Christ…for the past four years I've practiced karate so much so that it's become a reflex action. Then the first time I'm really tested, I sit there and take it like a piece of liver."

"What is it with you? You've led a Cinderella life. You've got everything any person could ever want. But that's not enough. You have to be stronger and tougher too?"

Adrian did not respond but instead stared out of the single small window that graced the room.

Jennifer put her hand on his shoulder. "Don't you understand? I love you the way you are. I don't need a caveman. And you don't have to put yourself on the same level as that gorilla who hurt you."

"I'm not."

"Well, it sounds like you are. Worrying about people thinking you're a wimp. That's dumb. If anything, the public's going to wonder about the goons they put on our police force."

Adrian didn't look convinced. "It was a one-on-one thing, him against me. And I didn't even put up a struggle. You can bet every newspaper's going to mention that I'm supposed to be good at karate."

"So what!" exclaimed Jennifer, losing control. "Who cares? So you didn't fight back — against someone twice your size. This is just male-ego bullshit!"

He started to raise his cast-covered arm in protest and then winced at the pain. "You don't see it, do you? I'm totally innocent, haven't done a thing to anybody, and this happens. What kind of society are we living in?"

"Well, now you know what the blacks have been up in arms about for the past few years. Getting shot for running radar traps. Being searched and harassed, often for no reason. More of them dead from police bullets than whites…even though they're such a small minority."

"Yeah," shot back Adrian, "but you always get people writing letters to the editor saying things like 'Our cops are tops; they've got a tough job to do.' Makes me sick, all of it. Might as well be living in China."

"Hold on a minute," Jennifer broke in. "So there are some bad eggs on the force; it doesn't mean every cop is a bloody criminal or something. You can't compare our country to China."

"Cops handing out their own justice — that's the first step." Adrian's stitched-up tongue was really starting to hurt now. The time for painkillers was nearing. "What happened to me is a loss of freedom for us all."

"That's not true. Police always overstep the bounds. For years it's happened…and sometimes they get caught. There's always the struggle — them asking for more power and civil libertarians demanding less. These are the checks and balances. It will never change. But I don't think our democracy is in any danger. In fact, we're all freer than we've ever been. The media says what it wants — even nasty things about your music, Adrian — as well as reporting police abuses. We can still talk about anything we like in this country without looking over our shoulder first."

"But is it really a free country if you have to worry about somebody coming up and practically murdering you with his bare hands…and this guy is on the side of the law?"

"Don't be so dramatic. I know you're in pain but don't twist this whole thing around. What happened to you was an isolated case. Every time people go out, they don't have to be afraid of a cop coming at them."

"Easy for you to say" — Adrian's voice was louder and angrier now — "because I'm the one lying here like I've been through World War Three. All I keep thinking is that I should've been able to prevent it. If I had another chance it would be different, that's for sure. Just another chance with that bastard..."

"I've got to go," Jennifer said abruptly, cutting off any further conversation, visibly irritated. Her sympathy was ebbing. While he may be in pain, she thought, it wasn't as though Adrian would be disabled for life. Other people suffered in silence. She stood up and leaned over the bed, kissing him on the forehead. "I'll be back to see you tonight. And don't keep going over and over it in your head. That won't help right now." She kissed him again and grabbed her suede handbag, which had been slung over the back of the chair.

After Jennifer left, a young Asian man came in carrying a tray with supper on it. He slid it onto the bedside table and made his exit quickly. Adrian could hear the trolley with all the meal trays stacked on it clattering down the hall, wheels squeaking and reverberating on the old cream-colored vinyl tiles. Then a nurse with a purposeful stride entered. She was an older woman with thinning, frizzy hair and thick glasses. Earlier in the day she'd helped Adrian with his lunch, cutting meat and spreading butter onto the white bread. He liked her manner. Now there were pills in the palm of her left hand and a glass of water in her right. Time to kill the pain and bring on a welcome stupor.

Once she'd gone, he was left alone to his thoughts. Adrian glanced about the dismal room; the light green paint on the walls was bordering on dingy, and there were dozens of lumps where old plaster had been repaired over the decades. The flowers his friends and fans had sent managed to liven it up somewhat though, like a splashy tie on a dowdy grey suit.

The last time he'd been in a room like this was two years before, when his father stubbornly fought the last stages of cancer. That wasn't how he wanted to remember his dad. It had been his father who encouraged Adrian to take up drumming, by buying him a pair of sticks and a rubber practice pad. Then a few months later, at six on Christmas morning, he saw it standing there: a stainless steel snare drum, made in Japan. It was a real instrument, not a toy. And with it an adjustable drummer's throne, with a cushioned black vinyl seat. Shortly after the holiday there were music lessons, the first of three years' worth, until Adrian could play better than his teacher.

By the time he met an aspiring guitarist named Cam Goodman in grade seven, Adrian knew what he wanted to do with his life. They formed a band and played songs by the Byrds and the Rolling Stones. Two years later, in high school, they ditched their bass player and teamed up with Alan Gershgorin, who was not only stronger on his instrument but had a strident, nasal singing voice too — the kind adults hated but kids loved. Soon the new band member had affected a stage name: Denny Yorke. So there they were: a power trio, just like Cream with Eric Clapton. A couple of years after that, Adrian dreamed up the name Tangent, just about the time they were getting their union cards and quitting school — much to their parents' chagrin.

Even now, after all the years of success, Adrian still couldn't get over the most fascinating part of his good fortune — playing for a living. Athletes get to do it too; so do some film stars. To actually do something you like so much, which comes so effortlessly and doesn't feel like work, even if you do work at it. For musicians too, there was the added benefit of sometimes finding a groove together or what was known as being "in the pocket," losing yourself in the music, when playing almost becomes a spiritual experience. On many occasions — in rehearsal or even onstage in front of fifteen thousand fans — he, Cam and Denny would find the pocket, would absolutely begin to soar together as though one brain controlled them instead of three, improvising here and there, changing the song's usual direction, immersing themselves in the music so deeply that the conscious world would disappear for a few minutes. Cam always called it an "eargasm," which Adrian thought was the closest thing to describing a sensation that every good musician feels and strives to attain.

Right now though, in the hospital bed, Adrian felt as though he'd never attain anything ever again. His body hurt right through the painkillers. Every time he moved even a little, wave upon wave of soreness ravaged him. Funny, he thought, as the pills really began to dull his senses, how little control he had over his life. Adrian Lee — of all the people living in the entire city — was chosen for a bout of misfortune, randomly selected to endure pain and suffering for no particular reason. Neither his wealth nor his prominent place in society had any effect whatsoever on the outcome. So here he was: disabled by the very people he thought should be protecting him. Now the drugs were taking hold, true downers, altering his perceptions enough to make him feel even sorrier for himself.

Lack of control. That's what was really eating away at him; the memory of the incident was repeated every time he moved slightly and pain stabbed some part of his beaten body. He hadn't been able to control the situation; he'd been defenseless, succumbed to his protagonist without even a struggle. Now there was frustration — and plenty of anger — building in him, trapped inside like a growing lump of bile.

***

Jennifer Lee wheeled her big BMW 735 into the driveway, behind the black Porsche with the dented right front fender, a neat pair of austere Teutonic automotive muscle contrasted by the classic British elegance of Adrian's navy-colored Jaguar XJS, which squatted aggressively beside them. She turned off the engine and removed the keys, glancing across the seat to her husband, who was staring intently at the Porsche.

"That's one thing I can be thankful for," he said, grimacing as he reached for the door. "At least the damage to the car is minimal — "

" — Do you need some help walking in?" Jennifer interrupted, changing the subject.

"Nope. I can manage." He edged out of the passenger seat slowly, bracing his cracked ribs with the cast on his arm, and pushing with his free hand, the same way elderly people get out of cars. He stood up straight, sucking in fresh air and gazing at the clear morning sky. While the breeze tossed his long hair about, he imagined what he must look like to any passersby or neighbors. Swollen black eyes, lumpy cheeks, bandages on his forehead and chin.

"Excuse me — Mr. Lee?" A raised voice from across the street.

Jennifer was almost at the door. She swung around immediately. It took Adrian a few seconds to rotate creakily so that he could put a face to the voice.

"What do you want?" he asked, tripping over his swollen tongue.

"I'm from the *Sun*," replied a dark, curly-haired man in his forties who sported a handlebar moustache and a loud sport coat that clashed with his blue jeans.

"No, sorry, not interested," said Adrian, nodding his head.

"Wait a minute," asserted the visitor, who was now at the edge of their driveway. "I've been waiting here since five o'clock this morning. We want to do a story about your side of things. You know, police brutality and all that. How about a minute of your time?"

Jennifer ran to Adrian's side. "You heard what he said," she yelled. "He's not interested — so piss off and leave us alone!"

At that moment Adrian noticed him. Another newspaper snoop. He was leaning over the roof of a car, about a hundred feet down the street, and he was wielding a camera with a telephoto lens. Adrian could just make out the sound of the motor drive automatically clicking pictures one after another. "Jenny, let's just get in the house," he said.

She walked with him up the stairs and unlocked the door. Even knowing he was being photographed couldn't speed up Adrian's body. Every step was painful, a grim reminder of what he'd been through — and who had done it to him. He stumbled along the hall as Jennifer slammed the door at the smiling newsman, who remained on the sidewalk by their driveway, notebook in hand.

Adrian eased himself onto the sofa in the living room. It was irritating the way he hurt more now, especially around his eyes and mouth and on his tongue; the more it bothered him, the more he relived Friday's nightmare — every confused detail of it, from being dragged out of the car to repeatedly being slapped and punched and kicked.

Jennifer strode from the kitchen into the room holding a glass of water and his medicine. "Here, time for your pills," she said. "You take them while I close all the drapes. The plants won't like it but at least we'll get privacy from those assholes out there."

"I think these doctors are going to make an addict out of me." He gulped loudly three times, having a difficult time getting the capsules down. "I'm starting to believe I can't live without these things. The pain just kind of takes over, and then after I've had them, I can function again."

"You need the stuff now, but give it another couple of days, once everything's healing. Then you'll notice a difference. You're just really sore right now. And I wouldn't worry about becoming an addict; with all the weed you've smoked, acid and MDA you've dropped and coke you've snorted over the years, you should be just about invincible by now."

"Very funny. I'll take recreational drugs any day over this shit. But right now I sure need it," he said, reaching out and running his hand up the side of her jeans to her hip. "My nuts are so bruised I won't be able to make it for a month."

Jennifer smiled and put her hand on his cheek as she stood over him. "Don't worry, I can wait."

He pulled her close to him and sunk his head into the soft flesh of her belly, sighing deeply. "I hate this," he whispered. "Why? Why did this have to happen to me?"

"Oh, Adrian, come on, it's not that bad. You're not a paraplegic or something. Think positively, about how lucky you are to be alive. You'll be your old self soon enough." She gently moved away from him and went over to the windows, yanking the curtains shut.

"You don't understand." He craned his neck to look toward her as he spoke. "It's not just the pain. It's this feeling of helplessness I had. I couldn't do anything; I was useless in the crunch. It's been eating away at me. I'm so pissed off I can't tell you."

Jennifer finished the curtains, flicked on a lamp and then joined him on the couch. "Is that what's really wrong with you? If so, Adrian, then you better realize just how dumb this sounds. Nobody outside of Superman could've done anything in your position. I think you're silly to even worry about such crap."

"You can call it crap. But I feel like half a man."

"I don't believe my ears!" She laughed out loud. "I don't want a macho man. Don't you even realize that by now? I want someone to relate to…someone to be my best friend. Someone to love me. There's no place in this scenario for a dragon slayer — some big man to stand up and fight for me."

He visibly bristled at what she was saying. "I think you missed my point."

"I did?"

"Anyway, let's forget it. How long until Maubach comes over?"

"He said he'd be here by eleven, so you can relax for an hour."

"Maybe he'll tell us how much we can sue that prick of a cop for."

"I doubt it," shrugged Jennifer, growing more than a little impatient with the conversation. "Steve won't be putting dollar-and-cents figures on the situation. He wants to find out exactly what happened so he can tell you where you stand legally."

"Maybe he'll tell me if it's legal to get a gun and shoot the bastard."

"I hope you're trying to be funny, Adrian. Because if you aren't, then you'd better see a psychiatrist instead of a lawyer."

He cracked a smile. "You're taking things more seriously than I am now."

"Maybe so…but then again, you should be the happy one today."

"Why's that?"

"Because seeing the lawyer is going to hurt a lot less than seeing the dentist."

"Maybe I won't shoot the cop after all. I'll shoot you instead." Adrian Lee started to laugh for the first time since the incident.

It was cut short by a ring from the doorbell.

"Who could that be?" moaned Jennifer, turning toward the hall.

"If it's that asshole reporter, tell him to leave or you'll call the police."

She strode over to the front door and glanced out the window for a moment, then unlocked the deadbolt.

"Hello…I'm Rita Barrett."

"I know," said Jennifer coolly, giving her a once-over, noticing the conservative blue jacket and skirt, and the way her dark skin almost shone against a white blouse. "Won't you come in?"

Adrian's eyes narrowed as the two women entered the room.

"I…" Rita hesitated. "…I'm so sorry for what happened."

"Well, you don't have to be sorry," said Adrian. "Christ, you pulled him off me. Probably saved my life."

"I'm sure you wouldn't have been killed."

"I know I would've."

The detective shrugged and let it drop. "Listen, I didn't come here today as a police officer. It's not an official visit."

Jennifer motioned for her to sit down. Rita moved stiffly toward a sofa.

"So why are you here then?" Adrian asked.

"I wanted you to know how badly Detective Bolan feels about this whole incident. You have to understand: Chuck is a good man. He mixed you up with somebody else. He wasn't himself either, because of some trouble we got into recently. It was an accident. He never wanted to hurt you."

"You're joking, aren't you?" Adrian laughed derisively. "You don't really expect me to have even one ounce of sympathy for that bastard, do you?"

Jennifer was squirming in her chair. "Adrian," she admonished, "calm down."

"Calm down! This whole thing is surreal. I get the shit beaten out of me, and she comes here to tell me what a nice guy this asshole is."

"He's a good cop," said Rita. "He's taken bullets in the line of duty. He's worked hard, so hard all these years." She felt tears begin to well up in her eyes, but fought them back. "I just hate to see his whole career go down the toilet because of this, when it was a mistake."

An awkward silence.

Adrian shifted painfully in his seat and leaned over toward the policewoman. "You know what I'd like you to do?"

"What?" asked Rita.

"Fuck off and get out of my house."

Jennifer's head snapped back. "Adrian!" she cried out. "You don't mean that." She turned to Rita, who was grabbing her purse and starting to rise. "He doesn't mean it. Really."

"You bet I do. You or any other cop sets foot in here again, and I'll have you reported. As for your friend, I don't just hope he loses his fuckin' job, I hope he rots in prison, like any other criminal."

Rita turned to Jennifer. "I'm sorry to have troubled you."

Jennifer was dumbfounded, mouth open, unable to find words. She jumped up from her seat to escort the detective out.

"And don't come back!" Adrian yelled behind them.

Chapter Seven

The constant clicking of computer keyboards and ringing of telephones were driving Chuck Bolan up the wall. He'd never spent so much time in Fifty-Two Division's relatively new, windowless building before, especially sitting at a desk doing absolutely nothing. Inside the modern police station harsh fluorescent lights cast an almost surreal keep-you-awake brightness; like a Las Vegas casino, it was impossible to guess the time of day without glancing at a watch. And while it was just as crowded as a casino, the surroundings were far less luxurious. But orders were carved in granite. He was to remain inside the station each day until a preliminary investigation into his behavior had been conducted.

Bolan leaned back in his brown, vinyl-covered swivel chair and put his feet up on the old wooden desk. He stared blankly at the tabletop, which was covered with chips and scratches — most of them etched into the surface long before he inherited the piece of furniture. All of the desks had been moved from the old station but now looked strangely out of place in such a contemporary setting, with its massive expanse of sterile grey concrete. He sighed out loud and put his hands behind his head, cradling it to relieve the tension on his neck — a place where stress usually hit him. Bolan felt like he was trapped under an avalanche without even a pin prick of light to guide him out. Everything had come crashing down on him at once, and he didn't have any solutions to his problems. One minute you're a hero, he thought, and the next you're a bum. Try to do a good job and be fair, even with some of the worst human excrement on the face of the earth, the kind the rest of society couldn't even imagine in their worst nightmare. Twenty-five years of it. And now in one lousy week you're washed up.

He felt a hand on his shoulder, which startled him. Larry Collins, another detective, stood looking down. He was a tall, wiry man with slicked dark brown hair and a Clark Gable moustache, unstylishly thin and carefully trimmed. It was the fifth time that day a policeman had come by to give Bolan encouragement.

After he'd gone, Bolan got up and made his way past endless symmetrical rows of desks and closet-sized offices to the front door, where there were newspaper boxes just outside. He picked through change from his pocket and bought all three morning papers — *the Globe, the Sun* and *the Star* — to find out what else had been written since the weekend. He swore under his breath at the front page of *the Sun,* with its bold headline: "Public Outrage at Brutal Beating of Musician." Even George Bush and the upcoming U.S. Presidential election took a back seat to this local story. He knew the continuing media coverage would make it even tougher on Sandra and their three children. Already, on Saturday afternoon, fourteen-year-old Nancy had come home very upset because other kids at the shopping mall were ganging up on her and making remarks about Bolan — which had probably come secondhand from their parents.

Back at his desk he read all the stories and editorials; they centered on police conduct in general and him specifically. At first he was shocked by the amount of space the incident had been given, but thinking it over he realized why: on weekends, when most reporters and desk editors are off, there's always very little news gathered — outside of the death of the Pope, a plane crash or a new war. Even the Saturday and Sunday editions are filled largely with material that has been prepared during the week. So Monday morning papers are always thin on news. But with a great local story like the police beating up a well-known musician, there was news galore, more than enough to be reworked all weekend, to rouse city politicians out of bed on Saturday for their usual fatuous comments, to repeatedly call Chief McMichael at his home and receive a "No comment" and to even quote university sociologists and other equally knowledgeable "experts" about the growing trends toward violence in modern urban society. Black-activist groups reveled in the story because — in one vicious stroke — the police had given credibility to their charges of harassment and brutality by law enforcers. When somebody who's not only white but famous gets roughed up, everyone takes notice. Yes, Bolan had really made the news that fateful Friday afternoon, and there were probably more than a few reporters who cursed him because they'd been called in on a sunny weekend to pursue the story even further.

The situation was grim — and he felt even grimmer. The night before he'd polished off three-quarters of a bottle of rye whiskey himself, after the kids had finally come home and gone to bed. Even though Sandra had a few herself, she'd been nagging at him incessantly to stop drinking, or at least slow down. Thinking about her brought a profound sense of guilt — the way they seemed to be drifting apart, not making love for three months, him out alone with the guys most nights. Funny, he thought, but a crisis like this should unite the family. Maybe he'd seen too many old movies.

He was still holding the newspaper up in front of him but not taking in any of the words. Something else besides guilt was hurting him too — his head — aching like a truck had run over it. He slid one of the drawers open and rummaged around for the little brown bottle of Aspirin, popping a couple just as

Rita Barrett walked up smiling, a wedge of partially chewed orange visible in her mouth.

"Here, want some?" she asked, offering half of it.

"Nah…I don't feel like anything."

"It's good for you. Vitamin C."

"No thanks, I said."

"You'll never guess what?" Her eyes twinkled and a broad grin spread across her face.

Bolan looked at her unsmiling. "What? I've been charged with murder now."

"No, no, grumpy. I haven't heard anything about that. But I just got word from the front desk that somebody in Thirty-Eight Division stopped a car making an illegal left turn. Seems they had stolen plates on a black Porsche 911. American driver's license too. They were taken into custody — and they're being delivered to us right now."

"So, what do you expect me to do — beat the shit out of them when they get here?"

Rita's smile was fading. "No," she said, "I just thought you might want to see them, that's all."

"Well, yeah…I might as well have a look. Lemme know when they're here."

"Sure, Chuck."

"Rita."

"Yes."

"Sorry. I didn't mean to get on you like that."

"No problem, man. I understand."

"I just feel so…so fucked over."

His partner nodded. "I know what you must be going through," she said.

"If only there was some way I could explain what happened so that musician would drop the charges." Bolan tapped his fingers lightly on the desk.

"Don't even think such a thing. The farther you are from him, the better off you're going to be. You're already in deep shit. So don't mess around. There's probably no easy way out, even though I wish there was." Rita's eyes were trained on him, gauging his reaction.

For a while after she left, Bolan just sat there staring vacantly into space. The throbbing in his head was beginning to subside. He pondered some immediate problems: how much money there was in the savings account and whether it would be enough to pay for the lawyer. He pushed the newspapers away and took out a scratchpad, scribbling numbers on a sheet. Then he leaned back for a moment, sighing and scratching the crown of his head where the hair had been carefully combed and hair-sprayed over a balding spot. When it came to money, his options were limited: slap a second mortgage on their house or borrow against his pension. Sandra's parents were retired, her father on a meagre fixed income after spending thirty years working in a dairy; his mother had nothing to spare either, especially after his father died a few years ago. Her old-age security was entirely eaten up just making ends meet.

Bolan continued his number-crunching, estimating what they would need to live on for four months and how much would be left over for the lawyer. He was lighting a Marlboro, wondering if he'd have to give those up, when the telephone rang. He grabbed the receiver quickly, as he always did. "Detective Bolan, Firearms Office."

"Time to see your special visitors," said Rita on the other end. "Come back here and find out who bent your nose."

"I'll be right there."

***

Although the room was large, it was claustrophobic because there were no windows and no break in the monotonous grey walls and ceiling. Just two desks and chairs and a coat hanger in the corner, and at least ten bodies huddling in close quarters talking in controlled, emotionless voices. Bolan had been in here many times for "shakedowns," when the suspect sat in front of the desk answering a barrage of questions with repeats thrown in every few minutes, designed to trip up someone who wasn't telling the truth. Sometimes the detectives would drag other chairs in from next door and sit in a circle around their prey, listening carefully to each word, hunting for holes in the story, asking questions over and over in calm voices, like an incessant broken record. Other times, like right now, they preferred to stand, looking down on the people they were grilling.

Bolan opened the door. He stood there sheepishly for a moment, shuffling his feet. The suspects were obscured from his view by all the officers hovering over them. As he paused there listening to the questions being fired at them like a machine gun, Bolan almost felt something in common with the man and woman who'd run him over. Perhaps it was because his turn was yet to come, when he'd have to stand before the cold face of authority; until now he'd never thought about what it must be like to be on the other side, to come into this room after breaking the law—or at least, suspected of breaking it.

Dreading this moment, Bolan moved toward the group and approached the desk. He couldn't believe his eyes. "Oh, shit," he muttered to himself.

The man was blondish and tall–an inch or two over six feet. He bore no resemblance to the musician. None whatsover. Suddenly he looked up, apprehensive, his eyes glued to the bandage that still covered Bolan's nose.

About twenty feet away, at another desk, was the girlfriend, who was answering questions put to her by a small policewoman with a steely gaze. Bolan stepped over for a closer look. She was probably in her late teens and had straight dark hair that hung lifelessly around her shoulders, almost wig-like. Even she didn't look anything like the musician's wife, who was fair and older.

The recognition of his error tore at Bolan now, making him feel even worse, like someone on the other side–a criminal.

"What'd you see, a ghost?" It was Rita speaking in a low voice as she walked up to him. He hadn't even noticed her approaching.

"Just a little shocked, that's all," said Bolan with a sigh.

"What amateurs," she whispered to him. "Already they've confessed to nearly everything. These two were in on the weapons with the others…and they all worked through somebody big — but neither of them will say who. Dumb punks."

"Dumb enough to suck us in good at the farm."

"Luck of the draw, I guess. Too bad it ended this way though. When I look at them, I can only think of poor Angela."

"Yeah, what a shitty mess this has all turned into. How dumb I was trying to get even with these assholes. God, I feel like a dope."

"Everybody makes mistakes, Chuck."

"Maybe so, but this is a big one I wish I'd never made."

Rita squeezed his arm gently. "I'm so sorry for you."

Bolan turned to her, shrugging and trying to smile. "When you first started, I figured you could learn a lot from me. Christ, look at me now."

"Don't be silly. You were a very good teacher…and still will be when all this trouble is over with."

He motioned toward the door. "I'm heading back to my desk. Wanna grab a coffee?"

Rita's eyes darted down to her wristwatch and back up again. "No, sorry, I can't," she said. "I'm teamed up with Gary Moses this week, and he's supposed to be here about now."

"You guys working on the Richardson thing?"

"Yes, same as you and I were. For all we know, our friends from the farm were probably bringing in his guns. Still no new leads either. Probably won't be. Nothing to go on. This man is made of Teflon, for sure. Car dealerships here and in the States. Probably chop shops for stolen cars. Maybe launders money after running guns. Biggest cross-border firearms smuggler. But Mister Solid Citizen, friend of politicians, all-round sleaze."

"Tough work, isn't it?"

"You said it would be a miracle to crack it…even in a year."

"Who knows, maybe you'll luck into a good lead," said Bolan, feeling left out. He desperately wanted to be part of the action, not sitting at his desk reading the papers.

As they both stepped out into the hall, a monotone male voice on the paging system echoed throughout the building. "Detective Bolan to the main boardroom. Detective Bolan."

"What now?" asked Rita.

"They probably want to give me shit for leaving my desk." Bolan grinned feebly and started off for the front offices.

He tapped on the boardroom door and then opened it a crack.

"Come in," said Chief McMichael, who sat alone at the end of the long oak table. "And close the door behind you."

Bolan pulled up a chair about halfway down the table, putting considerable distance between himself and his superior. He noticed that McMichael's pink face seemed somewhat redder today. The room reeked of his Georgio cologne.

"I was down here on another matter," the chief began and then paused to clear his throat. "So I thought I'd save you the trouble of coming up to headquarters."

"What for?" asked Bolan.

McMichael's small eyes looked directly at him. "What do you think? Special Investigations Unit has finished its work. I got the report last night. You've really done it this time. Like the guy who discovers his hair is on fire and uses a hammer to put it out. This was a no-brainer. Not only that, but now the media and politicians are all over us, trying to dig up dirt. They know about the farm and what went on there. The entire force looks really bad–thanks to you. Anyway, our investigation into the beating points all fingers at you. It's cut and dry. You assaulted a citizen without any provocation. So I have no choice. You're outta here, suspended without pay until further notice. And you better pray for a not-guilty verdict in the court case, because that's the only way you'll ever come back. Otherwise, you're finished. You'll never be a police officer again."

Chapter Eight

It was a street of small postwar houses and large shady maple trees. Behind one home, in the backyard, stood a dingy white clapboard garage just crying out for a new paint job. Near the peak of its sagging roof was a little window, letting light flow into a room that could be reached by stairs at one end. She was in there, curled up on her side with just her underpants on, like she was sleeping. Her body was stiff though, brittle-looking and white, except on her neck, where there were circles of blue and black. Horrible bruises. She was dead. Anyone in there would feel her death immediately, would sense it in the air without even looking, even if the acrid smell didn't get to them first. Her doll's face appeared as though it had been frozen in time, the round blue eyes wide open, a startled expression, the last look she ever gave, and to somebody unspeakably vile. It was summer, yet the sound of skate blades scratching ice could be heard clearly. There were other sounds too: children's voices as they played and then adults calling out, "Kirsten. Kirsten. Kirsten, are you there?"

Adrian still remembered every exact detail of this dream, even though it had happened six years before. He'd awakened sweating and crying at the same time, shaking all over. For about an hour Jennifer tried to calm him. The next two nights the same vivid dream haunted him, made him dread going to sleep. And he knew what it was about: on the way home from school a girl had disappeared from her street in the city's west end. She was in grade two. The police organized a huge search party with hundreds of volunteers, scouring the district one evening. A week after his recurring dream the body was discovered–two houses away from Kirsten's home–in a room above a garage. On the other side of the backyard fence was a park where boards went up each winter and the ground was flooded for a hockey rink. Adrian and Jennifer drove out to see the place, to find out if it matched the one in his dream. It did. Even though he'd heard that law-enforcement agencies often use psychics in their murder investigations, Adrian never went to the police about his premonition, fearful that he might be wrongly implicated in the crime or that the publicity might be harmful to his career or the band. To this day he still felt a sense of guilt because he'd done nothing.

Now here he was thinking about the missing-girl dream again, comparing it to the new one that was troubling him, trying to figure out what the yellow light, perspiring bodies and screaming baby symbolized–if anything. Why had these images been startling him out of his sleep a couple of nights a week for almost three months?

Outside it was a clear day with barely a cloud overhead, but the sun's brightness brought precious little warmth. There wasn't any snow yet even though the temperature had remained at ice-making levels day and night for the past week-and-a-half. He was glad to be ensconced in the warmth of his Jaguar, the twelve-cylinder engine purring through traffic. Everyone on the sidewalks was bundled in heavy overcoats and scarves to protect themselves from the wind's icy stab, which seemed capable of stripping paint. From downtown heading north, it would take about forty-five minutes to reach the offices of Tangent, and Adrian wanted to be on time for this particular business meeting. He'd been out shopping; picking up something new to wear always made him feel better about himself. This season cashmere was his inclination: the two Armani sport coats he'd bought were made of it. So was the oversized black Chesterfield coat with a velvet collar, by some Japanese designer whose name he'd already forgotten. Although it was only the last day of November, the stores were already made up for Christmas and some were even holding Boxing Month sales.

At a stoplight, he glanced around absentmindedly at various store windows for a few seconds before the green signal flashed and he made his left turn through the busy intersection. Suddenly he gasped in disbelief, wheeling the car to the right and into the first parking space he could find. Buttoning up his overcoat as he ran, Adrian rushed back to the intersection.

It couldn't be, could it? In the window of a travel agency was a poster. He almost shook with excitement. Everything was the same: the water, beach, hillside — even the birds. The question was, had he seen this poster before subconsciously, and that's how it came to be in his dream?

***

"Guess where we're going?"

"What do you mean?" Jennifer's voice came booming out of the Motorola speaker box on the floor of Adrian's car.

"I've booked us a trip over Christmas," he said, his head tilted slightly upward toward the microphone attached to the sun visor.

"Where to?"

"Cuba."

"Cuba? That is a surprise."

"Well, we're not going to be out in the middle of some pineapple patch, surrounded by peasants who want to overthrow Castro. Actually, I've booked us into this new resort they just finished restoring. It's supposed to be like the Great Gatsby or something."

"Sounds awesome — but why now? Usually we plan these things together."

Adrian hesitated for an instant. "It might do me good to get away after the…uh… incident. And you've been putting in more hours with volunteer work than you would if you had a paid job. Both of us need to reconnect. You're not bugged, are you?"

"Not at all. I think your impulsive behavior is really sweet." She laughed. "And know what else?"

"What?"

"I love you."

"I love you too," said Adrian in a low voice.

The trip actually was a bright spot on the horizon. During the past few weeks he'd experienced monumental change–all of it negative and with an impact that limited everything he used to take for granted: writing songs, playing his instrument and, most of all, his relationship with Jennifer. They hadn't made love since the incident, in spite of her repeated invitations and gentle prodding. She'd even suggested that he see a therapist, which infuriated Adrian. He didn't need any so-called experts to straighten out his life–at least not yet. Time would be the healer, not some meddling psychologist. But one thing was certain: his world was upside down, and he couldn't control it the same way he'd always done. There were nagging doubts inside him. For someone so used to orderliness, discipline and getting his own way, that was the ultimate punishment.

As he drove, a certain sense of apprehension was mounting. While his body had healed nicely and was getting back in shape — he'd worked out with weights, had a karate lesson with his trainer and practiced on his drums, all before noon today — the writer's block hadn't gotten any better. The more he dwelled on a lack of lyrics that stubbornly refused to percolate in his brain, the fewer ideas he got. Everything he attempted to write was unoriginal and lacking in creativity, certainly nowhere near the standards he always set for himself. That, of course, was the root of the problem — and why a meeting had been scheduled with Denny and Cam at their manager's office to go over the status of the new recording and tour. Adrian wasn't looking forward to seeing Reg Howarth at all, especially after putting him through the tangles of renegotiating dates in the studio and on the road — not once but twice already. With the recording postponed for at least another couple of months, the tour would be backed up even more. Instead of going out on the road in May–the beginning of the peak season–Tangent would be lucky to be in gear by July. There was a crew of twenty-eight to worry about, plus seven transport trucks and two buses to book, not to mention staging equipment, giant video screens, and computerized lighting. Reg had probably been going through hell.

Although technically he was an employee of the band, Reg was as much a part of Tangent as any of the three musicians. In the early seventies–after catching the band in a hard rock beer joint called the Gasworks on the main downtown strip–he'd approached them, offering his services and a chance to rise up out of the six-night-a-week grind in the bars. Adrian smiled to himself, thinking about Reg and how the fates had steered him to the band. He'd seen Reg many times when he was about twelve years old, long before Tangent. It was on a local television station, which carried repeats of wrestling matches every Saturday morning. Reg was known as Howlin' Howarth in those days because of the way he screamed like a rabid dog as he threw equally bizarre opponents onto the mat — and sometimes right out of the ring. Before and after matches, as well as during ringside TV interviews, he managed–in an earsplitting style–to live up to his "professional" name. All these years later, especially during Reg's heated telephone conversations with promoters or record-company personnel, Adrian was reminded of Howlin' Howarth. But what a tiger to have as a manager, someone so aggressive and protective of the band's interests.

The thing was, for all intents and purposes, Reg still looked and acted like a wrestler. He carried a considerable girth, about two hundred and fifty pounds spread around a frame that just nudged six feet. His stringy, reddish blonde hair was unstylishly long and combed straight down over his ears to near his shoulders. At least, that's what he did with the hair still remaining. Much of his dome was now shiny smooth so it was more of an overgrown friar's fringe than a true hairstyle, which hung about his collar inelegantly. Then there were the clothes: unfashionable three-piece suits. Reg desperately wanted to maintain the white-collar look of a respectable businessman, something befitting the manager of a relatively large music corporation — which Tangent was. A simple street-smart guy, he craved respect more than anything else and believed he dressed like a spiffy corporate executive, wanting the world to view him as cultured and savvy.

There was a distinct ache in Adrian's right elbow as he turned the steering wheel — probably from overdoing his workout earlier. Even a month after the cast had been removed, his flexibility and speed hadn't returned fully, which was pointedly obvious each time he sat behind the gleaming set of burgundy Gretsch drums and polished brass cymbals in his basement studio, going over specific rudiments and exercises that involved all four limbs working independently of each other. Yet the ache wasn't troubling him as much as thought of the meeting.

During the past couple of weeks Cam and Denny had been calling every other day, anxiously inquiring about Adrian's progress on the lyrics for the new songs. Although each of them professed to not wanting to put more pressure on Adrian, that was exactly what happened. He felt like he was letting them down, which only added to his worries and resulted in a complete dearth of ideas. No matter how often he went through his writer's notebook studying years of scribbles and inspiration, absolutely nothing clicked, and he'd be staring at blank paper and listening to Cam and Denny's rhythm track on tape for five or six hours. Only two songs were finished, and those had been in the can since early September — before the beating. Fifteen more of Cam and Denny's melodies were on a cassette tape in his library, awaiting words that would lift the songs out of a one-dimensional experience and paint vivid pictures in listeners' imaginations each time they played the new Tangent recording.

Traffic had thinned out considerably and he would be at the office in a couple of minutes. New housing developments lined each side of the street; up ahead a giant shopping mall had opened the previous year. Past the mall Adrian turned into a parking lot in front of a modern, grey, six-storey building that was unassuming to the point of being downright boring looking. An icy blast greeted him as he opened the Jaguar's door. Flat expanses of undeveloped, treeless land nearby allowed the wind to rip through the area. He turned up his collar and dashed between cars for the entrance, briefly noting that Cam's Range Rover and Denny's Lexus were in the lot already — because he was late for the meeting.

Stepping out of the elevator onto the fourth floor he could hear Reg's booming voice down the hall — even though the door was closed. As he passed by, Adrian thought about the tenant next to Tangent's offices, a company that distributed bottled spring water, and how they must loathe the sound of that voice by now.

"Hey, here's the man of the hour," announced Reg as Adrian walked into the reception area.

"Nice day, eh?" he muttered, unbuttoning his overcoat and glancing over where Cam and Denny were sitting on the sofa. He wiped his running nose.

Reg smiled. "Cold enough to freeze the nuts off a bridge out there, eh?"

"As usual," said Adrian, "your metaphors leave us speechless and enthralled."

"Damn right. Maybe I should be writing some of those lyrics instead of you."

"Good idea," chimed in Cam. "At least then we could finally record."

Adrian grimaced at their sarcasm, realizing they were already setting the tone for the meeting even before he'd gotten his coat off.

"Let's adjourn to my office," said Reg as he straightened his tie, a loud yellow number with burgundy diamonds on it, which didn't work with his brown herringbone suit and vest. He turned to their receptionist, a young woman with thick eyeglasses and short-cropped dark hair, who was still puzzling over the instructions included with her brand-new personal computer. "Julie, bring us a pot of coffee and the usual fruit juices for Adrian. We're going to be in there a while — and I don't want to be disturbed."

Inside Reg's spacious office they all plunked themselves into armchairs that were in a semi-circle in front of the imposing mahogany desk.

"How are Annie and the kids?" asked Adrian, looking over at Cam.

"Everyone's just rad," replied the other man with a grin.

Cam was the most easygoing and least intense member of the band. It showed too, in the extra pounds packed onto his rolly-polly, just-turned-forty body. A month before every tour, he would faithfully diet and take up some light jogging to get himself in shape. After that he'd let the frantic pace on the road keep unwanted weight at bay. His oval face was relatively unlined and retained a kind of boyish good-looking charm that was enhanced by the stylish blonde hair cropped short on the sides and long down the back. Of course, the hair was lightened by a stylist and augmented with a weave to cover the balding spots. Cam was quite sensitive about this. You could kid him about his ballooning weight or his blue-tinted contact lenses or almost anything — but never about his hair. Otherwise he was the picture of contentment and congeniality, as agreeable as a character off Sesame Street. On him, even four gold rings pierced through his right ear look innocuous, almost bland.

"That drive must be getting to you by now," said Adrian as Julie brought in the coffee and juice, carefully placing the tray on the edge of Reg's desk. He was referring to the country home that Cam had had built and moved into just after their last tour ended.

"It's no big deal," answered the guitarist. "What's forty-five minutes commuting when you don't have to travel in rush hour? I never want to move back to the city. In fact, I don't know how you guys stand it anymore."

Denny Yorke laughed derisively. "Yeah, tell me that when there's a huge snowstorm, or when Annie's sick of driving fifteen miles for groceries, or when the kids revolt against riding a school bus back and forth every day."

It appeared that Denny's mood was as black as the clothes he wore all the time. Right now he looked agitated, as though he hadn't slept well for a few nights. His hair was the color of ink, greasy and unkempt, swept back into a messy ponytail halfway down his back. Usually there were dark circles under his equally dark eyes, but today the bags seemed to be taking over his cheeks too. No wonder his glasses had colored lenses. This afternoon he seemed extra twitchy too. Adrian knew that Denny — a driven person like himself — was upset about the delays with their recording session and tour.

"Let's get things going here," said Reg after they'd all poured their coffee and Adrian was sipping from a bottle of papaya juice. "You guys know that I've been busier than a one-legged man in an arse-kickin' contest. Arranging, rearranging, re-rearranging and just generally fuckin' with schedules. Some of the promoters are getting nosy too, wondering what's up, why we're on and then we're off — and if our drummer is finally all right after his run-in with the cop. I just bullshit them, tell them we're juggling dates around the world to make a better plan. But it won't wash much longer."

"Why don't you just put out the word that we're all tired and want to be home with our families for a while?" Cam asked.

"Oh, sure. And then what the fuck is the record company gonna think when word gets around? They'd be hotter than the left cheek of Satan's ass. I don't have to remind you guys that the contract we signed with them calls for an album this year — and a tour to plug it."

Adrian moved about anxiously in his chair. "Okay," he said, "it's my fault. I take full responsibility for it."

"We're not here to point a finger at you," interjected Denny. "We just have to get it out in the open and come up with a solution, that's all. Let's face it — we're not getting any younger…and who knows how long we're going to fill seats. I'll tell you, I'm getting worried."

"Let's not be melodramatic about this," said Adrian.

Denny pointed a finger at him. "Fuck you. I'm not being melodramatic at all. This is serious. We're talking about our future here. I for one don't want to see the bubble burst after all these years. We've got to get our act together — and soon."

Reg nodded in agreement. "Denny's right. You let me know when you think the songs will be finished — a realistic guess — and I'll get on the horn and arrange everything for us."

"I don't know when they'll be finished."

"Whaddya mean? Look, pick a date. Even February, for Christ's sake. I can work with that."

Adrian bristled. "You don't get it, do you? Writing lyrics isn't like shitting. When you have trouble, you can't just pop a pill and everything begins to come out again. Ever since that cop almost killed me there have been problems."

"Do you feel all right," asked Cam, looking genuinely concerned.

"Yeah, pretty much. I've still got really sore ribs but at my age they'll take a long time to heal. My playing's coming along though."

"Then what the fuck is the problem?" demanded Reg, his voice growing louder and face getting redder.

"I have a mental block, a writer's cramp. I'm not the first and I won't be the last person to get one either. Certainly other bands have taken time out. Look at Def Leppard. It takes them four years to put out new albums."

"That's a different story. Their drummer lost his arm in a car accident and had to learn to play all over again. Somehow I don't think writer's block has the same ring to it."

Cam came to the rescue. "Lay off, Reg. You're not helping things."

Their manager looked exasperated. "Why don't you try something different? Maybe write some straight-ahead rock stuff, ya know, like Van Halen."

"Okay, we'll do something like Van Halen," scoffed Adrian. "That's their thing, and they do it well. But I can't write lyrics about high school high jinks."

Denny laughed, loosening up a little. "What about me? You think I could sing stuff like that? I couldn't get away with it when I was twenty-five, let alone now."

"You're not getting any younger — any of you," said Reg. "So let's be realistic, guys. Tangent peaked in eighty-two; that's when you were the hippest of hip. We sold the most records then. Packed them in every arena. Doubled our attendance figures. Six years later those days are gone. Not that we're starving or anything. But now there's a whole new sound. I'm worried that if you don't put out something and tour with it, then you're gonna drop faster than a whore's pants on payday."

"Bullshit," broke in Adrian, shaking his head. "So we were trendy for a time. Big deal. We were popular before that — and we've been consistent ever since. Tangent has never been a mainstream band. And it's not the mainstream that leads the way in any art form — film, painting, photography, literature. We were a harbinger — and we're still trying to be."

Reg perked up. "This is good stuff you're talkin' about. Maybe you could work it into a song."

His ingenuous remark caught Adrian off guard for an instant; the other two band members were both smirking.

"I'm not kidding. And maybe you could do a song about this writer's block thing. Or how about police brutality, what it feels like to have the shit kicked out of you?"

"Reg, give it a rest," said Adrian. "I know you wouldn't care if I wrote something that sounded like the Pet Shop Boys — as long as you had a song."

Denny was fidgeting with a pen. "Where does that leave us now?" he asked. "We've got to have some kind of plan."

Adrian nodded, worn down and ready to acquiesce. "I know. January looks good. I might be going down south, and the change of scene should help. Get a fresh start. If possible, the last songs could be done by the first or second week of February."

"That's four months behind schedule," noted Reg. "We could always condense the rehearsal time a bit. Speed up recording. Hell, maybe don't go to Switzerland for this one. Stay in town or go to Quebec or New York. We could lean on everybody. Squeeze out some time here and there. Have those assholes turn the video around in a couple of weeks. Christ, we pay enough. They'd give us special treatment. Then maybe we could still be touring by the end of June or early July — and even start it all in Brussels as planned."

Cam mulled it over. "Sounds good. The only thing I'd be careful of is cutting down our recording time. I don't mind rushing the mastering, the video, the cover art and all that stuff but the initial recording is the heart of the project. There's no use putting out something that's not up to par just so we can get on the road in a hurry."

"I agree," added Denny. "Once the lyrics are fine-tuned, I still want to make the best record we've ever done."

Once the lyrics are fine-tuned. The thought sent shivers through Adrian. But he'd committed himself now. Reg would proceed to book the entire tour. Usually the pressure of a deadline was like wind sweeping over a fire, stirring it up and bringing new turbulent life. The result was he always got the job done, a prodigious outpouring at the last minute. But that was then, and this was now. Weeks and weeks of twelve-hour days without producing even a decent chorus had left him despondent and beaten. His recurring nightmare was waking him twice a week. Jennifer wanted him to get professional help; he couldn't make love. In fact, his brain was so bereft of ideas he couldn't even conjure up a decent enough fantasy to get himself off. Was he on a gradual descent toward a breakdown — all because of that cop beating him?

For the next two hours he tried to get his mind off the songs and pay attention to Reg, who was going over some contracts they would be signing at the lawyer's office the following week, as well as making arrangements for a meeting with their finance director and accounting firm to review the audit and year-end statements. And of course there was the usual day-to-day business that Reg insisted on taking them through, like salary increases for the office staff, which royalty cheques had come in and for how much, what equipment was going to cost for rentals on the next tour and so on. As usual, their fan mail had been sorted into three piles, ready for each of them to take home, glance at and dictate short snappy replies that would be typed onto band postcards.

Finally their manager got the hint and wound things down when he glanced over at Cam, who by now had a severe case of the nods, his head rolling forward and back as he kept jerking himself awake. The others wanted to go out for a quick beer in a nearby restaurant but Adrian begged off.

It was getting dark as he left the office building and felt the raw nip of this wintery evening. Even with his coat bundled up around him, the icy wind lashed out and worked its way inside. On the road, rush hour traffic was getting irksome, and it seemed that of the million red tail lights glowing ahead, all were attached to cars with drivers as impatient as he was. What nerve, it occurred to him, to feel so diminished, so troubled and beaten, when people like Reg have bounced back from overwhelming distress — like losing his wife to cancer and daughter in a boating accident — and carried on without even flinching. Or Cam's struggle in the mid-eighties to kick a deadly habit of hitting speedballs — a potent mix of heroin and cocaine. So how did his mishap with the police detective and ensuing writer's block measure up on a severity scale? Like a pinprick on an elephant's ass, as Reg would've put it. Adrian felt a little embarrassed and wondered what Denny, Cam and Reg were saying about him right now.

***

Turning onto his own street, Adrian could see a car parked at the roadside up ahead, partially blocking the entrance to his driveway. As he approached slowly, someone got out of the cream-colored Oldsmobile, a large hulking form silhouetted by a nearby streetlight. Adrian knew who it was immediately. He wheeled his Jaguar around the other vehicle and stopped a few yards away. Buttoning up his overcoat, he stepped out into the cold and wind. The figure approached him.

"I was wondering if we could talk," said Bolan, vapor from his breath steaming into the night air. He was wearing a wool hockey toque pulled down low over his forehead.

"Who the fuck do you think you are!" Adrian spat the words out.

"Look…" the detective began, pausing to sniff a runny nose and fish for words, "…it was an accident. I just want you to know how sorry I am."

Adrian was beginning to lose it. Here was his foe, the bastard who had inflicted such pain and left him messed up emotionally, standing a few feet away begging forgiveness. "What do you want me to do — drop the charges?" His voice was louder.

Bolan seemed taken aback. "No, that isn't why I came. It was to let you know how badly I feel about what happened."

There was no containing the rage inside Adrian at this moment. "You're a fucking pig!" he screamed. The instant he'd finished speaking, Adrian lunged at Bolan, his arms extended with needle fingers aimed at the other man's eyes; at the same time, he swiveled his hips and brought one straight leg up for a groin strike.

But the policeman was ready; years of experience had taught him to never let his guard down. His head darted sideways, easily avoiding the fingers, and his knee smashed Adrian's leg out of the way, stifling the kick and sending him off balance to the frozen ground. Bolan stepped back. "Get a grip," he said firmly. "Obviously we're not going to talk, are we?"

"You bastard!" Adrian thundered into the wind. He pushed himself to his feet as Bolan turned around and began walking back to the Oldsmobile. "You can't do this, coming here and harassing me. I'm gonna see my lawyer. Just wait."

Chapter Nine

That night by ten o'clock it seemed as though they were the last tourists alive. Everyone had cleared out of the dining room quite soon after the meal, obviously feeling the effects of fresh air and sun. Adrian and Jennifer were the only ones there, sitting in the dim light amidst the clattering of clean-up; they left and wandered over to the bar at the opposite end of the building, in another room. Like the dining area, it was a throwback to the thirties, full of art-deco touches like red leather and chrome, with marble floors. From any of the bar stools there was an unobstructed view out to the patio and down the hill to the ocean — although very little could be discerned in the darkness, just heard, because of the pounding of the breakers rolling in. The breeze played with their hair, as they sipped twelve-year-old dark rum — like a fine brandy almost.

Their second full day in Cuba had been uneventful: lying motionless in the December sun on a secluded stretch of beach half a mile from the resort and then eating grilled lobster tails during a buffet lunch. Hard to believe how two days had made such a difference, cleansing Adrian's spirit, even allowing him peaceful nights of sleep — undisturbed by the tormenting dream. He felt good too, completely healed, even the fractures in his right arm and ribs, those stubborn hangovers from the drubbing three months before.

Beside him, Jennifer was smiling, her face almost glowing from the sun, salt and wind, her natural linen dress billowing with each gust. Adrian was reminded of how much he truly loved her. This trip was knitting them together in ways that just wouldn't have happened back home.

"Coming here was such a good idea, Adrian." She echoed his own thoughts. Leaning over and grazing his arm lightly, Jennifer pulled him closer for a quick kiss. "It was the sweetest, most thoughtful thing you could do."

He felt a twinge of guilt, since his impulsive decision to visit Cuba hadn't exactly been altruistic, to say the least. However, he felt vindicated somewhat because Jennifer was so happy now. Almost everything had been perfect so far. Right from the start, in Havana, a car had been waiting for them at the airport — so they didn't have to board an air-conditioned bus with the other tourists. A big old black Mercedes, the limousine was used for diplomatic purposes, but their travel agent had managed to secure a ride to the resort in it — certainly a luxury in a country so short of fuel.

The driver gave them a tour of Old Havana, with its nine hundred historic buildings from the sixteenth and seventeenth centuries. Adrian couldn't get over the rickety American automobiles from the fifties sputtering along congested streets in a surreal scene: classic cars against a cityscape of antiquity. Once they'd left the city, traversing a highway that ran beside the ocean, there were horses, ox carts and bicycles. Factories belched smoke in distant little towns, and miles of plantations and tiny scrubby farms lined the side of the road. Off the highway, at the resort, opulence became the order of the day, and theirs was the finest accommodation — a villa that had once been a guest house on the giant estate.

Just one nagging difficulty. Earlier that day, after returning from the beach, Jennifer had peeled off her bathing suit and pressed up against Adrian, kissing him and gently stroking his damp hair. He nuzzled her neck, inhaling the sun's scent on her skin, took her wrists and raised her arms overhead, and pushed her back onto the bed, his hips grinding into her, kisses penetrating her. But when Jennifer reached down past his muscular abdomen and slid her hand inside his bathing suit, feeling for him, what rested in her palm remained as lifeless as one of the jellyfish on the beach, even as she continued to fondle it.

The recollection stung him even now, twelve hours later. His body stiffened, and he shifted uncomfortably on the bar stool.

Only one other person was around, besides the two waiters in their crisp white shirts and powder-blue vests and pants. Adrian stared at the stranger for an instant and then nodded a greeting. Like most Cubans, the man wasn't very tall and looked to be in his late forties or so, in relatively good shape and with strong Latin features. He got up and came over, saddling himself on the stool beside Jennifer, giving her a rather indiscreet once-over, his dark eyes dropping to her shoulders and then lower, focusing on her breasts, which were outlined relatively clearly through the thin dress she wore without a bra. She swiveled toward him and whispered, "Why do all of the men here talk to my tits?" Then she turned and met the stranger's eyes with her own, a look of disdain quite evident on her finely featured face. That was one of the things Adrian really loved about her: the twenty-four-carat cool, the way she could put people down with just a glance from those steely eyes. Neither of them said anything, assuming that this man didn't speak English.

Finally he took the long, well-chewed Monte Cristo cigar out of his mouth. "Hello," he said in almost perfect English, "I'm Ricardo Sosa, the manager of La Sorpresa." Then he smiled so broadly that even his bushy black moustache seemed to turn up at the sides, as though it were taking orders from his pronounced dimples. They each shook his hand and introduced themselves. Both of them were startled that this curious-looking fellow was actually the person who ran the resort. Adrian couldn't take his eyes off him for a moment, noticing how eclectic he looked, with a droopy navy jersey and baggy pants of the same color, black well-worn running shoes and, most curious of all, a Toronto Blue Jays baseball cap on his head. Then there was his face: twinkling and somewhat bloodshot eyes that smiled right along with his mouth, oily dark skin and black slicked-down hair.

Ricardo Sosa, as they were soon to find out, was a man of many parts. Their conversation at first was stilted, filled with bland statements about how nice it was to be somewhere warm, how lovely all the blossoms looked and smelled, how they were having a super time, how well all of the Cubans had treated them and so on — the usual innocuous chatter of people who've only just met. After a couple more rums the talk began to have some substance, fleshed out with overtones of politics: my country versus your country.

"I know the revolution helped once upon a time," Jennifer told Sosa, "and children don't go hungry anymore and everybody gets medical care...but that seems to have changed. Now it looks like there's not enough food or medicine. And human-rights abuses just go on and on."

The Cuban shrugged, quite obviously aware that two of his employees — the bartenders — were within earshot. "You would have to know what it was like before," he said. "Then you would appreciate what we have now."

"What a pat answer," Jennifer said. "Castro practically stands alone in the world. He's defied the odds. And he's still having dissidents beaten and thrown into jail."

"How do you know this?" asked Sosa. "You have no proof...only the propaganda that's spread in your biased media."

Adrian was amused at the banter between the two of them and how ballsy his wife could be. "You're trying to tell us there are no political prisoners," he remarked. "In a small country with over one hundred prisons. Come on now, we've heard there are five thousand political prisoners. How many do you think there are?"

"I couldn't tell you," answered the Cuban. "But certainly counter-revolutionaries who try to overthrow our government shouldn't be allowed to wreak havoc upon the society."

"Well, people are allowed to speak out in our society," piped up Jennifer. "We haven't fallen apart yet because of it — and 1988's almost over. We have plenty to eat, and we can travel anywhere."

"I can travel anywhere too. In fact, in May I'll be visiting your country, for a conference in Montreal."

"Maybe you can leave," said Adrian, "but most people can't. Your human-rights record in Cuba is dismal."

"Tell me this: why does the United States continue its embargo against us when it makes glaring exceptions with countries like China, whose human-rights records are many times worse than Cuba's?"

"That's just the stupid U.S. foreign policy," replied Jennifer. "Bush is no better than Reagan. And they don't need you. Cuba's nothing. China's another story. I read it's going to be the world's biggest economy in the nineties. But despite the American embargo, there's still no excuse for violating freedom of speech and basic human rights."

Sosa held his hands up in front of him. "Hold on," he said smiling with his cigar clenched between stained teeth. "Enough of politics for now. I have a much better idea: come to my cabana for a drink. I have wonderful scotch that some generous Canadian visitors so kindly gave me. The touristos who have returned for a second time never seem to forget me when they visit their duty-free shop."

Adrian glanced at Jennifer, who gave him an affirmative nod. "Sure," he said, "we're game for a nightcap."

During the walk downhill from the bar, amidst fragrant flowering bushes and stately palm trees silhouetted against the starry night sky, Ricardo Sosa seemed to loosen up a little when he spoke. "I hear from others that you are well known...a music star," he ventured to Adrian.

The musician blanched visibly. "I guess word gets around."

They veered to the right, down another pathway in the opposite direction of the resort's main building. Partially hidden by a thatch of trees were four or five modest white buildings — obviously lodging for the staff. Sosa approached the largest of them. Stepping inside the cabana, in which every light had been kept blazing, he threw his baseball cap on the bed and pulled up a couple of chairs. Adrian noticed the room was filled with Canadian goods, like men's colognes, disposable razors, nail clippers and a host of other odds and ends. There were also a number of Canadian and American magazines strewn about on the dresser, on the extra bed, even on the floor. It appeared the Cuban was a voracious reader, what with Spanish-language books everywhere too — thick hardcover reference texts, like those from university libraries. Add in the clothes tossed haphazardly over furniture and spilling out of the open door to the closet, and at the very least the room was in shambles. Amid all the clutter though was a well-stocked bar: bottles of four different brands of scotch, two kinds of Canadian whiskey, gin, Russian vodka, vermouth, brandy, port and — as would be expected — half a dozen Cuban rums.

"You should go into business for yourself," said Jennifer sarcastically. "This bar definitely rivals the one in the dining room."

"Don't forget," Sosa answered with a grin, "I have to live here. I don't merely want to exist." He poured twelve-year-old Macallan scotch into three tumblers, filling each of them, and passed them to his guests. "I propose a toast, because you are so special."

"Why are we so special?" asked Adrian, taking his glass from the Cuban.

"Because," he went on, "you are the first rock and roll star to visit La Sorpresa."

Jennifer laughed out loud, shaking her head. "Give me a break. Pretty soon you'll find out he's just another complaining Canadian…and not nearly as famous as your bearded leader."

"There's very little chance Fidel would ever stay here." Sosa took a hearty swig from his glass, gulping noisily as he did so. "He has a beautiful summer house."

"Just your basic elitist revolutionary," said Adrian.

"So how did you learn English so well?" asked Jennifer.

"I took my bachelor's degree at Yale."

Her interest was piqued. "What was your major?"

"Anthropology. I'd already begun studies at the Universidad de La Habana — or Havana, as you say — when I was fifteen. Of course, I took English there too. I can still see myself then: very fresh, very young. I don't think I even needed to shave."

"Why Yale?" she queried.

"I don't know. My parents thought it best for me to attend a prestigious American school. So I finished up there…and, of course, left Connecticut to return to my homeland just before my eighteenth birthday."

"Let me guess," said Jennifer. "To help out in the revolution, right?"

"Exactly. When it was over and our country was free, I studied medicine at the Sorbonne, and later psychiatry."

Jennifer's eyes widened. A university dropout, she was a bit of an academic groupie, in awe of those who pressed on. "My God, that means you're fluent in French as well as English and Spanish."

"Oui," he smiled. "And there is a little German and Italian in there as well."

"So you were a practicing psychiatrist?" asked Adrian.

"Oh yes, for many years after I returned. I took some time out for postgraduate courses in anthropology and a little teaching but had my practice until two years ago, when I took this job."

Adrian looked around the small cabana and back at the Cuban, who had taken on extra dimension now. "Why did you stop to run a resort?"

"To be truthful, my own mental health was suffering. After many years my marriage was like an infected wound. Finally I decided to amputate. It's not so bad, since the children are grown up now. But also I had pushed myself for a long time, not just in my practice but in my anthro...an — " he slipped over the word, probably a result of the scotch — "anthropological studies and doing special work for the government. You must realize that my practice had been extremely demanding too. After the social turmoil generated by a revolution, there were many, many people who needed a psychiatrist. I helped to set up four mental health hospitals. There was a shortage of good medical care before and for a few years after the revolution. But Fidel saw to it that this was corrected. For some time we had one of the best medical systems in the world...until recently."

Adrian shifted in his seat and leaned over to place his empty glass on the floor beside him. "Running this resort seems like an odd career change."

"The job was given to me. I had been off work...close to a nervous breakdown. Tourism had been flourishing for about fifteen years since we opened the country to foreigners again. To Fidel, tourism is very important — and so are the people entrusted to deal with the visitors. It is like public relations. And especially today, in these difficult economic times, running a resort is much more important a task than in your country. So I was put in charge of La Sorpresa. It is a good job, not so taxing as my other duties had been, and I enjoy it much. And as you can see, this is the finest, most exclusive resort in the country."

Jennifer glanced about the room. "This is your home?"

"Oh no," replied their host, a broad grin spreading across his face. "Every month I go back to my house in La Habana for four days. And the resort is not open all year. From September until April it's for Canadian tourists. From June to August, top party officials get free vacations here. And I am not around very much."

Sosa got up and poured more drinks and then went on about his background, about growing up in Santa Clara — a city a hundred and sixty miles southeast of Havana — where his father owned sugar plantations and factories that made electrical equipment like fuses. After returning from university in the United States, he spent night after night with young leftist intellectuals and became politicized. They plotted the demise of the regime of President Fulgencio Batista. Sosa and his friends printed up newsletters and organized anti-government — and anti-American — rallies, something that was strictly forbidden.

"You couldn't demonstrate against Batista," he explained. "One time I was picked up by the police in a friend's room at the university in La Habana. There were four of them, big brutal men. They took me to a police station for questioning. Then afterward they marched me outside to the back. One of them drew his pistol. I thought this was the end, I was going to die. Instead, he fired it beside my head. The others did the same thing for twenty minutes. Now I'm deaf in my right ear. They beat me very badly too, kicking me over and over with their boots until I looked like a slab of beef."

Jennifer was visibly moved by what she was hearing, perhaps because she'd recently seen police brutality firsthand. "That's horrible."

"Not really, because there is a happy ending. A group of us went back two weeks later and blew up the police station, killing everyone in it. You see, we really were radicals in those days. After seeing hunger and corruption and American imperialism, we wanted a total change."

"Was it really that bad?" asked Adrian.

"Worse than you could ever imagine, my friend. Starvation and sickness were everywhere. Beggars in all the streets. Women forced into prostitution and unnatural acts…like having sex with donkeys in nightclubs for the amusement of American tourists. Unlimited gambling twenty-four hours a day. The government was in place only to protect the interests of the United States and all its companies here — companies that wouldn't pay a living wage to the Cuban workers and took all of the profits back home."

Jennifer sat wide-eyed. "Your education helped you see what was going on," she said, "and what should be done about it."

"Yes," Sosa answered, "we were transformed into true revolutionaries. After bombing the police station I went back to Santa Clara in hiding. It was then I talked to my parents for days, telling them what Fidel's rebels were doing in the mountains of Sierra Maestre, how change would soon come — and how it would be swift. I persuaded my father to accept it when it happened, to turn his land and factories over, which he did later. Not that he liked it, of course. Now he is dead, bless his soul, but he was a member of the party for many years. Other rich people did the same thing…the right thing."

It all seemed a little unreal: the country, the man and the atmosphere in the room at two in the morning, the mystification probably heightened in direct proportion to the liquor consumed.

"You mention your studies a lot," Jennifer said to the Cuban. "I take it anthropology still interests you."

"Very much," he answered, relighting his worn-out cigar for about the tenth time. His words were becoming slurred and his eyes involuntarily half-closed.

"During my holidays I continue with them...but just for enjoyment. I'm not publishing anything in scholarly journals, if that's what you mean."

"What's your specialization?" prodded Jennifer.

"Oh, primitive religions mainly. I'm fascinated by the sophistication of them...their complicated structures, the belief they instill in people — sometimes even their amazing results. I will tell you something: when you learn even a small amount about them, you stop laughing at the idea of a witch doctor."

Adrian looked at the other man incredulously. "What...you mean you believe in some of this hocus-pocus?"

"That's a very unscientific way to put it," said Sosa, "but I don't believe or disbelieve; I simply examine, attempting to use as much objectivity as is available to me under the circumstances. For instance, one time at a conference in the Philippines I watched people supposedly in a trance walk across burning coals that we'd just roasted a pig on. Afterward I examined their feet. As a medical doctor — and simply as an onlooker — I was astounded; there were no marks on the soles...nothing even resembling a blister...just some ash. I had seen them walking with my own eyes. The fire was easily hot enough for third-degree burns. So who knows how powerful the mind really is? I say that as a psychiatrist. Like most people on earth, you both have probably wondered what the rest of our brain — the ninety percent we don't use — actually does. Well, I think the possibilities are endless...and have been since the early days of human evolution."

"I certainly believe in the power of the mind," said Adrian, "but I'm not sure what I've seen about toothless witch doctors in National Geographic counts for a lot."

"You must look at the broader picture and not simply focus your skepticism on aboriginal tribes. Remember, even in Europe long before the Dark Ages, sorcery was the first practice of medicine, religion and psychiatry — all rolled into one."

"But what's your focus then?" asked Jennifer.

"I'm interested in many things but mainly I concentrate on those in Central and South America, which all have their roots in the Yoruba of Nigeria and spread here with the slave trade. Of course, the most famous is voodoo. It has been done to death in books and movies...shreds of fact mixed with misconceptions, so now it is almost humorous. No one takes it seriously. Perhaps that is why Adrian used the term 'hocus-pocus' earlier."

The musician perked up at the mention of his name, trying to throw off his drunken haze. "Even with my limited knowledge, I know there's a lot of ridiculous superstitions attached to any primitive religion. Don't tell me you believe in them."

"Not all of them. But as I said before, there are many things I cannot explain. Ever since I've been young I've known about Santeria, and after years and years of studying it, I find there are just as many puzzles as when I first started."

"What is Santeria?" Jennifer asked.

"It is a religion here in Cuba," replied Sosa. "I'm probably one of the world's most knowledgeable experts — simply because so few people know about it. Santeria stems from Nigeria just like voodoo in Haiti as well as other primitive religions in Brazil and Jamaica. The idea is the same but the gods are called by different names, and so are the methods and rituals."

"And it's still practiced?" asked Adrian.

"Most definitely. By thousands and thousands of people. In Florida and New York too, wherever there are Cubans in exile. You don't just erase a cult that's been so deeply ingrained for more than three hundred years. Even near the end of the last century there was a move by officials to rid this country of Santeria. You see, there were some priests who were notorious for their child sacrifices. So the clean-up began — a purge really — and after a time it was reported that Santeria, this savage heresy in a Catholic country, had been eradicated. What a joke! In the mid-fifties there was a black woman, a noted scholar named Lydia Cabrera, who discovered that Santeria wasn't gone at all — it had just become more of a secret society. Nothing had changed."

"This is fascinating stuff," said Jennifer, trying her best — and failing — to sound somewhat sober. "So there are still sacrifices and secret rituals today."

"Yes, of course. Santeria is a growing institution, practiced in all the rural and urban areas on this island. Animals can be sacrificed, and many times graves are dug up, with certain bones and the brains removed from newly buried bodies. Just recently I read that police in Miami discovered an altar with animal remains, Santeria symbols and a human skull on top of a goat's severed head. It happens all the time in Florida…and most cases go unreported. Last year there were the Matamoros killings in Mexico, where dozens of bodies were dug up near a Santeria altar."

Sosa stubbed out the few remains of his tortured cigar. "This kind of thing has gone on all over the world and throughout every age. It knows no religion or race. From the most ancient European civilizations to primeval jungle villages, there has always been the Great Darkness, the one who steals souls, whose face shows no reflection in a mirror or water, and who inspires absolute terror. Have you ever wondered why demonology seems to have a single thread woven through cultures that have nothing else in common?"

"Probably because underneath," replied Jennifer, "we all have the same fears and taboos."

"Precisely," said the Cuban. "That's why there are so many common elements in religions around the world too. And Santeria is no exception. In fact, some aspects of Catholicism crop up among the African beliefs. It is a definite hybrid."

"Sacrificing children doesn't sound very religious to me," remarked Adrian.

"Certainly not. The santero, or priest, who practices Santeria has been schooled in the art of white magic, in the purity of the religion. What priest would ever admit to being a practitioner of evil? A good santero can cure sickness, drive out evil spirits and influence the morality of those who follow him."

Adrian smiled ruefully. "What about a bad one?"

"Ah, yes. There is always another side; the side of the Great Darkness. Not so long ago, in a fishing village a few miles from here, a santero was possessed during a ceremony in front of a hundred worshippers. Two children, a young boy and girl, were near the altar, dressed in white robes and faces painted white, ready to witness the spirits rise as the drums beat. Obeying the priest when he summoned them, the two stepped forward. The santero pulled his blade out from his robe, slit their throats and hacked out their hearts, drinking blood that ran out of them. This hideous crime was kept secret for many months."

"Why didn't anyone report it to the police?" Jennifer asked, wide-eyed now.

"Fear, of course. You talk, and perhaps an evil spirit will enter your body and take you slowly. This kind of fear is much stronger than the fear of police and judges. Colombian drug lords use religion to keep the people in line. Mexican drug traffickers do too. All kinds of Santeria good luck charms and mysterious necklaces have been found on drug smugglers. It's like the Godfather with his extended "family" that he takes care of — but only if they obey. And God help those who don't."

"Oh, shit," said Adrian, glancing at his watch, "it's almost four. The sun will be coming up in an hour-and-a-half. We'd better shove off, Ricardo." He signaled to Jennifer and began to get up. "Thanks for the drinks."

"My pleasure." He started to rise but then dropped back into his chair. "Wait a moment," he said, motioning to them, his hand held up in a rather lacklustre fashion, floating unsteadily. "I may have given you a wrong impression about Santeria. It is not just about sacrifices and murder, you know. Before you leave, let me tell you a short story, which was also the reason why I became interested in Santeria."

Jennifer was game. "Sure, what's another few minutes; we're all going to be tired and hungover anyway."

"When I was twelve and growing up in Santa Clara, a woman moved in nearby. She was from La Habana and had come to my town with her parents, who were quite wealthy. In the city she had been promised to a man for marriage, and when they packed up and left, he was terribly angered and upset. This young woman, who was nineteen at the time, began experiencing fainting spells and rages. They got worse. Her eyes would glaze over and her body would quiver. She would snarl like a rabid dog. Once I saw her like this in the street. Other times she would howl in a very strange voice, with a much higher pitch than even a wolf. She went to the best doctors in La Habana. But all medical and neurological tests revealed absolutely nothing. Then back in Santa Clara she started to fall into violent rages, screaming and lashing out — so bad that servants were often called in to restrain her. At other times she would go through periods lasting about ten minutes when she appeared to be in a state of cataleptic shock, not even able to feel a pinprick and with her pulse and respiration dropping far below normal, to dangerously low levels. Then she would recover until the next fit. But they came sooner and sooner. During a rage she would scream out that she was going to die, that she had been visited by a spirit who told her so. Despite their education and social standing, her family believed it was the suitor who had sent some dead soul to haunt the poor woman."

There was a pause while Sosa lit another seven-inch cigar, puffing a number of times and filling the cabana with curling blue smoke.

"What happened after that?" asked Jennifer anxiously.

"Well, the parents called the police in La Habana to check up on the boyfriend who she'd been promised to before. They went to his house but he wasn't there. In a chicken yard out back though they found an altar. There were Santeria herbs, sacred stones, freshly killed chickens and some unidentifiable old human bones. The police said some graves in the area had been disturbed.

"So the parents searched for a santero. They found one in Santa Clara, a bookkeeper in an office, who had been born in a small village. He came with his tools and symbols to prepare a ritual. My father and some of the neighbors were asked to come and be part of the ceremony, to lend support for the tormented woman. Before going, my father had doubts about it. He was a practical businessman, one who did not believe in spirits.

"After he had gone I crawled out my bedroom window and followed. Only one room in their house was lit, so I went and stood outside, near a window. Sometimes I moved to it and looked inside for a moment. There were about thirty people, including the servants, and they all started to chant when the santero told them to. The woman, who was sitting on a chair, began to chant too, but different words, and then her voice grew stronger, and she jumped up and began swaying. From her mouth came the same words over and over, screaming them now, so loud it was earsplitting. And I looked at her face — it was so white, with such deep black eyes. It was the face of death for sure...or so I thought then. For a boy my age it was most frightening. When I looked inside at my father, as he kept repeating the chants, I saw dread in his eyes as well. The woman fell to her knees shaking, tearing at her clothes, her body sweating and trembling as if in convulsions, and she no longer screamed but spoke in her own voice, the one we knew. She stated that three dead souls haunted her and that they would leave. Halfway through her sentence, another voice took over. I can still clearly remember its sound. Like a growl, it filled the room — and it wasn't in Spanish. Possibly it was an African tongue because the words were jumbled and meaningless to me, yet certainly resembled a language of some sort.

"Suddenly she was thrown back, as if someone had struck her, and her head hit the floor very hard. Everyone ran to her then, except the santero, who kept chanting. The woman's eyes opened, and she spoke in her own voice.

"Before I ran back to my home I looked at the santero, watched him picking up some small dark objects off a desk and placing them into a little sack. And then he passed out. Off I went, my heart racing with fear and my mind full of questions.

"My father said nothing of the ritual. The woman's own personality returned, and she recovered completely — but she could not remember anything that happened at the ceremony. I wanted to know more. It was like a thirst in me. Even when I was home for a visit from university a few years later I talked to my father about the ceremony. He would not speak of it. I asked some of our neighbors who had been present that night what was in the little sack. They just shrugged and said nothing."

After a moment Adrian stood up and stretched. "So what was in the sack?" He wanted to know before they left.

"Not now," said Ricardo Sosa wearily, smoke mingled with his words. "Another time."

Chapter Ten

She couldn't have been more than nineteen or twenty years old. With hair obviously dyed coal black to contrast with her absolutely untanned alabaster skin, she looked like a silent-screen star. At the moment she wasn't wearing any clothes, except for a pair of black stilettos that exaggerated her long slender legs even more. Of course the nail polish was Gothic black, as was the lipstick on her tight thin mouth. The music — her choice, the same as it was for every one of the fifty dancers when they were onstage — was a vicious-sounding mix with elements of rap, thrash metal and techno tossed together. But who was listening anyway? About four hundred pairs of eyes followed her every move as she knelt down and slid onto her back, thrusting her legs straight up and apart. One hand toyed with the nipples on her small breasts, stroking them, tugging at them for a few seconds and then slowly moving down between her thighs. All of her pubic hair had been shaved smooth, so there was little if anything left to the imagination when she glided a forefinger back and forth over her protruding sex. Two gold pierced rings dangled from one vaginal lip, gleaming under the soft red-tinged stage lights. Lying on her back she pushed on the floor with the palms of both hands and swept her legs up behind her head, rolling into a rearward somersault, and landed on her feet in a standing position. As the song faded, the dancer approached the brass rail that fenced in the stage, turning around, bending her upper body forward, and did a deep stretch, grasping her ankles and peering out upon the audience, smiling from between her parted legs, fully aware that most of the men seated at tables weren't looking at her face.

A syrupy disc jockey's voice boomed over the fading music. "Gentlemen, let's put our hands together for Brandy! Isn't she something else? Give Brandy a big hand. And remember, she's available for table dancing too — just ten dollars, and she's all yours."

Above the din of half-hearted applause, Chuck Bolan was just sitting down and yelled to a waitress who was wearing a thong and halter top. When she came over to the table, he — and the three men who were already seated — ordered a round of bottled beer.

Another night at the Lancaster. Bolan knew many of the faces by sight: the letter carriers from the post office nearby, the car salesmen from the Chrysler dealership, a few seniors from the old-age home down the street and, of course, some off-duty members from the police station that was here in the west end of the city, a tough working-class junction bordering Lake Ontario. He nodded a greeting to his drinking companions at the table.

"Hey, Chuck," asked Doug Warren, a desk sergeant at the station nearby, "what's forty feet long and smells like pee?"

Bolan shrugged.

"Line dancing in a seniors' home."

Unimpressed, Bolan managed a faint smile.

"So, what's up?" asked Warren, a man whose short-cropped hair, thick neck and broad shoulders made him an obvious standout as a cop. "Anything new today?"

"Not much. Out on my ass until further notice."

"Son of a bitch, eh?" mumbled one of the other men, a young constable with boyish good looks.

"Not just that," continued Bolan, "but I saw the dirtbags who started the mess in the first place." He subconsciously ran the fingers of one hand across his scarred nose before pulling a cigarette out of the pack.

Warren's eyes widened until they looked like a fish's. "Betcha' wanted to give it to them, eh?"

"Nah. That was the last thing I felt like doing. The slime bucket didn't even look like the guy I flattened. So I'm in this shit knee-deep, I can tell."

"It's a tough situation," said Warren, "but it's gonna work out okay, Chuck. You did a great job blowing away the bastard who shot Angela. The whole force is behind you. Tell you what…I'll treat you. That'll take your mind off all this trouble."

Bolan leaned back in the chair, relaxing his sore neck muscles for the first time that day. When the beer came he poured it quickly into a glass and chugged back over half of it in three gulps. With no food at breakfast and lunch, only running on coffee and cigarettes, he felt the alcohol swiftly spread over him. Maybe he'd have a burger later or make a sandwich when he got home.

A stripper walked attentively through the maze of tables toward Bolan. She stood so close to him that he had to spread his legs bullishly. Elsewhere in the enormous room about thirty other women stood patiently by tables waiting for someone new to take the stage and the music to start. This particular dancer was wearing a camisole — and nothing else. She smiled at Bolan and the other three men.

"Hi, I'm Ginger," she said.

"That figures," mumbled Bolan.

"Pardon?"

"Nothing," he replied, wondering why all strippers seemed to have one of three names: Ginger, Brandy or Tiffany.

"So, what do you do?"

"I'm a policeman."

"Wow, that's radical."

"It has its ups and downs."

"Well," she cooed, running one hand down his chest and onto his belt buckle, "I sure do like the ups."

The other three men were grinning. Bolan smiled politely as a Blondie song came on the sound system at an earsplitting volume and the dancer rubbed against him. She ran her fingers through long, ash blonde hair that had been dyed and permed too many times. Her young face was finely featured and quite attractive, big ingenuous eyes and full, pouty lips; but the effect was diminished by bad teeth that looked as though a dentist had never seen to them during her childhood.

As the woman was grinding slowly — certainly not in time to the music that was playing — she pulled the camisole over her head, revealing huge breasts like cantaloupes, firm without the least hint of sagging, so rigid they seemed to defy gravity itself. She bent over, purposefully grazing Bolan's face with them ever so slightly. Like many of the strippers in the Lancaster — and everywhere else, for that matter — she'd had cups of plastic implanted to greatly augment what nature had provided. She actually pushed one giant breast up and sucked on her own nipple for a moment, as the men from Bolan's table and others nearby took in this spectacle intently. Then she leaned back, the strong scent of her perfume overpowering even the smell of cigarette smoke that hung in a thick blue haze. Her right hand slid down between her legs; she used her forefinger and middle finger to tug lightly and then spread herself. Bolan could see the dark razor stubble where she trimmed the upper reaches of her thighs and shaped the remaining hair into a heart. Long fingers with frosted false nails slid back and forth. After a moment of that she swiveled around and crouched, her back to Bolan's chest, her face looking up at him, hands reaching overhead to caress the sides of his head.

He didn't know how to react; he felt like a center-shot, with everybody around him staring. It was weird, a nude woman curled up on him while he was fully clothed in a public place. Maybe there was the slightest tingle within him…but he certainly wasn't turned on. A few years ago he would've been bursting through his pants but not anymore. Nothing seemed to get him hot these days — not Sandra, and definitely not this dancer who was trying so hard to make him hard. Bolan looked at the table dancer, who had turned to face him and was kneeling, a hand on each of his thighs. As the song ended she stood up straight, her crotch barely two inches from his face, and pulled the camisole back down.

"Was it good for you too?" she asked, smiling down at him, hoping that he'd spring for another table dance so she wouldn't have to move around. But really she knew better; men in groups usually didn't go for repeats. It was guys sitting by themselves, often at the back where it was darker and more private, who would sometimes pay a hundred dollars or more to the same woman for one dance after another. The only time the stripper would leave was to do her show onstage, and then she'd come right back to the mark, so he could press more cash into her hands.

"That was very nice, thank you," said Bolan politely, the way a kid talks to a school teacher.

The dancer stepped down off her stool and reached across the table, where Warren had placed a ten-spot. "Thanks," she said, becoming very businesslike all of a sudden and scanning the room for another paying customer. As she raised the stool over her head, she looked down at Bolan again. "You're a cop, eh? Did you hear what happened to the drummer of Tangent?"

"Uh...yeah...I guess so," he stammered, caught off guard, his heart finally racing but for the wrong reason now.

***

It was dreary outside with a driving frozen rain and blasts of frigid wind. The wet-slicked avenue shone under the glare of streetlights and neon storefronts, just the way streets did on the TV show Miami Vice — only here it was heart-stoppingly cold. As he sped along, Bolan's mood was as dark as the moonless night. Earlier that day he and Sandra had arranged a second mortgage on their house to cover his legal fees and lack of a paycheck.

A tiny ray of light penetrated the darkness of his thoughts. The lawyer claimed there was a possibility Bolan might win the case, by focusing on the rocky period he'd been through and the effects of prescription medication on his behavior. Bolan viewed this with a not-so-small dose of police skepticism. As much as he'd been disenchanted with his job frequently — sometimes even loathed it — he desperately wanted to keep it, and not let everything he'd worked for and the years of struggling for promotions to be stricken from his life after one mistake. Sandra and the kids were considerations in this matter too; their lives had been tossed into turmoil as well.

He stopped for a red light and lit up a cigarette, thinking about his sullen behavior in the Lancaster, how he hadn't spoken more than three sentences in four hours. Conversation at the table had been directed around him; his friends knew his state of mind and left him to brood. Bolan had turned to the hockey game on the giant TV screen, but the Maple Leafs were losing badly to the Detroit Red Wings. That's when he left.

The interior of his Oldsmobile had just warmed up to a comfortable level when he turned into the driveway in front of the thirty-year-old bungalow, with just its street number distinguishing it from the other thirty-year-old bungalows up and down the avenue. As he got out and absentmindedly stubbed his cigarette on the sidewalk — something Sandra repeatedly asked him not to do — Bolan felt guilty for staying out drinking when he should've been home with his family. Never before had he felt so cut off, so utterly alone and unsure of where he was headed. Why, he asked himself, couldn't he communicate his feelings? Instead he barricaded himself with walls that even Sandra wasn't able to break down. And not being on the force now meant he didn't see Rita every day, the only person who could prod him into talking about what was happening in his head. But what would he talk about: his absolute dread of being in court? He thought about the dozens of times he'd been in crowded courtrooms, as a witness or investigating officer, oblivious to the fear, despair and despondency written all over the faces of the defendants. Now their anguish came back to haunt him because his turn was yet to come. How was he handling his fears? In the worst way possible, taking long solemn drives and invariably ending up at the Lancaster. The beer didn't help either; if anything it made him dwell on his problems even more, so that by the time he returned home at night — just like now — he was in an even deeper state of depression.

And he had to be up early the next morning for a job interview. It was embarrassing to think about, a security guard at less than half his usual salary, after a quarter-century of police work. But he was going to need the money in the months to come; and it was either that or go on unemployment insurance, something he relished even less.

Since the porch light wasn't on he had to fumble with the key for a minute. After finally unlocking the door, he padded inside quietly with that extra-careful gait people take on after they've been drinking, like someone crossing a stream on slippery stones. He slipped off his nylon jacket, the one with the kids' league hockey crests on it from his coaching days, and hung it in the hall cupboard with barely a sound in case Sandra was sleeping.

"Well, it's only ten-thirty." She was in the living room. "What's the occasion? You're home so early."

Bolan stiffened as he walked. "For Christ's sake, don't start on me. I really can't take it anymore."

"And I suppose I can."

"Lay off, okay? I don't want to fight. I don't even want to talk." He stood over her, arms crossed, body language echoing his words. She was sitting in her favorite easy chair — a dark blue, crushed velour recliner with a high back. Her bathrobe was tied loosely over a slightly diaphanous nightgown. In her lap a magazine lay open. Her dark eyes were red around the edges.

"What's happening to us, Chuck? Tell me. We're growing farther and farther apart when we need to be closer than ever — to get through all this trouble."

"Yeah."

"There's a helpful response. Clamming up won't fix anything. If you keep bottling up your thoughts, it's just going to make things worse."

"I'm not bottling anything up. You know the facts as well as I do."

"Oh, shit," she said, sighing out loud, "you don't have to talk to me like a cop. I'm your wife, remember? Anyway, I'm not talking about the trial or even you going for that new job. I'm talking about you — and the way you're behaving lately. Going out alone, staying out late, coming home drunk. Nobody — the kids or I — can get you to say anything half the time. So what's happening?"

"Not this again. We go through this goddamned shit night after night. Nothing's changed. I'm depressed, that's all. And I feel like getting out and relaxing with the guys. Tonight I watched the hockey game."

Tears were beginning to well up in Sandra's eyes now. She tried breathing deeply before she spoke to force them back. "You don't have to go out every single night. It makes me wonder…" She let the sentence dangle.

"Wonder? About what?"

"I don't know. It's strange, that's all. You out night after night. Always with the guys."

"Aw, c'mon." Bolan reached inside his shirt pocket for the pack of Marlboros. "What do you think: in the middle of this mess in my life, I'm going out looking for a fuck somewhere? Christ, I've got enough stress on me right now. That's all I'd need."

"But where do you go and spend so much time…with the guys?"

That caught him off guard. He wondered if his face were getting flushed. Sandra didn't know he hung out at the Lancaster. Feelings of guilt and embarrassment swept over him like a kid accused of cheating on a final exam. Suddenly he felt tainted, as though he reeked of another's woman's perfume. Should he tell her? "At Courtney's," he lied, popping a cigarette between his lips. "You know, that sports bar off Lakeshore, the one near the McDonald's."

Sandra nodded, staring directly into his eyes. "What's the attraction there? You can drink beer at home too."

"It's not just beer. All the guys are there. Giant screen too. You know, it's a chance for me to get out."

"You're out all the time. Even before you were suspended, none of us saw very much of you. And since then — "

" — What is this?" he said, taking the offensive as he strode across the small living room and plunked himself down onto the sofa. "I can't even go out anymore without you thinking I'm up to something."

"Don't give me that. Even when you're home you stay cooped up drinking beer all day. You could at least spend time with the kids…or even go out and rake the leaves or something. But you'd rather be alone, feeling sorry for yourself. Well listen here, mister, you'd better start thinking about the rest of us and get your life together."

"I know, I know," he said, getting up again. "I am trying to get my life together."

"It doesn't seem like it. And you really haven't thought about me and the kids, about how hard it is for us. The phone's always ringing with reporters asking to talk to us. They even try to get at the kids on their way to school, asking for interviews."

"They do?"

"Yes. And not only that, but seeing their father's name smeared in the papers every second day has made it hard for them, especially Nancy. She can't take the comments from her friends. Now, with all this new stuff about the farm and what you were doing there, it's gotten worse…for all of us."

"Yeah…you're right," he sighed. "I've really left you in a mess, haven't I?" He leaned over and touched Sandra's shoulder. She began to sob. Standing there motionless, Bolan watched her cry for a minute. "I'm so sorry," he said, his words faint, almost inaudible, like a whisper in the wind.

She got up and wrapped her arms around his waist, burying her head in his chest. "This is no way to solve your problems," she said, sniffing.

After she went down the hall to the bedroom, he flicked off the lamps and pulled the floral-patterned drapes open, glancing out at the dark, rain-swept street. Drawing a last lung full of smoke, he stubbed his cigarette in an ashtray and ambled out of the living room, turning off lights and checking the stairs to the basement on his way — anything to kill some time. Stopping at Melissa's and Nancy's room, he was about to open the door and check on them but thought better of it, in case one of them was awake and had been listening to the conversation. Down the hallway a needle-thin crack of light escaped under the door to his and Sandra's bedroom.

Evidence of a night of beer drinking was irrefutable as a pale stream that never seemed to end splashed noisily into the toilet bowl. Bolan brushed his teeth and undressed, holding his clothes in a heap under his arm like a football. He stared into the mirror. Was that really his face, with the thinning hair on top and lines etched so deeply in his forehead? Was that really him behind those eyes? Did he even feel young inside anymore, or had his ambition and ideals been trampled upon too many times? Right now the image in the mirror was beginning to reflect the torment he felt inside.

He tiptoed into the bedroom, eyeing Sandra, who was lying on her back in the queen-size bed. Dropping the bundle of clothing on the beige broadloom, he climbed in with her, switching off the bedside lamp. Bolan rolled over and lay close to her, soaking up the body warmth, and ran his hand lightly across her shoulders.

She turned to him, and he kissed her lightly on the forehead.

"Chuck," she whispered, "are we going to make it through this?"

Chapter Eleven

For the past five days, in the late afternoon when the sun's heat had diminished somewhat and as the moist breeze swept in from the ocean, sweetened by oleander and hibiscus blooms everywhere, Adrian played squash with Ricardo Sosa. Really it was a hybrid version of jai alai and racquetball played on an old court with walls thirty feet high — but only three of them — and one side open to a manicured lawn, where the ball would rebound.

Usually they sweated through six or seven games, all of which were controlled by Sosa, even though Adrian sometimes came within a point or two for a few rounds — something he suspected the Cuban was doing on purpose just to keep his interest from ebbing. Which was the case right now. Even though Sosa had almost a decade on him and Adrian was back in near-athletic shape, he couldn't catch the Cuban. Finesse was something Sosa didn't lack; during the game he controlled the center of the court, making Adrian do all the work. And when he did have to run — which wasn't often — Sosa was exceptionally fast in the sprint, pouncing on any shot that was halfway challenging and effortlessly returning the rest. Although he puffed heavily in the heat, showing some strain on his cigar-smoke-clogged lungs, he barely paused after each point before serving again. His brown body, clad in only a baseball cap, swimming trunks and running shoes, was still firm except for a flabby paunch, with taut strong biceps and calves, a sign of the excellent condition the Cuban must have been in most of his life.

Just two points behind near the end of their fourth game, Adrian strained to reach the ball before it ricocheted out onto the grass and suddenly stumbled, falling sideways on his arm, dashing it against concrete and putting himself in absolute agony for a few moments. He lay immobile, completely enervated and in considerable pain, his back propped up against the scratchy, damp wall of the court. He'd known that morning his right arm — the one fractured and in a cast just a couple of months before — was acting up, giving him occasional jabs of discomfort while he did push-ups. But he'd worked through the pain, and everything had seemed fine until now.

"Are you certain you are all right?" asked Sosa, who had a genuinely worried look on his face. "Perhaps I should examine you." He knew about the broken arm and beating from a conversation with Adrian a couple of nights before.

"No, no, I'm fine. Really, the pain's almost gone now. I guess I just overdid it, that's all. You know what it's like, Ricardo. Healing takes a lot longer when you get older…and maybe my arm just wasn't a hundred percent yet."

"You should listen to your body more often and pay attention to the warning signals, my friend. I think you are too competitive, putting intense pressure on yourself for no particular reason. That's how you open yourself up to injury. So there will be no more squash for a few days, okay?"

Adrian nodded as he looked up at Sosa, who was standing over him. Funny, he thought, how that other part of the Cuban — the doctor and psychiatrist — had just replaced the resort manager and squash partner. Even his voice had taken on the "I know what's best for you" tone, a mainstay of physicians — even those who drank too much and inhaled strong cigar smoke all day.

A few feet away, sitting cross-legged on the court, was the woman who had ridden over with Sosa on the tandem bicycle. The Cuban had introduced them but Adrian already knew her name was Maria, having seen her around the past week, noticing she did paperwork and acted as a sort of management assistant to Sosa, often taking instructions from him. Adrian wondered if she spoke English, since she'd been so quiet during the squash match and after he'd hurt himself. There was something rather alluring about her — even though she wasn't particularly striking to look at, at least in a classical sense. Her broad nose lacked definition and seemed insignificant on the oval face. The forehead was protuberant too, and its largeness was amplified by the fact her brown hair was fine and limp, hanging languidly down to the tips of her shoulders. Many women would probably get a perm, Adrian thought, but she obviously wasn't overly conscious of her looks. She didn't bother tanning herself — in fact, she was quite pale looking — and her appearance could best be described as devil-may-care, just a few notches from sloppy.

Yet there was a definite attraction, something that was quite obvious judging by the number of males who turned their heads for a second look when she passed by. Perhaps it was her manner, the apparent air of total independence, as though she couldn't give a damn what anybody in the world thought of her. There was an undisguised self-confidence too — almost haughtiness — that was evident every time she smiled, showing all of her bright straight teeth.

"Let's forget about the cerveza today," said Sosa. Usually the two of them adjourned to a beach bar after their games. "Before I leave for La Habana to visit my children, I have to check on the preparations for tomorrow. There is to be a special Christmas dinner on the water — six turkeys roasting over an open fire, something we have never tried before."

"I was going to suggest skipping the beer anyway," Adrian said as he slowly got to his feet, groaning a little as he did so, and cradling his injured arm. "I feel like lying down for a while in our villa. But later, before dinner, why don't you drop by for a Christmas Eve drink?"

"Thank you. I will." Sosa smiled and turned to Maria, speaking in Spanish. She got up. "I'm going down to the beach now," he explained, looking at Adrian again, "so Maria will give you a ride back to your villa if you like. And make sure you rest that arm for a few days while I'm away." He picked up the rackets and ball, and strode off, stopping a few yards away, awkwardly balancing the equipment in one hand so he could light a cigar.

Adrian watched Maria out of the corner of his eye as she walked the bicycle toward him. The only sounds at that moment were the shoosh of tires meeting concrete, along with the distant squawk of a turkey buzzard, barely audible in the hills. Even taking a breath seemed to invade the stillness. She stopped beside him and waited until he'd grabbed the handlebars and swung onto the seat behind hers, his feet touching the ground to steady the bicycle while she got on.

Turning to him, she pointed at his arm. "Hurt," she said, with just a hint of a smile, her green eyes flashing at him.

"Si," he replied, one of about fifteen Spanish words he knew, most of them having to do with food or drink or washrooms.

Maria boldly ran her fingertips over the arm, barely grazing it. The feeling was exhilarating. "I know who you are," she said haltingly, over-pronouncing each word. "You are famous."

"Really." He tried to sound nonchalant.

Still smiling she turned around, and they began to ride across the scrubby parched grass to the stone path, wobbling rather precariously a couple of times as the front wheel fell into ruts.

A few minutes later, nearing the villa perched by itself on the gentle bosom of a hill, they passed a dozen tourists coming from the main building and heading to the bar, freshly showered and decked out in whites and pastels, florid faces shiny from after-sun creams. Maria steered the bicycle around them, weaving in and out along the winding path. Adrian just pedaled, occasionally glancing to each side at the flowers and towering palm trees, but mainly focusing on the young woman in front of him: her broad shoulders, the exposed stretch of skin between the blue halter top and shorts she was wearing, and the backs of her soft, fleshy white thighs.

Was there something stirring in him? His heart beating faster? He honestly couldn't tell, and rationalized it as possible over-exertion or even the pedaling. The way he'd felt the past few weeks, any throbbing between his legs would be the best — and probably least expected — Christmas present imaginable."Oh — we're here already," he blurted out with a start, as Maria hit the brakes while he was still pedaling. So immersed in his thoughts, he hadn't noticed they were in front of the villa. He got off the bicycle, thanking her for the ride. She looked straight into his eyes and laughed; he didn't know why.

***

A couple of Aspirin and a steaming bath had settled the throbbing in Adrian's arm. He and Jennifer were sitting in the spacious living room of their villa sipping twelve-year-old rum with ice.

"This seems like as good a time as any," Jennifer said, getting up abruptly.

"What are you doing?" asked Adrian.

She went into the bedroom. He could hear her shuffling around in her suitcase. She returned with a long black leather pouch and handed it to her startled husband. "Merry Christmas," she said and then bent down to kiss him. "I know these last few months have been tough for you. But just remember how much I love you."

He kissed her back, this time deeper, and then undid the tie at the top of the pouch. Reaching in, he felt something familiar, and withdrew a pair of drumsticks — but nothing like his usual hickory signature models that he got free and went through at the rate of about four pairs a week. These were hand-lathed out of the darkest ebony with mother-of-pearl tips that shimmered even in the dimly lit room. Adrian was almost speechless. "I can't believe it," he whispered. "They're even my size." He'd played thick sticks with large tips since his high school days, long before microphones were used to amplify drum kits, when the instrument had to be attacked to be heard over the electric guitars.

"Do you like them?" asked Jennifer.

"Oh, God, I love them."

"You can really use them too if you want."

Adrian nodded. "I can see that…they're perfect…a piece of art. But I'd rather have them mounted, on one of our walls at home. Where did you get them anyway?"

"I got the name of somebody in New York who could make them. He even asked for the model you use, so he could buy some."

Returning them to their pouch, Adrian jumped up out of the chair and went to the bedroom. He came back with a small box wrapped in silver paper with metallic red stars on it.

Jennifer tore away the wrapping and flipped open the powder-blue jewelry box. She gasped for a second at the sight of it: a platinum ring crowned with a perfectly cut two-carat emerald, surrounded by a cluster of small diamonds.

"I know you don't like showy jewelry," Adrian said, sitting down beside her, "but I couldn't resist this one."

"It's absolutely breathtaking," she responded, sliding it over the fourth finger on her right hand. "I can't wait to have it sized when we get back."

Adrian pulled her toward him and pressed his lips over hers. "Merry Christmas," he murmured. He began to kiss her again when the sound of footsteps interrupted. Then tapping at their door.

Jennifer pulled away from him. "Who could that be?"

"Oh, shit, I forgot — it's Ricardo."

She looked exasperated. "You invited him on Christmas Eve…after playing squash with him this afternoon? And we've been at his place almost every night this week."

Adrian got up and went to the door.

"I trust I'm not disturbing you," said Sosa.

"Not at all."

"How is the arm doing?"

"Much better, thanks. I'll be fine tomorrow."

Sosa smiled. "You're so predictable. Take my advice though — and take it easy."

"Come on in and sit down," said Jennifer, who had risen to greet their guest.

"Thank you. I have only a couple of hours before the bus ride back to the city." He pulled out some matches from his pants pocket and relit the ever-present cigar. "It's very rare to find people here I can talk to and genuinely want to be with, if you don't mind me saying."

Jennifer looked puzzled. "Why us?" she asked. "You meet people every week."

"I can only remember one or two occasions when I felt so close to touristos after just a few days." The Cuban sat down on the sofa and took the drink Adrian offered to him. "You both have a natural curiosity…just as I do."

"Well, your stories about Santeria are fascinating," said Jennifer. "Adrian and I never thought much about any religion before."

"There is more here than simply a religion. In Santeria, the Yoruba of Nigeria dealt with psychology and even parapsychology, using knowledge accumulated and passed on over thousands of years."

"The more you talk to us about Santeria," said Adrian, "the more I'm beginning to think you actually believe in its spirits and dead souls — just like you did when you were a kid watching through the window. Where's your scientific objectivity in all of this?"

"Don't worry, it's still there. Haven't you ever seen or read something that defied logic? What about psychokinesis, where people make things move by thinking about them? Scientists all over the world have witnessed and studied these acts. And then there are clairvoyants, who are almost in the mainstream now — even used by police to solve crimes. Seers and fortune tellers are abundant in every country on earth, no matter how rich or poor, or what political system happens to be in place. You are an intelligent man, Adrian, but do you actually deny the existence of things like mental telepathy when you know so little about them?"

"No, I don't, not at all." There was a long pause. Adrian felt a flutter in his stomach as he remembered his own prophetic dreams — and why he decided to come to Cuba in the first place. "Somehow sacred stones and drums and witch doctors and all of that other hocus-pocus seem so...well...primitive and unscientific."

"That is your prejudice. To a person who has never been to a Catholic Mass before, the entire ceremony might be like natives pounding drums and dancing around a fire."

"But blood and herbs and drums and stones. It's a strange combination."

"Is it?" asked the Cuban with a sly smile. "Perhaps there's a parallel here too. In the Catholic religion the blood of Christ is symbolized by wine in Communion; burned palm leaves are used on Ash Wednesday; and there is consecrated stone in the altar. Not to mention the singing of psalms. Doesn't the combination of elements in Catholicism seem strange?"

"Listen," said Jennifer, "I wouldn't even call Santeria a "primitive" religion. In fact, it all seems rather complex — sacred stones, special herbs for different gods and all those sayings — what are they called?"

"Orichas," answered Sosa, before finishing the last of his rum.

"Oh, yes, orichas. Anyway, tell me the truth, Ricardo. I know you've studied Santeria, but have you ever practiced it?"

"No, not ever. I only observe it. But there are many questions I cannot answer. A wide gap exists between the logic of science and what people strongly believe in. Faith knows no logic. So it is difficult for me to make judgments."

"That's a roundabout way to answer a question," commented Adrian. "Don't be so abstract. Do you believe in the powers of Santeria or not?"

Sosa slouched in his seat and ran a hand through his slick dark hair. "There are many things I cannot dispute," he replied. "I know about the power of the sacred stones used in rituals — wherever that power comes from. The stones may be just a medium…a tool, if you will…much the same as tarot cards are for a gifted clairvoyant. But there is a power of some sort there nonetheless."

"What kind of power?" asked Jennifer.

"Well, I have talked to many santeros, and they have told me very strange stories about the stones. The most powerful were brought over from Africa during the slave trade by natives who had swallowed them. Then they were passed from santero to santero for hundreds of years. They have told me about how they tried to dispose of the stones, throwing them into the street or even the ocean, and having them reappear in their houses or at the altar."

Adrian interrupted. "But exactly what is this power?"

"It's something that protects the santero and members of his cult, and lets the gods manifest themselves. But the stones must be fed at least annually, starting with the sound of the drums, and then by washing them in special herbs and the warm blood of an animal. A santero is educated in performing this ritual properly — because the gods must be fed and summoned in the right manner. It is essential."

The musician shook his head in disbelief. "And you call them priests," he scoffed, "when they sacrifice living things and wash in the blood."

"Remember, every santero claims to practice white magic…and most of them do, I think. Although to defeat evil, you also have to know how black magic works, or else your powers of good will not be effective against it. So, in Santeria, as in most things in life, it's the grey areas that prove most effective — somewhere in the middle between good and evil. But each santero knows that the farther you head toward blackness, the more powerful you feel and stronger the attraction…and closer you are to the edge, to the unearthly horrors of hell."

"That's what you told us about the first night we met," said Jennifer. "The Great Darkness, human sacrifices and drinking blood."

"Precisely," nodded Sosa, rising slowly out of his chair and heading toward the liquor bottle. "For a few santeros it becomes a fatal attraction. They are transformed, inflated by the power — sometimes even literally. Witnesses say that the priests actually increase their size as a spirit rushes into their bodies, swelling with the power like a blowfish. I have heard about them plunging their hands into a beating heart while the person is still alive…and then drinking the blood. They slice off knuckles and toes, and the penis too, of course, and suck the brains out of the skull."

"Oh God, stop it," moaned Adrian. "Here we are before dinner on Christmas Eve, and you're telling disgusting stories about the Anti-Christ."

Sosa finished pouring his drink and turned around to face the other man. "We are not talking about your average santero here, who is basically good and believes in the white magic. But these horrible things have happened…and I am sure they will continue to forever."

"So what else is involved, besides the feeding of the stones?" asked Jennifer.

"One more important element: resguardo. These are charms and beads that have been treated with herbs and blood over the years. They have come in contact with the sacred stones. By wearing these on the body, a person is protected — and no danger can come near. Drug dealers from the Medellin Cartel in Colombia have had resguardo on when they've been arrested. A believer from Cuba who has lived in New York for twenty years might put resguardo around her sick child's neck to speed up the healing and prevent further illness. Of course, these are both examples of using resguardo for external dangers."

"There are internal dangers too?" queried Jennifer.

"Most definitely. The saints can also work against you, especially if you haven't fed them properly or used the correct orichas. To the followers of Santeria, unleashing a spirit is very serious business, and not to be taken lightly. I've heard that if the saints are not pleased, then there will be evil possessions instead of good ones, causing pain and suffering. The evil spreads too, infecting others far removed. Wearing the resguardo can help protect you against this kind of backfire."

Adrian tilted his head back to finish the last few drops remaining in his glass. Then he looked straight at Sosa. "Do you really believe all this? A straight answer, please."

"I'm not sure," answered the Cuban hesitantly.

"Well, I'm sure of one thing," said Jennifer. "I wouldn't want to be at the mercy of some strange, unpredictable power that I couldn't control."

"Neither would I," added Sosa in a solemn voice. "Neither would I."

***

Both of them sat there sipping cognacs, while revelers all around them managed to drown out the sound of the surf, their stomachs bursting after dining on mango and scallop salad, slightly smoked marlin, fire-roasted turkey, seared lamb and rich Cuban ice-cream. Christmas night of all nights, Adrian and Jennifer had been chipping at each other, the tension gradually building.

"You just don't get it," she said. "I'm not even torn between a career and a family — because I have neither."

He shrugged. "Hey, I didn't make you quit university. You could've gotten your Master's."

101

"I can't believe what I'm hearing. You practically pushed me out of school, telling me I'd never need to work, and that I could really help out taking care of our house and cottage and social calendar. I thought it was just a matter of time until we started a family."

"Your memories certainly don't jibe with mine. Anyway, what about CANFAR and all your work with the AIDS thing?" Adrian's eyes were glazed over, his mind somewhere else, at a packed stadium on a clear warm night, looking out from the stage past the lights into the audience where thousands and thousands of lit matches and disposable lighters are winking, held aloft by the wildly cheering crowd. He and Cam and Denny are totally in the pocket, playing their guts out, anticipating each other's moves perfectly, letting the song build to its shattering climax.

"You're not even listening to me, are you?"

"Something about a baby, wasn't it?"

Jennifer exploded. "Maybe we'll never have children," she lashed out, "because you're so fucking wrapped up in yourself you'll never be able to make love again!"

She leapt up from the table, threaded her way through the boisterous crowd and then headed down the beach, deliberately kicking sand with each step she took. The trip had been planned to bring them closer together — and for the first couple of days it actually had. Until Adrian began seeing so much of Ricardo Sosa. If it weren't squash, then there would be late-night bouts of drinking and talk that always ended up as marathons. As much as she respected Sosa's intellect, her tolerance of him was diminishing. What a relief that he'd left for Havana to spend three days with his family. She'd imagined that Adrian would almost be falling into her arms. Instead, it ended up like this, with Yuletide fireworks.

Nightfall had blanketed the beach; she squinted in the darkness to make sure a jellyfish wasn't underfoot, a natural land mine to the unsuspecting. About two hundred yards away she could still hear the tourists plainly, their joyful drunken voices carrying over the water. She stopped by some white pedal boats and sat down on the edge of one, scratching her ankles furiously. The sand fleas were getting to her. Once the sun's heat abated, they started hopping, biting with a ferocity that far outmatched their size — not much bigger than a grain of sand. She cursed herself for wearing a dress and sandals, for deciding to walk on the beach in the first place, even for bothering to scratch because it only made the bites itch more on the worst Christmas of her life.

Suddenly a sound gave her a start. She glanced over to the water. It was Juan, the lifeguard at the resort. He was sitting alone in a dinghy that had been pulled ashore. She hadn't even noticed him. Now he jumped out of the boat and was walking, hands in the pockets of his white jeans, which were all he happened to be wearing. She'd seen him many times since their first day on the beach. Occasionally he could be found at his lifeguard's post, but more often he ignored his job and joined some of the other employees — who were ignoring theirs — for a game of volleyball at the staff quarters. Or else he headed to the resort's main building to flirt with the women working in the office. A couple of times about mid-morning, Jennifer had spotted him swimming in from the reef after three or four hours of snorkeling, his sack full of lobsters, crabs and small fish he'd speared.

Others at La Sorpresa treated him with a good measure of deference, something Jennifer had noticed immediately, having seen people do the same thing around Adrian for years. She asked Sosa about him, and the mystery was unraveled: Juan was a former Olympic athlete, like others who worked on the beaches in many resorts around the island. He was a young middleweight boxer who had competed at the 1980 games in Moscow, finishing just shy of a medal. Greatness was predicted for him four years later at the Los Angeles Olympics — but then Cuba followed Russia and Eastern European countries in boycotting those games, so he never got his shot at the big time. But in Cuba he was obviously a star, which is why he strutted around so pompously, like the last man on earth.

Jennifer looked at him standing a few feet away with his back to her, seemingly watching the receding tide. His white pants appeared luminous, a stunning contrast to the rest of his body, which had almost faded into the night's blackness. During the day she noticed the depth of his tan, the way his naturally dark Latin skin was evenly bronzed almost everywhere, from his rusty blonde hairline to the tops of his feet.

Not wishing to give him the pleasure of thinking someone was looking at him, she reached over and began scratching again, clawing away at her itching ankles and lower legs, which were beginning to drive her mad. Juan turned around at the same time and smiled, scuffing his feet around in the sand and staring straight into her eyes.

"Fleas," she said, realizing right afterward that he probably didn't understand English. She couldn't recall ever seeing the husky lifeguard talking to tourists.

He approached and without a word went down on his knees in front of her, taking one of her feet lightly in his hands. A little alarmed and definitely uncomfortable, Jennifer stiffened and swallowed hard. Then Juan dug deeply into the sand, up to his elbow, where it was moist, and spread it on her ankle and calf, sliding his hand back and forth gently, allowing the cool mud to cake on.

She looked down at his thick sturdy wrist and brown hand, with its oversized, rock-hard knuckles. Although he was probably an inch shorter than she was — five foot eight or so — Juan was still massive looking, with huge sloping shoulders and wide back muscles that seemed to roll under the skin with each movement of his hand on her leg. He put down one foot and lifted the other; already the itching had subsided where the sand had been applied. Her mind was racing abstractly; she didn't know what to say or do. So Jennifer sat there mute but smiling vacantly, trying desperately not to admit to herself how good it felt, the smooth strokes up and down, the delicious ooze of the mud — another man's gentle touch on her body. His face now peered up at hers, the eyes and teeth jumping out of the darkness, some of the tousled shock of hair falling onto his forehead. She looked at his strong chin and lumpy aquiline nose, wondering how many times it had been broken in the ring. He swept some more cool wet sand onto her leg and flattened it with his palm, sliding his hand up and down again; this time though his fingertips kneaded the skin slightly on the back of her calf and then crept farther up within a inch of her knee. She was about to pull away but at the same instant he stopped and put her foot down. Jennifer felt a burn rush to her cheeks when she noticed that her dress was up around her thighs and that her legs were parted.

With the grace of a dancer, Juan sprang up, turned and started walking down the beach, hands in his pockets again. Unmoving, Jennifer watched him for half a minute — and then the noise from the Christmas festivities intruded, sparking her senses. She'd forgotten about everything for a while: the fight with Adrian, the dinner, even where she was. The experience had enveloped her, but as she got up, reality set in again. Raucous sounds from the party echoed along the shore. Now the local band had started playing, with murderous renditions of Cyndi Lauper and Billy Ocean tunes. The flickering glow from fires licked the beach and water around her. As she walked back, the experience seemed so strange, because only one word had been spoken the entire time: fleas.

Chapter Twelve

"I always feel a little sad a couple of days after Christmas," said Rita, pouring herself another cup of steaming herbal tea from a hand-painted porcelain pot.

"Why's that?" asked Bolan. He sat across from her on the floral-patterned sofa in the small living room, awkwardly cradling a cup and saucer in his lap.

"Because I get so excited with the buildup. And then when it's gone so fast, I'm all let down." She glanced over to the corner where the Christmas tree stood, twinkling lights casting a warm glow about the entire room and the pine scent still fragrant even after a week indoors.

"Yeah. I guess I used to feel that way too. Maybe as you get older, things change."

Rita sipped her tea and looked into his eyes. "Did you have a merry Christmas, Chuck?"

"Sure. It wasn't bad," said Bolan, nodding and tapping his fingers on the sofa arm. "Sandra and the kids enjoyed themselves. Visited relatives. The usual festive stuff. Kind of weird not drinking though."

"I know what you must be going through. But I'm proud of you. It's a big step, just quitting cold turkey."

"Over the years I had my fill. So it's not so bad, I guess. I feel better in the morning. It's easier to get up and face the day."

"Well, that's an improvement right there."

"Yeah, I suppose. And I'm not as down about everything. Sandra and I are getting along better too. I know it sounds kind of corny…but I can see again why I married her."

Rita was beaming. "When times are tough, it's good to know who really loves you — and who will be there when you need them."

Afraid of becoming maudlin, Bolan cleared his throat and straightened up in his seat. "I'm coaching peewee hockey again," he said, changing the subject, "filling in for a neighbor of mine who got a job transfer. Keeps me out of trouble."

"That's great. I didn't know you used to coach kids' hockey."

"Yeah, when Derek was young I was behind the bench with his team. Then I kind of stayed on even when he got older and moved to another league."

"Sounds like you're really getting your shit together."

"As best I can."

"How's the job been working out?"

"Whaddya think…boring as hell. I sit on my ass all night looking out over an empty factory. The only time there's any action is when the company calls, checking to make sure I'm there. I guess some guys are cut out to be security guards — but I'm sure not."

Rita broke into a broad grin. "I'll tell ya though, you are the biggest security guard I have ever seen. Usually they're midgets or little old men who couldn't blow away a fly. Have you ever noticed?"

"Tell me about it. Those guys are my partners now." Bolan grabbed his pack of cigarettes off the pine side table and shook out some. He motioned to Rita, who smiled and reached over for one.

"Well, in spite of your problems, it's nice to have a couple of days off over the holidays."

"I dunno. Whenever there's free time I think too much about all the shit I'm in."

There was a pause as Rita exhaled cigarette smoke with a noticeable sigh. "You know, I went to see Adrian Lee."

"You did?" Bolan looked incredulous.

"Yes. It was just after he got home from the hospital."

"Why?"

"Why do you think, Chuck? You're a decent human being, and I don't want to see your career ruined because of an accident."

"Really nice of you, Rita. Thanks."

"Don't mention it."

"So what's new at work?"

Rita laughed. "This is amazing."

"What is?" asked Bolan.

"You've actually been here an hour and never talked shop until now."

"Christmas only comes once a year."

"Well, because you've been a good boy, I should let you know the latest."

"Fire away."

"You know the black man from the farm and in the parking garage?"

"Intimately," replied Bolan, remembering how he literally squeezed information out of him.

"Well, I've been working on him. He's up for accessory in Angela's murder. But he's beginning to trust me. Crown prosecutor says she'll consider some kind of plea bargain if he helps us nail Richardson. So he's been singing for us."

"That's great news. Good work."

"It's a start," said Rita, "but we haven't gotten far. You know how Richardson has half a dozen car dealerships — here and in Montreal and Buffalo and Syracuse? Seems weapons sometimes come across the border in boxes of auto parts. So we followed up and got a search warrant. Emptied every box. Took apart the truck. Nothing. Could be they were tipped off. Richardson's got mob connections, so there must be informants."

"Hey, I'm impressed. You're really diggin' in there, Rita."

"He's slippery and well-insulated…but we'll get him."

Bolan glanced at his watch. He pulled on the Marlboro and then watched a thin rope of blue smoke spiral upward. There was silence for a minute or so. He put his cup and saucer on the table and shuffled around. "I guess I should be heading out."

"So soon?"

"It's almost nine…and I don't want a late night."

"That's too bad," said Rita, getting to her feet as Bolan did. "Trevor should be home from basketball soon. He wanted to wish you the best of the season."

"I'll catch him next time."

In the hall, Bolan zipped up his coat and pulled a wool toque from the pocket. Rita opened the front door and poked her head out, marveling at the stillness of the night and the large cotton-ball snowflakes fluttering in the air like feathers. Half a foot of white blanketed the ground.

"Thanks for the tea, Rita," Bolan mumbled as he squeezed by her out onto the porch.

"Did you like it?"

"It takes a little getting used to. Ask me again in a couple of years."

She laughed. "See you later."

"Have a happy New Year."

"You too, Chuck." Before he could get away, she pulled him back by the shoulder, gave him a hug and pecked him on the cheek. "Take care of yourself. And give my best to Sandra." As he reached his car at the curb, she yelled out to him: "Drive carefully."

Chapter Thirteen

It had been blustery and unsettled all day; but though the dense grey clouds were threatening and obscured any direct sunlight, there wasn't any rain. The beach was so chilly and windswept it was uncomfortable to be without a jacket. So like most tourists, Adrian and Jennifer kept close to their villa all afternoon, sprawled in lounge chairs on the patio, reading, talking and nodding off.

Although she'd tried to coax him into joining her for a walk, Adrian declined. He felt unusually lazy, unable that morning to even muster the energy for his karate workout. When Jennifer left he took a ten-minute cold shower, which did drive some of the sluggishness out of him. Afterward, standing in front of the mirror, he dragged a comb through his tangled wet hair and listened to the gusts of wind rattling the louvers, creating a kind of drum roll that filled the cabin — so much so he hadn't noticed the knocking at his door. The second tap-tap-tap was louder and in quick succession, almost official sounding. Hastily tugging on his jeans he ran out of the bathroom and down the hall toward the door.

"I hope I'm not intruding," Ricardo Sosa said, smiling slightly and cradling a big brown paper bag to his chest.

"No, no, not at all." Adrian yanked open the door. "Come on in."

"Thank you," the Cuban said, stepping forward. He was wearing a windbreaker, white shirt, navy dress pants and black leather lace-ups — a startling change from the running shoes and shorts he was normally seen in.

"How was the trip to Havana?" asked Adrian, motioning for the other man to sit down.

"It went very well. At Christmas, even my ex-wife and I manage to get along. I visited with my sons, and went to see my daughter's residence at the university. You must understand that as much as I like it here in La Sorpresa, the cabana cannot compare to my house."

Adrian nodded and sat down in one of the plush living room chairs, his bare upper body reacting to the cool air with goose bumps. "Well, you made it back in time for supper," he said, forcing the conversation a little.

"The bus made a quick trip today." Sosa appeared a little ill at ease too, somewhat like the first night when they met him in the bar. "Sometimes I do not return until ten or eleven if there are many people at the stops along the way."

His own way of life was so different, thought Adrian, with four automobiles, a wad of credit cards and the freedom to travel easily anywhere he wanted. Here, it took three or four hours to go forty-five miles. "Jenny's gone for a walk," he offered, for no particular reason. "She'll probably be back in a few minutes."

The look on Sosa's face showed he was feeling like an intruder. "Oh, I'm not going to stay. In fact, tonight seems a perfect time to read in my cabana — after I make sure the resort is running as it should." He paused. "I brought something you might be interested in from La Habana." Grasping the bag from the top, he handed it to Adrian.

"What is this?" The musician reached inside and pulled out two drums, like bongos almost, about nine inches in diameter and twice that in length, with well-worn hide stretched over the round wooden frames.

"You are a drummer, my friend, so these are yours. They are the smaller ones used in Santeria rites. Now you have your own sacred drums."

Adrian was truly flabbergasted. "Thank you...but...I don't know what to say. Really, I can't take these from you."

"Of course you can. I have no use for them; they were given to me by a friend many years ago. Now they just add to the clutter in my library. But you are both a musician and someone who has shown an interest in Santeria — so thcy arc yours."

Placing them between his legs, Adrian used the heel of one hand and the fingertips of the other to bang out a rhythm. Because of their length, the drums were exceptionally loud, and the hollow sound was particularly penetrating. He lifted one up and examined the crude yet effective instrument, admiring the craftsmanship that had gone into its fabrication. It was worlds apart from the sophisticated, glittering drum kit he used — but performed exactly the same function.

Sosa cleared his throat, which got the other man's attention. He handed Adrian a small cloth sack, a filthy-looking shade of brown with dark stains all over it. "These are to go with the drums, a memento of your trip to Cuba."

Adrian took the sack, untied the drawstring and turned it upside down over one of the drum heads. Thirteen ruddy stones — the largest about the size of an Oreo cookie — fell out in a clatter. Little bits of caked dirt, dried blood and weedy-looking substances lay around them. They were repugnant to look at but Adrian didn't let it show. "Christ," he said quietly. "Sacred stones. How did you get them?"

"An old santero I knew gave them to me," Sosa replied. "It was a few days before he finally succumbed to cancer. I had been visiting him at his home, because he refused the care in a hospital, even though his death was painful and drawn out."

For a second Adrian thought of his own father's struggle near the end. "It doesn't matter whether you're in a hospital, does it?" he mumbled. "Because the result is still the same."

"Well, he had been a friend of mine for fifteen years, and had helped me in my studies about Santeria. So I wanted his suffering to be minimal. But he wouldn't allow me to administer morphine, even though his pain was horrible. While he was still quite lucid, he asked me to take the stones, probably his most valued possession. Supposedly their saint is Shango, the warrior."

"This is so...so weird." He fingered a few of them and rolled them around in the palm of his hand. "Have you...have you fed them?"

Sosa roared as though he'd just been told one of the world's funniest jokes. "And you asked me if I was a believer!" he chortled. "You are some skeptic indeed."

"I was just wondering," said Adrian defensively, embarrassed now at his question. "I wasn't sure whether all this stuff on them was from you."

"Of course not. I don't have rituals by myself. I am not a santero. You don't seem to realize it, but I study and analyze using accepted scientific methods."

Adrian was stung a little by the Cuban's schoolteacher tone. "I know that," he began defensively, "but...you know...there's that part about them being treated every year or so."

Again Ricardo Sosa laughed. "Since my friend died only six months ago, there's no need. I don't mean to offend you but this conversation and your reaction amuse me. A few days ago you assumed Santeria was just some silly superstition, and were curious to know whether I believed in these rituals."

"I was wondering, that's all. Anyway, there's something spooky about having these sacred stones in your lap — especially when you don't know whose blood has been poured on them for hundreds of years."

"Is it any different than seeing, say, a mummy in a museum?"

"Well, I've never taken one out of the glass case and brought it home."

Sosa smiled. "Remember, they're only stones."

"Really, I don't know how to thank you. You're truly a generous man."

"Hah!" exclaimed Sosa. "My ex-wife should hear those words. She would tell you a thing or two." He paused briefly. "But as I said before, these objects mean little to me. Over the years I have witnessed countless rituals. For someone so jaded, the drums and stones hold no particular interest anymore. You will appreciate them much more than I do."

"Don't worry, they'll have a special place in my home."

"You must already have rooms full of souvenirs from your travels."

"A few knick-knacks and some art, but not as much as you'd think," Adrian lied, feeling guilty about his worldwide shopping sprees.

"Why not? You seem to be quite interested in other cultures."

"To tell you the truth, I don't think about much except playing when I'm on tour. You're so tired from the travel, and then most of your spare time before the show is spent doing sound checks and giving interviews."

Sosa nodded. "Since this trip is your vacation, you can take time out to see things you'll always remember. And I have just the occasion — if you are interested."

"Yeah, sure I am. What is it?"

"Something very few touristos have ever seen. Tomorrow is your last full day here. If you wish, you and Jennifer can come with me to Guanabo. In a house near the village it will be the third and final night of a Santeria ritual — and the feeding of the stones."

Adrian's eyes widened and his stomach fluttered a little; he remembered Sosa's story from childhood, of peeking through the window and witnessing the exorcism of an evil spirit from the young woman. "You mean we can see the whole thing for ourselves — they'll let us in?"

"Certainly. I am known around there, and you could attend with no trouble."

"I'd love to go. In Guanabo, eh? Is that the place a few miles along the south road?"

"Si. But we will be on the outskirts of the town. I have been to this house before."

"This is too much. Jenny wanted to see what really goes on in Cuba, and now she's got the chance. What a finale to our trip."

"In a way, our country may provide a more memorable experience for you than most other places you have been."

"No kidding."

Sosa pulled out a cigar and lit it so he wouldn't have to outside in the wind. He smiled at Adrian. "I'm glad you wish to come. It will be interesting for both of you. Anyway, I must be going now. My suitcase is not unpacked, and the evening meal is almost upon us."

After he left, Adrian lunged for the closet to find a sweatshirt, socks and shoes, to cut the chill creeping through his body. As he laced up his black leather running shoes he glanced across to the chair opposite him, where the drums were. On top of one lay the sacred stones, scattered about where he'd left them. They looked so benign, so ordinary, like something out of a muddy garden. He smiled to himself at how spooked he'd been when Sosa first handed him the sack and he'd spilled them out. Funny though, as he stared at them now, there was a flutter deep inside his stomach, an indescribable sensation that bordered on eeriness.

Suddenly there was a crash. He practically jumped out of his chair.

"Oops, sorry." Jennifer's voice. "Door slammed behind me. Lots of wind out there." She strolled over toward him.

"Christ," he gasped. "You scared the shit right out of me."

"Oh, that's not true. You're probably still full of it."

Adrian smiled at her, getting up out of the chair. "Very funny."

She moved closer and kissed him on the mouth. Her hair was disheveled, a mess of tangles, and her cheeks were baby pink. It struck him how she was almost glowing, which added to the beauty of her face. The past couple of days, after making up, had been like a tonic for both of them. She started to pull away but he yanked her back for another kiss, this time deeper and longer.

"What a nice evening for a walk," she said afterward. She let go of Adrian's waist and stepped back a little, glancing about the room for a second. That's when Jennifer noticed them.

"What are those?"

"Like duh. They're drums."

"I can see that…but where did they come from?"

"Ricardo brought them for me from Havana. They were his. He says he doesn't want them anymore."

"Great. Now you can feel indebted to the guy. Is there anything in the world he won't do for you? Maybe you should ask him for his house. I'm sure he'd give you that too." She took a few steps across the room to the drums and then halted abruptly. "Yuucckk!"

"He gave me those too."

Jennifer picked up one of the largest stones, rolling it between her thumb and forefinger. "These are rather disgusting, aren't they?"

Adrian shrugged. "They're sacred stones."

"I know."

"Well, they're not supposed to look like diamonds."

"Don't worry; they'll never be mistaken for precious stones…especially with all this guck all over them. It's an odd gift, you must admit."

Adrian picked up the sack they'd come in and began to put them back, like a kid with his marble collection, scooping each stone carefully off the drum head, along with the bits of withered, dirt-like herbs, blood and whatever else that had been caked on and dislodged. "You wouldn't say that to an archaeologist."

"But you're a drummer, not an archaeologist. And if I'm not mistaken, you've never shown any particular interest in archaeology ever before."

"Who knows though — maybe they're valuable."

"Yeah, sure," said Jennifer with a chuckle. "I've never heard of a run on sacred stones, have you? Anyway, you have no documentation. There's no indication of how old they are, where they've been used, how many times, whether they're really from Africa or not. A real archaeologist would know all that stuff."

"One thing's for certain: these suckers look authentic."

"They're horrible-looking. See the blood all over them? The thought of it just turns my stomach. Why don't you throw them away? You won't have to tell Ricardo."

"You're probably right," agreed Adrian, tossing the sack onto the chair. "They do look gross. I'll pitch them later." There was a pause. "There's something else too."

"What?"

"Ricardo has invited us to see a Santeria ritual with him — to witness what really goes on."

"When…tonight?"

"No, tomorrow."

"I thought we were going to the Tropicana together to wind up our holiday."

"Yeah, the Tropicana. But…I don't know…I thought you'd be more excited about the ritual, that's all."

"I went through bureaucratic hell to arrange a car for us, so we wouldn't have to take the bus to Havana with all the tourists. Do you have any idea how hard it is to get a car and driver to come out here in the country?"

Adrian put his arm around her waist. "I know you went to a lot of trouble. But after everything Ricardo's told us, don't you think this would be a once-in-a-lifetime experience? Certainly it's something I could use in my lyrics."

"I can understand you wanting to go," said Jennifer, smiling weakly.

"Are you disappointed?"

"A little. But, to tell you the truth, I'm not into blood rites on my last night here. Would you mind if I still went to see the show?"

"Not at all. And you're not mad because I'm going out with Ricardo again?"

She put her hands on his shoulders and nuzzled his face. "No," she whispered. "I know this means a lot to you. We'll have a great day tomorrow and catch up with each other in bed. Unless…"

"Unless what?" he asked.

"Unless I find a good-looking Latino who's hung like a whale."

Adrian laughed. "Hey, I'm not sure I can use any competition right now."

Chapter Fourteen

The moon was their beacon, illuminating stretches of the narrow asphalt road ahead and bathing the valleys on either side in ascetic white light. The spindly trunks of palm trees were silhouetted against the night sky, rising tall with a smooth curve high above the scrubby grass. Other than the crickets' incessant song, the only sound was the sibilant patter of bicycle tires gliding on the pavement.

Adrian was glad for a clear night but its stillness bothered him. Usually a breeze rolled in about seven or eight, cleansing the air and dropping the temperature a few degrees, yet there hadn't been one this particular evening. So the air hung over them like a blanket, humid and heavy, without any movement whatsoever. He was sweating profusely as he pedaled the tandem bicycle. On the seat in front of him Ricardo Sosa was panting like a hound as they struggled up a steep hill. The Cuban's shirt was soaked through too. When they neared the crest, both of them stood up off their seats to get more leg action on the pedals and keep up the momentum.

Over the top and onto a flat section of road, their speed increased four-fold as they moved in silence, riding to an easy rhythm now. Gradually the fragrant air took on a foul odor that seemed to increase in strength every few feet. Adrian knew they were nearing the garbage dump, which was off to one side and down a little path. The week before he and Jennifer had almost been bowled over by the smell when they'd ridden to the village. It seemed even worse tonight.

"Here is where we burn trash from the resort," said Sosa between heavy breaths, his voice muffled somewhat since he was facing ahead while he spoke.

"You're kidding!" exclaimed Adrian in mock surprise. "I had absolutely no inkling, none at all." He smiled at his own sarcasm, and was about to prod his friend with more when —

— Howls. Loud and near. Getting louder.

Suddenly as Adrian turned his head to the right in the direction of the sounds, there was a blur of white leaping at them out of the darkness. His heart jumped into his throat.

Instantly Sosa reacted, veering the bicycle sharply, right toward three animals, closing in on one and viciously kicking it, sending the cur rolling and yelping into the drainage ditch beside the road. The others ran from them, still howling, blending into the night almost immediately.

"Wait!" yelled Adrian. "Stop the bike!" His heart was thumping madly, and he was visibly trembling.

They both braked hard. Sosa turned to him after they'd ground to a halt. "Nothing to fear," he said calmly, taking off his Blue Jays cap and fanning himself. "Just wild dogs. They are everywhere, living off garbage. But they rarely bite, although they do have infections and carry diseases. Probably these ones were hoping we would feed them. Sometimes in the evening we come here and shoot them so they won't go looking for food at the resort."

Adrian nodded. "It's all right now," he mumbled. "Just gave me a jolt, that's all. Let's go."

He didn't confide in the Cuban, didn't want to tell him about his recurring dream, the one that had haunted him a few months earlier and brought him to this country — and was mainly responsible for the panic he felt right now after seeing the dogs. I've done this before, he thought. It's exactly like my dream, exactly like I've lived it already.

An overwhelming dread spread over him from this déjà vu; even ten minutes later he was still jumping inside, staring at the pavement as he pedaled, not seeing anything, just thinking, preoccupied with the dogs, their ghostly shapes springing from the blackness, just the way he'd seen it so many nights in his sleep. A coincidence — it had to be. Then he began to wonder about Sosa, this enigmatic man to whom he'd grown so close in fourteen days, someone who had little interest in Adrian's musical career or success but bore him gifts and seemed to seek his favor. It was almost as if the Cuban knew about this particular dream of his, aware of what they would encounter later this night, about everything that was to be, about his entire life.

Stop it, he told himself; you're getting paranoid, filling yourself with ridiculous thoughts, making a big thing out of nothing. He shook his head, as if that physical action could literally remove the doubts and fear in his mind.

Not far ahead — perhaps three-quarters of a mile — was a scattering of houses on the fringes of Guanabo: dwarfed flat-roofed dwellings constructed of concrete blocks, or else older homes of wood, sagging and dilapidated, with thatched roofs. They were barely visible but for the glare of the moon and a few lights burning. It was here that Sosa cut the bicycle to the right, heading onto a dirt road dotted with ruts and bumps. The ascent was gradual at first, for about two or three hundred yards, but once they rounded a chiseled corner the hill loomed steeply over them, dark and portentous, blocking out everything in their view.

The Cuban turned his head around as he gradually back-pedaled to brake. "We should walk the bicycle from here. It's quite difficult to ride up."

Both men stood in silence for a moment after dismounting, wiping the sweat off their foreheads and finding their breath. Then Adrian heard them.

Drums.

They'd just begun; a light tapping in the distance, a simple repetitious beat that he memorized easily after hearing it only twice. It grew louder as they pushed the bicycle up the incline.

"Are we missing something?" asked Adrian, feeling giddy and apprehensive now, like a bungee jumper seconds before the big leap.

"No, not really," replied Sosa. "The santero has taken the stones out and put them on the altar. Now he is chanting orichas, and the drums have begun — as you can tell. But they will be much noisier soon. Sometimes this chanting goes on for an hour. So we are in no hurry, my friend."

While they were nearing the precipice, Adrian looked down one side at the village sprawled below, discernible only by the lights inside the houses, a honeycomb of yellow specks. He glanced back to the road and found that Sosa was up ahead, leading the bicycle by the handlebars. Running to catch up, he moved to the other side of the bike, resting his hand on the seat and helping to guide it.

"Not far now," said the Cuban.

Adrian nodded but was only half-listening. The drums' steady throbbing was infectious, working its way inside him; he was aware of his fingertips lightly tapping out the Afro-Cuban beat on the bicycle seat. As he neared their destination — and after the incident with the dogs and overwhelming sense of déjà vu — there was something else he was conscious of too: his heartbeat.

***

So this was it, Cuba's own version of Niagara Falls: the Tropicana. How tattered and dowdy it seemed, thought Jennifer, sitting alone at a table a few feet from the stage. She was close enough to notice the mends in one dancer's black mesh stockings. Various costume changes each brought a new array of hats, frilly low-cut gowns with high slits and even elbow-length gloves, all looking like hand-me-downs from some forty-year-old Dean Martin musical. Aside from the big band, which did play its Afro-Cuban rhythms exactingly — and had a killer drummer Adrian would've liked — the overall effect was about as tasteful as a statue of Venus de Milo with a clock in her navel.

Ninety percent of the customers in the nightclub were tourists who'd been bused in from one resort or another. Of the few Cubans there, three of them had already been to Jennifer's table, leering and hitting on her in the most obvious manner — only to be duly rebuffed in an equally obvious way. She took another sip of champagne, then aimlessly slid the stemmed glass back and forth on the table, guiding it with her forefinger, making patterns with the condensation that had dripped from it. A musical number ended, and she was so immersed in her thoughts the sound of applause didn't even register at first.

The entertainment hadn't served to lift her spirits; she felt lonely but had no inclination to join tourists at other tables. Jennifer wasn't sure if she'd really wanted to come tonight or was simply taking a stand, making a statement to Adrian by not joining him. Sometimes it was difficult to accept how her interests and opinions — her life — were almost deemed to be of less importance than his. Although on the one hand she enjoyed their standard of living and being with a man who was always the center of attention, on the other she absolutely felt smothered by the sublimation. Only when she was with colleagues from her volunteer work did she feel her sense of person and self-worth become evident. The rest of her life was spent around people who fawned over Adrian: music journalists, disc jockeys, concert promoters, record-company reps — not to mention the general public, whenever somebody recognized him. She'd adapted to all of this, including the years of touring for months at a time, drifted with the flow and in return had a life of more freedom than most people could ever imagine. She regretted ever taking Adrian's last name as her own; for five years she'd toyed with the idea of going back to using her family name but hesitated, wondering how Adrian would react after all this time. The bother of dealing with government bureaucracy to legally change it was a factor too.

Even aside from the name, there was always an imbalance. Sure, they had a cleaning woman who took care of the house and washed the clothes, but Jennifer handled everything else. Yet it was she who always took second place to Adrian's work, his hobbies, his problems. At parties, she was always introduced as "Adrian's wife, Jennifer." No matter how much she'd let her husband have the spotlight, no matter how much her own desires — including having children — were shifted to second place, it wasn't good enough. She thought about Adrian's impotence and inability to write lyrics, the waves of helplessness that had rolled over him after the mishap with the policeman. There was so much more to it than just a beating, mere physical punishment. The real damage had been to his sense of manhood, to his male ego, that strange genetic gearshift driving all men — even those who don't appear macho at all. Here was a person totally in control of his life, supposedly secure within himself, blessed with abnormal talent, rewarded more than anyone deserved to be, and one incident that bruised his maleness could destroy his image of himself, render him as vulnerable as a lost child.

But, in spite of all this, for the past fifteen years there was no one else she'd rather be with. She loved Adrian fiercely.

Conga drums pounded from nearby, startling Jennifer out of her thoughts. Dancers flooded the stage in yet another change of costume: three-foot-high headdresses plastered with rhinestones, long pink and white plumes attached to their hips and scanty bikini-like tops and bottoms. She glanced around at the faces in the crowd, loosened up now after a few drinks, applauding and cheering at the stage show. Everywhere around her people appeared happy; at the next table a woman had her arms draped around her spouse's shoulders and was kissing his neck.

***

The house came into view near the top of the steep incline, very plain-looking, like the other rectangular concrete dwellings in the area, although somewhat larger. It was an anti-climax for Adrian; he'd been expecting something ominous and oozing mystery, if not like Transylvania in an old-time horror flick, at least resembling the Bates Motel in Psycho. Instead, there was this featureless low building with bicycles lying in the grass around it and a couple of beaten-up cars parked nearby.

But what the house lacked in atmosphere was more than compensated for by the drums. They were deafening now as the two men leaned the bicycle on its side and proceeded toward the doorstep. Aside from the drums, what Adrian noticed as they approached was the heat: steamy air blasting out the open door, tinged with the soupy scent of body odor and rum. He hesitated for a few seconds, letting Sosa walk past him and inside. Then he followed, suddenly feeling a little sheepish about barging in on a religious ceremony.

The room had no furniture, not that there would've been space for any. There were no lamps, just a single naked lightbulb dangling from the ceiling over to one side, leaving it quite dim everywhere else. Seated on the concrete floor, crammed into every available inch, were eighty or ninety people, half of them black. They were repeating a single oricha over and over, but the sound of their voices was lost to the pounding of the tom-toms. Some of them were swigging dark rum and passing bottles around. Adrian stumbled in, wading through sweat-drenched bodies, keeping his balance by lightly touching their swaying shoulders as he moved, attempting not to disrupt anyone. He scanned the room for Ricardo Sosa without any luck. Squeezing himself between two plump women who appeared oblivious to his presence, he sat down cross-legged. Turning in the direction of the thundering sounds, he caught sight of the drummers — a man and a woman — almost hidden among the crowd, him pounding with his bare hands and her flailing away with thick long sticks, bigger and rougher than any Adrian had seen before. The woman used tom-toms almost identical to the pair Sosa had given him; she was really giving them a workout, sticks raised above her head and violent swings. Her black arms looked stronger than most men's. Beads of sweat flew from her head and shoulders onto a ragged red dress she wore. The man beside her, a tall mulatto with creamy brown skin and a rumpled white shirt, used much larger drums — the size of garbage cans — but whacked them with his palms and fingers, keeping the same seven-stroke beat. Although its tempo wasn't constant, gradually speeding up as the volume increased, the same seven strokes were repeated continually, never faltering: boom ba-boom ba-boom boom boom. As the beat got louder and faster, the people on the floor chanted more noisily and began to clap their hands.

A dozen feet from the drummers in the center of the room, behind a crudely built wooden altar, stood the santero. His bald head glistened with perspiration, eyes wide and bulging, their whiteness jumping out against the dark skin and robes, flashing like the eyes of a stirring horse. He looked up to the ceiling, raising his arms as he did so, his whole body quivering, sending a steady stream of ripples down his robes. He was chanting, lips moving constantly, but his voice was drowned by the drums. The noise was enough to numb anyone's senses, and the air itself seemed to vibrate with the pulsating.

Then the santero closed his eyes and brought his arms down quite suddenly.

Instantly there was calm. The drums died at once. All of the people sat motionless, as though a fuse had been pulled out of their bodies — so much power before and so still now. It was eerily silent.

Adrian was still looking around for Sosa, and found him about thirty feet away jammed into a back corner with others. He'd taken a little pad from his pocket and was jotting in it. He glanced up for a few seconds, catching Adrian's eye and smiling to him.

The drumming began again very low, almost inaudibly, a light tapping but the same beat. His hands inside a large bowl on top of the altar, the santero mixed wrinkled dried herbs and caked blood with water. Next he submerged beads in the solution. Even as he slid a long gleaming knife from under his robes, the priest didn't pause or look up for even a second. His intense concentration was obvious; he paid no heed to the congregation, even though every eye was upon him. He dipped the wicked-looking blade into the bowl and removed it slowly, setting it on top of the altar too.

The stones were next. After the stained brown cloth had been unwrapped painstakingly slowly and with an abundance of dramatics, he bathed each one separately. The sacred stones had the Cubans mesmerized, their eyes fearful-looking and mouths dropping open. A few gasps could be heard above the drums' tapping.

When every stone had been bathed, the bowl was taken away and a black box placed on the floor beside the santero. Leaning over, he reached down to get something from it and then stood upright again. He started to chant, and as he did so the drumbeat surged. The priest kept repeating the same phrases over and over; many in the crowd rose to their feet and began to chant along with him, their bodies swaying to the drums' loudening throb. Adrian stood too so he could see but his view was partially blocked. That flutter in his gut he'd experienced earlier on the road had returned — along with a sense of déjà vu again. He didn't know why but his whole body felt as though he'd been injected with adrenaline, and his heart seemed to be keeping time with the drums.

A woman was up at the altar now beside the santero, unwrapping a small bundle swathed in white. Adrian stood on his tiptoes to get a better look. The priest watched the woman intently. A baby about six months old appeared from the blanket's cocoon, abruptly awakened. His eyes were open wide but not comprehending anything except possibly the noise and unfamiliar surroundings. He started to scream, his face contorted, tiny arms and legs flinching. The woman placed him on the top of the altar.

Adrian couldn't see the baby anymore — but he'd caught a glimpse of the little pained face. Suddenly it felt like a brick had made contact with his brain. The bulb strung from the ceiling. Its harsh yellow light around the room. The small windows without any glass in them. Darkness outside. Oh my Christ! Everything's the same. Everything here was in my dream. In the hospital, trying to describe it to Jennifer, the memory of it so vivid. He'd seen the future — or been through this before.

But the baby, where was the baby? They weren't going to, were they? "No!" he shouted at the top of his lungs, his voice audible only to those closest to him. "No! Stop!" He pushed aside one of the women next to him and started to shove his way through the throng. By now the gathering had been transformed into a frenzy; people were stomping on the floor and screaming out the words to the chant, fighting to be heard over the drums' ever-rising volume. He banged into one person after another, thrashing about wildly, forcing his way toward the altar, crying out for them to stop. As he shoved through, two men fell out of their trance and tried to restrain him. Adrian lashed out with a perfectly placed elbow, catching one of them in the solar plexus, followed by a savage knuckle blow just above the bridge of the nose. Before the other man had time to react, a side snap kick was delivered with lightning speed to his groin area, knocking him off his feet and onto a swooning woman.

Adrian was getting closer to the altar, yanking people out of his path. He could see the santero — but couldn't believe his eyes. The man seemed to swell, to actually grow larger, as he raised the knife above his head. "No, not the baby!" cried Adrian, desperately lunging forward.

The blade came down swiftly.

But it severed a rooster's head, not the baby's. That's what he'd taken from the box. Immediately the santero pressed his mouth to the bird's neck, turning and twisting it for a moment until he threw his head back triumphantly with the wishbone between his teeth. He was crazed-looking, like a madman, eyes bugging out of his head, chin dripping crimson. Warm blood squirted from the gaping stub of a neck and over the stones. Dropping his knife to the floor, the santero used that hand to cradle the baby's head, and allowed a few drops of blood to mark him just above the eyes. During this baptism, the dead bird's feet quivered and wings flapped for another few seconds. Then it was still.

But the room was alive, the drums deafening, the chanting at a fever pitch. All around Adrian people were staggering, some falling over, their eyes open, staring blankly straight ahead, speaking in strange voices, hyperventilating. Everyone was screaming now, moving faster and faster to the beat, ignoring those who'd passed out and were writhing on the floor. But the men Adrian had struck weren't under the influence anymore; they were trying to push their way through, yelling in Spanish to people nearest them, explaining what had happened. The trouble was, Adrian could barely move now in this delirium. He was being swept along with it, the drums' pulse and continual chanting ricocheting off his brain, pulling him in deeper and deeper, his body swaying back and forth, as though he were off the ground, floating like he was inside a bubble. At the same time there was an incredible sense of strength, of being invincible, unbeatable, the most powerful person on earth. It was a gloriously pleasure-filled sensation. Yet part of his brain was calling out to him: get it together. You're in trouble. Outside the bubble, everything was in slow motion; people were pointing at him and talking about him, he could tell. But it was easier just to ride with the flow, to bounce and nod and reel. Gotta get out of here, gotta get air, gotta breathe. He felt a tug in the pit of his stomach, and it moved straight to his head, like there was a tube inside him for it to travel up. He was inhaling and exhaling heavily, so heavily he started to feel dizzy — but it wasn't really quite dizziness. It was something else, something he'd never experienced before. That floating sensation totally engulfed him, and he could see the frantic people thrashing around, only they seemed to be getting shorter. He was looking down on them and still rising; the tops of their heads were down below and the lightbulb was near, so close he could almost touch it. But blackness was closing in too, and a small rational corner of his brain was barking desperate orders at him: go back. Go back now — before it's too late. It was happening; he was speeding through a cone-shaped tunnel, a dark grey one, and he was traveling so fast through this vortex that it was impossible to comprehend a beginning or end to it. You must come back right away.

A fraction of a second later he could see the people around him on the floor again; but everything was blurry, although slowly growing clearer, and he was gasping for air, panting, feeling feeble now, the strength drained from him, his legs wobbly. He swung around spastically, banging into hot gyrating bodies, their sweat sticking to him, trying to head toward the door. To his right and closing in fast was the man he'd kicked. Adrian's stomach was churning and real dizziness was overtaking him as he groped through the crowd. But it was too late — he was going to faint, fall face-first to the cement, because the room was swirling, spinning the way a carnival ride did once when he was ten and got sick to his stomach.

What happened next was so unexpected that at first he assumed his head was playing more crazy tricks. But no, somebody was tugging his arm, guiding him through the crowd. Then there was warmth around his shoulders, a soft warmth on his neck and a firm grip holding him up, leading the way through a maze of twisting, turning people. His vision clearing, he turned his head — and saw it. That smile, that proud self-assertive smile.

Maria!

She was there, pushing him outside into the cool air. She must've been there all along, he thought, must've seen him and knew he needed help.

"Hurry," she whispered with a thick accent. "You must hurry." She was practically dragging him now.

With each second Adrian was letting more and more of the real world back in and regaining his strength. He broke into a run even though his legs were still shaky. The sound of the drums was muted somewhat and no longer head-splitting, fading behind him. Maria kept up the pace, leading him through knee-high grass and toward the edge of the precipice overlooking Guanabo. Adrian could see lights on in many of the homes down below. They kept walking along the edge of the bluffs for ten minutes, putting more and more distance between them and the house. The ritual must've ended because the drums stopped, the echo throughout the valley ceased, and there was peace.

Adrian turned away from the edge and faced the woman who still had an arm around his shoulders as if to steady him, which was a charade really, since both of them knew he could stand easily now by himself. She stared up at him, the moonlight adding a spark to her large round eyes. Next there was a delicious grin. He was struggling in a net of tangled thoughts, at once trying to figure out what had happened at the ritual, where Ricardo was, what Jennifer might be doing right now, and most of all, why he was burning inside for this woman, a guardian angel if there ever were one. Her large forehead was near his chin, and he couldn't stop himself; he pressed his mouth to it, tasting the salty perspiration, and then wrapped one of his arms around her shoulders, hesitating at first, not sure of himself, afraid of offending or even frightening her. "Gracias," he murmured, thanking her for the help, attempting to downplay the significance of the kiss — even though he so badly wanted more.

But it was as though she could read his thoughts. Suddenly she used both hands to clench his long hair, yanking his head down to her level, planting her open mouth on his, biting hard at his lips, forcing her tongue into him. Taken by surprise, he was slow to react at first, just hugging more tightly, hanging on for the ride. Their kiss seemed to last a millennium, as dozens of different thoughts collided in his brain. Then she became the focus of his senses: her taste, smell, sound and touch. He felt almost adolescent again, like this was one of his first real kisses. First there was the ritual. Now another dream was unfolding around him — a lot less threatening than the last one, which had certainly been the strangest experience of his life.

They were both teetering on their feet, gasping for air and exploring each other's mouths. Then without warning she tore away from him, giggling, and leapt onto the ground, lying prostrate, her face in the grass. Instantly he was on top of her, his need so urgent now, painfully pressed against his jeans, a throbbing ache that seemed to be getting stronger every second. Adrian's open mouth glided down soft hair to her neck and along her shoulders to the top of her dress. It was like he wanted to swallow her whole, to possess every inch of her, to taste and savor it forever. Reaching down, he tugged at the light blue dress she was wearing, and she responded by raising her hips so he could easily pull it up around her midsection. Then his mouth was there, biting her skin through the panties and kissing the small of her back ever so lightly. He could feel Maria's breathing getting deeper.

Still on her stomach and as if to give him a hint — or a helping hand — she took hold of her panties and slid them down part way; he got up on his knees and finished the job, pulling them right off, then separated her legs and lay down between them, his face nuzzling her inner thighs. The moonlight illuminated her generous backside, two white globes moving up and down slowly as he touched her. He kissed and licked her haunches, squeezing each side with his hands, spreading them, tongue running along the crevice in the dampness of her hair, gently stabbing at her most hidden place, the taste pungent in his mouth. Moving down farther between her legs, he wanted so much to touch her sensitive little trigger, but even with his chin brushing the grass, he couldn't reach. Obviously she knew what he was thinking because she moved up and rolled over at that exact moment, her legs straddling him. Amidst the dark moist tangles a thin white string dangled, like a luminous inchworm.

"Wait," she whispered, turning onto her side away from him to remove it. When Maria rolled over again, her face had that broad grin. Adrian wasn't sure whether she was embarrassed or simply finding humor in the situation.

His fingers opened her, and there were dark smears — the second time he'd seen blood tonight. He put his mouth there, tasted it, and then moved up to find her tiny pleasure point among the thick brown curls. While he played with her, she began to moan slightly and whisper the odd word in Spanish, which he couldn't understand. Nearing the peak, her fingers clutched at his hair and nails dug into his temples. Adrian was oblivious to it, his own hips grinding into the ground, completely tuned in to her sensations, the way every muscle tensed as she came, quivered for a few seconds and then loosened.

Afterward they were both on their knees kissing, his face still wet from her. She motioned for him to stand, and he got up slowly, almost groggily, still off somewhere else, lost in her orgasm, the memory of it fresh in his mind. She slid her hands around behind, gripping him tightly, and pressed her face against the bulge in his jeans. He couldn't take much more. Faster — he wanted her to go faster before he burst like a water balloon. Her fingers fumbled with the buttons on his fly. With his pants open, she could see it sticking straight up past the Calvin Klein underwear band, pulsing in spasms, as though it had a life of its own, trying to spring free of the restrictive clothing. A single touch of her hand was like an electric jolt to Adrian, he was so sensitive. Finally his sword was unsheathed, the months of frustration and angst behind him now, and he could revel in this supercharged moment. Her mouth encircled him, barely moving at first and then slowly into his rhythm. But it was only for a few seconds.

"No, no," he gasped, gently moving her head away from him.

She cupped one hand over the end and used the other to touch him as the most intense surge he'd ever experienced seemed to go on endlessly, wave after wave, as though all of the fluids in his body were running out of him in a single gusher.

"So much, so much!" exclaimed Maria afterward, examining both her hands.

"It's been a long time," he said, out of breath, wondering if she understood.

They both lay down on the bed of flattened grass and took off their clothes. After only a few minutes of hugging, deep kisses and fondling her large breasts, Adrian could feel desire rising in him again.

"Oh, no," laughed Maria.

"Oh, yes. But don't worry, it will never happen this fast again — except in my dreams." He rolled on top of her.

"Wait," she said, pushing him off and reaching for her purse.

"What is it?"

"Here." She handed him a condom.

"So you're a rubber maid, eh?"

She looked at him quizzically.

"Forget it," he said. "A feeble attempt at humor."

Twenty minutes later, while they were laying side by side, Maria took her hands off his hard, muscled chest, reached around behind her head and unsnapped something, handing him the string of tiny beads she'd been wearing. When Adrian hesitated, gawking at them in his palm, she took the beads and strung them around his neck.

"Protect," she said slowly, obviously a word she'd only recently learned.

"Resguardo," he told her.

"Si. Resguardo." She took his arm and put it to her cheek, looking serious now. "You will need, music man. Keep resguardo on."

Quite suddenly, a sound, low and guttural, a growl. Adrian realized he was the source of it. "Excuse me," he said, puzzled and embarrassed. "Maybe I didn't chew my dinner well enough."

Maria was laughing — but not at his joke.

Adrian looked down. He was hard again.

***

After paying the driver generously for her return trip from Havana, Jennifer stood alone at the entrance to La Sorpresa, gazing heavenward at the full moon and billions of stars that lit up the clear night. She glanced at her watch — almost midnight — and, craving fresh air, decided not to go back to the room right away. But she didn't want to walk on the beach either because of the ravenous sand fleas. An obvious spot seemed to be down the hill, part way to the beach, a private place where there were gardens of honeysuckle.

Once there, she flung off her sandals and felt around with her feet for the softest grass. Sitting all by herself was starting to become the norm, she thought, instinctively pulling the cotton wrap skirt up under her bent legs, and then smiling at what she'd just done, preserving her modesty when nobody was around. After a few minutes she lay back and stared up at the sky. A few stray blades of grass tickled her underarms, an area the silk tank top didn't cover. Restless, she sat up again, back straight, propped up by her arms. She gazed at the shrubs in front of her, the tops of which were painted a rich cascade of scarlet and lemon yellow, visible even under moonlight. After the hustle and blare of the nightclub — not to mention her own edginess — Jennifer was finally beginning to uncoil, lulled into relaxation by the gentle splash of waves as the tide went out, by the sweet-scented air and the peacefulness around her.

Abruptly her trance was broken when a blossom sailed into her lap. Looking up, she saw Juan, the lifeguard, his teeth flashing as he smiled down at her.

"Buenos nachos," he said.

"Buenos nachos," she greeted him back, wondering how he'd managed to come so close without her noticing.

He knelt down beside her, staring right into her face, which Jennifer found unnerving, but wouldn't give him the satisfaction of knowing that — so she looked right at him too. What kind of bloodline did he have, she wondered, with a blonde mane, such light hair for someone with dark brown eyes and so swarthy? The moment of silence was becoming uncomfortable now; Jennifer's mind raced, trying to recall some conversational Spanish, enough to talk even a little. It was no use though, since her command of the language was limited to the usual tourist phrases. Nervously she fidgeted with the red flower, twirling it between her fingers. It struck her how absurd this situation was, him hovering over her, both of them unable to speak, probably an idea in his head that he was going to make love with her — especially considering that she hadn't exactly dissuaded him on the beach a few nights before.

Quite slowly and deliberately he slid one of his bronze hands across her lap and put it around hers, squeezing so that she almost squashed the blossom. His thumb and forefinger massaged her wrist and stroked the back of her hand. The torn and wrinkled flower escaped her grip and fluttered down onto her skirt. Feeling awkward, she glanced down at it for a moment, noticing how in the darkness it resembled a blood stain. When she looked up, his face was very near to hers. In fact, she could clearly discern two scents on him: beer and some kind of lime aftershave.

Still on his knees, he leaned forward, the fingers of his other hand running delicately through her hair, grazing her forehead faintly, then down over her eyes and nose and onto her lips, barely making contact, tracing a profile of her face. Jennifer's pulse was racing; she didn't know what to do — or what Juan would do next. His fingers were so thick and strong, and he kept touching her lips with them, parting them slightly as he moved his hand. When one finger actually made contact with a front tooth, she shut her eyes and closed her mouth on it, tasting his skin for a few seconds. Then without notice he put both hands behind her neck and tugged Jennifer nearer to him so that her head nestled in his shoulder, and she could feel his mouth on her ear and temple, the warm breath caressing her hair. She brought her arms up and pushed against his chest in a half-hearted protest, feeling the ripples in his steely upper body. Grasping his arms, she noticed the swell of his massive biceps, which seemed as though they were going to split the sleeves of his white shirt any second.

Juan squeezed harder and pressed his mouth over hers — something that Jennifer hadn't expected to happen yet. His skin against hers felt moist, sticky even, from the humid air. He was nibbling on her lips. Quite inadvertently she let out a sound resembling a moan as she panted for air. This seemed to be a signal for him because one of his hands immediately went for her breast, tugging at it roughly, pinching the nipple through silk. His breathing grew heavier, in short spurts almost as though he were in the ring, and his exploring mouth lightly bit and sucked her cheek, then traveled down onto her neck.

She'd fanned the sparks, and now there was a fire in him. But Jennifer didn't know how to pull back, and although it would never show, she was in fact a little frightened — as well as excited. For the past fifteen years she'd been with only one man, someone whose touch was familiar if not predictable. Here she was in a foreign land with a complete stranger, and she couldn't even talk to him.

At that moment though, conversation was the last thing on Juan's mind. His squeezes were tighter and his kisses and bites harder. Clasping each of her wrists, he heaved Jennifer onto her back and lay astride her, grinding his hips into hers. She could feel his hardness pressing, urgent and seemingly uncontrollable. Hands still pinned above her head, she felt his mouth engulf hers like some cavernous creature with a mind of its own and a weapon: a tongue that was growing more insistent, no longer curious and gentle, but stabbing as if he were trying to prove he could reach her lungs. Then one of his hands suddenly left her wrist and slid like lightning down between her legs, yanking up the skirt around up her hips, forcefully enough that his fingers scratched her skin. He reached inside her panties, ripping them easily, since they provided a small resistance, splitting them down the seam so she was now completely exposed. A finger went directly into her without any warning, without any tease or coaxing.

Jennifer cursed herself for being wet — a result of her arousal a few minutes before — because she knew it would only serve to further encourage him. She was caught between entirely contrary feelings: on the one hand, thrill and excitement, which were beginning to wane as his behavior became more unsavory and downright savage; and on the other, fear and apprehension at having reached the point of no return.

His prodding of her ceased. Then there was the muffled sound of a zipper. That's when Jennifer forced her mouth away from his and shook her head. "No," she cried out, wrenching her arms free and pushing at his shoulders. "Get off me — now!"

Shocked, Juan pulled back, mouth wide open, looking like he'd just been told his mother was dead. He pushed himself up into a kneeling position, shaking his head, the startled look replaced by one of genuine questioning. His breathing was still heavy, and sweat covered his forehead and the underarms of his shirt.

Neither of them moved for a minute. Then Jennifer raised herself into a sitting position, straightened her hair and looked over at him. "I'm sorry," she said, knowing he probably understood those words. "But it just wasn't right. Not now anyway."

The Cuban shrugged, glancing at her warily out of the corner of his eye, like an animal that's just been beaten and, full of doubt, is prepared for what might happen next. He stood up and undid his shirt, throwing it on the grass next to her. Sighing loudly, he took two steps away and crossed his arms, peering in the direction of the beach.

Jennifer said no more, just looked at him, his face and upper body in profile, in silhouette against the blazing night sky. It was odd, she thought, because the situation should've been remarkably uncomfortable — yet it wasn't. She didn't feel threatened by him anymore; even he seemed quite calm, despite his obvious frustration. Inside her though still remained a twinge of hunger, a gnawing that made her second-guess the decision to go no farther.

The Cuban's eyes shot over to her for an instant and back to where he was gazing, toward the water's edge. Then, moving quite slowly and deliberately, he reached inside the open fly of his white neon-bright jeans, pulling out what was now limp, and began to urinate. Moonlight reflected off the steady stream as it hit the grass in a patter. Jennifer was glad to be sitting slightly uphill. She watched him resolutely, refusing to be intimidated or embarrassed, playing his game. Twice he looked over at her, and instead of meeting his eyes with her own, she continued unflinchingly to focus on his crotch. Afterward he spent an inexorably long time shaking out the last drops. Next he turned to face her, with it still dangling like a snake in front of him, dark against the luminescence of his jeans, looking somehow disembodied, not part of him anymore. Jennifer suddenly began to feel uncomfortable, like a peeper. She noticed a hint of a smile on Juan's slightly parted lips. His hands were at his sides, thumbs hooked in the front pockets of his jeans. Without even touching himself, he was beginning to grow hard. Perhaps it was her watching him, she thought, a little nervousness and titillation creeping over her at the same time. His foreskin receded as the shaft grew taut and smooth. It was curved, almost like a boomerang. She'd never seen a bent one before, not like this anyway, arched proudly in front of her, the head pointing upward at an angle, the same direction as the moon. A strange fantasy came to mind, of feeling her way along a row of naked aroused men in the darkness, touching one after another until she found him, because this boxer had more than one hook.

Chapter Fifteen

That morning, before leaving the island, Adrian felt almost hungover, as though he were recovering from too much of something, his mind overloaded with the goings-on of the night before. For some reason he felt strong, confident and impassioned now, fully in tune with his capabilities and primed to take on any challenge, no matter how demanding. His recollection of the previous night's events was still vivid, especially the sense of "floating" over the crowd he'd experienced and the magical rush that had come with it: like all his body fluids were boiling and coursing through him at tremendous speeds, pumping him up like a balloon. No drug had ever given Adrian such a high, had even come close. And somehow everything that happened there — including the liaison with Maria afterward — had served as a spark to ignite his spirit and destroy the feebleness, which had infected him like a plague since September.

It was all so confusing. How did a Cuban religion and his dreams tie in, he wondered? He needed to find out more about Santeria. Ever since the ritual he'd been going over and over countless riddles, trying to fathom how his dreams had foretold the experiences he had in Cuba. He only let Jennifer in on a few facts about the previous night's events: that he'd almost passed out during the ceremony and had a sensation of floating over the crowd. Naturally she seemed quite concerned, worried even, and warned him about any further delving into Santeria.

Of course, Sosa had been worried too after the ritual. Adrian was walking along the road to the resort when he'd caught sight of the Cuban. For nearly two hours Sosa had been riding the bike all over the village, as well as up and down the road, searching for his tourist friend. After Adrian called out to him, the Cuban seemed relieved to find him in good shape. Adrian explained that he'd been overcome by the heat and noise, and had left the house to get some air and start back down the hill to the resort. He made no mention of Maria.

The sun shone burning bright after breakfast as Adrian and Jennifer waited in their villa for the limousine to arrive. Sosa joined them to say goodbye, as invigorated as ever despite his lack of sleep.

"Here," said Adrian, passing him a plastic bag, "I want you to have these."

Sosa peeked inside and pulled out a Versace silk shirt and Nike running shoes — obviously items unavailable in Cuba. "I can't take your clothes," he said, smiling a little and shaking his head.

"Sure you can. I want you to have them…because you've given me a lot. And I'm pretty sure our foot size is the same."

"I am truly flabbergasted, Adrian," Sosa said, his fingers running over the sheen of the silk. "Thank you. And if there's anything I can do for you…"

"I want to learn more about Santeria."

Jennifer's mouth dropped.

The Cuban cited an article in a scientific journal, which he claimed was the most comprehensive information about Santeria in the English language. There were other references too, including a book in Spanish with the words to many orichas. Adrian jotted down the titles in his little notebook — along with the date in May and the hotel where Sosa would be staying in Montreal for his conference.

A bellboy arrived in a golf cart with a trailer to pick up their luggage. The limousine was waiting by the lobby.

On the plane, barely speaking to Jennifer or anyone else, Adrian experienced a virtual mental outpouring — an overflow really — as he madly jotted down one idea after another for songs. He was so caught up in it he refused the microwave-heated surf 'n' turf they were serving in first-class.

Surprisingly, the trip through Canada Customs hadn't fazed him on this occasion. Like other rockers, he was subjected to an intensive search after every excursion out of the country. In fact, on various tours he'd found it easier to get into Russia, Hungary — even China — than back into his own country. It was as though the customs bureaucrats thought every pop star was a drug abuser stupid enough to smuggle some home. As soon as they saw his passport he was taken aside, then to another area for a complete luggage check and sometimes even to a small inspection room for a strip search and rubber-glove probe. But this time the predictable hold-up through customs hadn't dampened his enthusiasm in the least; it seemed as though nothing could hold him back anymore.

By the time they arrived back at their house about nine o'clock, Adrian was still riding a rush of exhilaration, like someone who's been lost for a long time and suddenly finds the path again. He could hardly wait to immerse himself in the music, to experience the explosive purge of pent-up thoughts that had accumulated since he'd been at the ritual.

Dumping suitcases in their dressing room, he went straight to work in the den. Jennifer planned to unpack and then go to bed.

Later, aiming the remote control at the cassette deck, he punched off the music that was pouring out of headphones into his ears. In front of him on the burgundy leather blotter atop his century-old rolltop desk were hastily scribbled, crossed-out and rewritten words: the lyrics to a song. Adrian slid the headphones — which he wore when Jennifer didn't want to be disturbed — from his ears and then copied the composition neatly onto a fresh sheet of paper, reading it once more as he did so. Afterward he glanced over at the grandfather clock ticking away in the corner, wedged between oak bookcases. Four in the morning. It was time for a breather, to escape his thoughts for a little while; and then he would come back refreshed for one final go at the verses and chorus, singing to himself along with the music, to make sure what he'd written meshed perfectly with the melody.

Despite the late hour, words had come easily to him tonight, and he knew they were good. Standing up, he leaned back and stretched his arms out to each side, breathing deeply, then joined his hands briefly to crack the stiffness out of his tight knuckles. The dozen or so newspapers caught his eye, stacked neatly on an antique filing cabinet near the window. Natalie, their cleaning woman, always did this when they were both out of town. He sauntered over to the pile and leafed through a few sections, thinking about how irrelevant old news is, when the top story a few days before is so quickly out of date, so utterly dead. Even bread doesn't get stale as quickly as a newspaper.

Just about to walk away, Adrian noticed something on the front page of that morning's Globe and Mail, obviously meant to be a "light" item, sandwiched in among longer, more important stories:

Miguel Michardo of Miami is due this week to appear before
the U.S. Supreme Court to defend the right of his Santeria
Church to sacrifice chickens and other animals during services.
A supporting brief by the Presbyterian Church says: "One
can get Chicken McNuggets in Hialeah, Florida, but one may
not kill a chicken for religious reasons."

He was absolutely astounded at the sheer coincidence. The same day he arrives back in Toronto, thousands of miles removed from Santeria and caught in the frozen vice grip of a long harsh winter, there's an article in the paper about this obscure religion, which probably only a handful of Toronto's two-and-a-half million residents even know about. In fact, if he hadn't gone to Cuba, Adrian never would have heard of it either. Only now he felt like some kind of expert on Santeria — especially after the night before last.

When he finished reading, the page slid through his fingers, and he stood there for a moment switched onto replay, thinking about the ritual, the santero, the baby, the rooster. Shaking off the memory he left the library and tiptoed to the bathroom along the creaking hardwood floor in the hall. He removed his brown suede wingtips and padded from there into the large walk-in closet and dressing room that adjoined the master bedroom. Opening the door a crack and allowing a sliver of light to escape, he peered into the darkness of the room. Jennifer rustled under the covers.

"Adrian," her voice said weakly, still ensconced in the depths of sleep but worried-sounding nonetheless. "Is that you?"

"Yeah."

There was such a long pause that Adrian believed Jennifer had fallen back asleep. Then she raised her head up and squinted at the clock radio on the bedside table."Oh God, look at the time. What are you doing?" Her words were spoken with that drugged-sounding, out-of-breath whisper, the way people do when they're not fully conscious.

"I've been writing. Got a whole song finished, believe it or not. At this rate I'll have the other fourteen done in a couple of weeks."

"Hmmm." She was nodding, trying to fight off the sleep.

Shutting the door to the dressing room behind him he walked in, eyes adjusting to the blackness as he made his way to the window. Pulling the curtain aside a few inches he peered down at the street below where gently falling snow was being melted by road salt. Without even a hint of a breeze it was one of those postcard winter scenes: fat snowflakes dancing a little as they dropped onto rooftops and evergreens. A couple of houses still had on twinkling colored Christmas lights, despite the hour and even though it was already a couple of days into the new year.

Jennifer stirred behind him. "Are you coming to bed now?"

"Soon," he replied in a low voice, "after I go over my song again."

"You're crazy. It's almost time to get up."

"Well, don't bother waking me. I've got to finish, no matter how long it takes."

"Fine with me." Her words were trailing off.

Adrian moved back toward the big brass bed, arms outstretched in front of him so he wouldn't run into one of the posts if the shadows played tricks on his eyes. There was a crack of brightness under the door, just enough light for him to make out Jennifer's shape in the bed. He leaned over and touched her shoulders lightly. Her arms reached out to him, encircling his neck. She pulled his face onto hers, and he nuzzled and kissed her delicately on the cheeks and neck. Even this fleeting contact had an effect on him; already the crotch of his pants was tight. He couldn't believe it — hard in twenty seconds flat.

"Good night," she whispered, giving him a last kiss and then turning onto her side.

No use pressing the issue when it was this late, he thought, wondering whether some quick relief in the bathroom by his own hand might suffice. He walked back into the dressing room and closed the door softly. Jennifer's luggage had been unpacked and put up on the shelf neatly. His bulging suitcase and garment bag were still slung over a chair, where he'd dumped them. For a moment he stared at the mirror on the wall opposite him to admire the bronzed unshaven face and golden-streaked shaggy hair. Looking into his own eyes he saw strength and determination where there had been none a short time ago.

Then he turned his attention back to his bags. Once unzipped, the large suitcase overflowed with clothes, shoes, books, a shaving kit and toiletries. Rolling up all his laundry like a big snowball, he walked over to the hamper and dumped it in. Next he removed a sweater and sweatshirts — and the drums, which had barely fit. In a flap at the back of the suitcase were boxes of wooden matches, his Swiss Army knife, tanning lotions and Maria's resguardo. Adrian looked closely at the string of tiny blue beads, many of which were smeared with a ruddy substance but that didn't particularly detract from their appearance; in fact, the two colors complemented each other. He stood there for a minute, holding the beads and thinking of an explanation. Well, he could always say that Ricardo had given them to him. Sooner or later he knew Jennifer would ask, so it seemed perfectly logical to say Sosa had insisted — especially after Adrian had offered up his clothes as a gift.

Adrian stuffed the beads in his pants pocket and dug into the suitcase again, pulling out a few magazines and books, and near the bottom some pairs of socks he hadn't worn. Then his heart jumped.

The stones!

There was the sack. He stood there dumbstruck, mind racing, trying to put thoughts in order. But he was sure he'd thrown them out a couple of nights ago, after he'd shown them to Jennifer and agreed with her that they had to go. When they'd finished dinner Jennifer returned to the villa; he stayed behind at the bar. I was positive I took them outside after I got back, he thought. Jenny was sleeping, and the sack was on the chair where I'd left it.

But perhaps his mind was dulled from the after-dinner rum. Maybe he hadn't picked them up after all. Yet why did he distinctly remember stumbling around in the dark and tossing the sack into some shrubbery where it wouldn't be seen? Obviously that recollection wasn't correct because the stones were in his suitcase right now. Over the years he'd been drunk and stoned more times than he cared to remember, but never had his mind worked against him like this — not just blacking out but actually twisting the facts, making him think he'd done one thing when really he'd done another. Adrian picked up the sack, poured a few of the stones onto his hand and rolled them around in his palm. So now there was another mystery. One by one he slipped the stones back into the sack and tugged the drawstring taut. Picking up the drums he went through the bathroom and headed down the long hall toward the library.

It was in the second drawer on the left that Adrian stashed the sack and beads. All of the drawers on that side of the desk contained items relating to his career, like newspaper and magazine articles about Tangent, keepsake letters from fans, early promotional photos of the band and little souvenirs from their tours over the years. Jennifer knew what he kept in these drawers, and it would be rare for her to ever go through them.

Leaving his chair he flopped onto the carpet and picked up the sacred drums, once again examining their crude construction, the way rough goat skin had been stretched over the shell and a wooden hoop nailed on to hold it in place. Looking at them brought back a memory of the big black woman covered in perspiration hammering on the heads with incredible force, bringing her arms down as though she were trying to destroy them instead of playing, totally caught up in the rhythm that was pounding through the room. Even if she had been mesmerized by the ritual, her passionate playing was something familiar to Adrian. Sometimes when he practiced, the same kind of feeling would sweep over him too. Of course, in playing percussion well, control is absolutely imperative; it's what separates the amateurs from the professionals. The best drummers are almost effortless in their movements, showing little if any strain no matter how fast or hard they're playing. But because of the nature of the instrument — something you flail with sticks — every drummer at one time or another lets go. Even now Adrian would occasionally practice something as rudimentary as a single-stroke roll, an ordinary one-two, one-two, which would get progressively faster. Or he would bring in both bass drums, the balls of his feet kicking the pedals faster than any Olympic sprinter's feet hit the ground. Veins would bulge out of his arms, and his mouth would distort with the strain, but it was a kind of mental and physical high. Perhaps that was why he enjoyed working out on a heavy bag or speedball, punching out combinations over and over, faster and harder; the rhythm of boxing seemed similar to that of drumming.

When he played drums during a solo, the crowd would get involved in the pounding, almost hypnotized by it, cheering wildly at the conclusion. And that was no different from the people at a Santeria ritual, who were caught up in the drums too. Both drummers in that hot house created a pulse that invaded the souls of everyone there — including himself. How ironic, he thought, because he was a drummer too. Yet he'd been affected just as much, or perhaps more so.

But that's what he was rewarded so handsomely to do: connect with people through music, so much so you take them onto a different plane. All of the laser shows, giant video monitors, dry ice, flash pots and banks upon banks of speakers were just window dressing. In essence, rock and roll was still as primitive and gut-tugging as howling at the moon — and had a lot in common with the tribal drummers of Africa and, much later, the black-inspired American rhythm and blues.

Adrian tapped very lightly on the tom-toms with his fingertips. Next week, he decided, would be a good time to have Tangent's drum technician come to the house and mount these onto his practice set in the basement. The thought of it made him smile: that really would be marching to the beat of a different drum. High tech meets Old World.

He got up off the carpet and sat in his chair again, ready to go over the lyrics one more time, his mind clear and more objective after the little break. Holding the paper up in front of him, his eyes ran over the words quickly, and he nodded approvingly, allowing himself a slight self-congratulatory smile. With the headphones back on and remote control in hand, he rewound the cassette to the beginning of the music and then punched the "play" button. As the melody filled his head he sang along in a low voice, barely reading the lyrics, since he'd memorized them by now. His new song, Full Color Bend, was complete.

> When you stop soaring, begin to lose height
> Excuses or denial won't set things right
> Can't cough up what you used to be
> Because it's phlegm that surfaces, not destiny
>
> If the mind is set, the heart will follow
> No pill ever too bitter or big to swallow
> Blinding weakness always robs you of light
> Must reaffirm what you are, regain lost sight
>
> Call on the strength within
> Always fight to win
> So what's the sin?
> Do a full color bend
> Supercharged spirit
> The means to an end
>
> Banish those demons of imagined inadequacy
> Power surge your soul, lash out defiantly
> What ceases to exist is matter over mind
> Weakness afflicts others, never again your kind

Call on the strength within
Always fight to win
So what's the sin?
Do a full color bend
Supercharged spirit
The means to an end

Chapter Sixteen

Chuck Bolan threaded his way through the noon-hour crowds congregating in the basement food court and shopping concourse of a gleaming glass office tower. He was oblivious to everything around him: the neon signs and garishly colored paint to liven up a windowless environment, the clatter that echoed off hard floors and walls, the combined scents of fatty fast food — Chinese, fried chicken, burgers, pizza, deli. None of this penetrated his consciousness. Right now Bolan's focus was on the upcoming meeting with his lawyer.

Riding the escalator to the lobby, he could feel tension in every muscle of his body.

Not drinking for the past month had deprived him of an outlet for stress. Even a nightly walk — before he left for the midnight shift on the security desk — didn't allow him to unwind sufficiently. This healthy life wasn't all it was cracked up to be, he thought, as he double-checked the suite number on the lobby directory.

After whooshing up forty-nine floors so fast it felt like his stomach got left behind, he exited the elevator into the plush elegant offices of Baker, Thomson. It was almost eerily silent in the reception area. As he stepped up to a marble-top reception desk, Bolan glanced at the leather sofas, oriental rugs and paintings that he was helping to pay for.

"I'm here to see Barry Brodsky," he said curtly.

"I'll let his secretary know you're here." The woman behind the desk was fiftyish and attractive in a severe kind of way. "You can hang up your coat over there, Mr. Bolan," she said, motioning to the double doors just off the foyer.

He slid into one of the sofas and picked up the morning paper off a glass coffee table. To read he had to hold it out almost at arm's length. For the past year he'd been avoiding the inevitable: glasses.

A few minutes later, Brodsky's secretary appeared and led him to a small boardroom, where he waited some more. Finally the door opened and a bull-like man strode in, almost as tall as Bolan, large-boned with broad sloping shoulders. What little neck he had spilled over his stretched white shirt collar. His full head of black hair was coarse and unruly; even though it was just past noon he already looked in need of a shave.

"Nice to see you again, Chuck," he said, hand outstretched even before Bolan could rise from his seat. Spreading out some papers on the boardroom table, Brodsky got down to business right away. "As I told you on the telephone, the court date's been set for February the third. That gives us less than a month. I tried but couldn't get another remand."

Bolan shrugged. "Maybe it's better to get the thing over with now."

"Not necessarily. The longer the wait, the less people remember. Everything gets a little fuzzy as time wears on. That's to our advantage when we have them up on the witness stand. Makes it easier to discredit their testimony."

"What's our strategy going to be?"

Brodsky leaned back in his seat and cracked his knuckles. "Well, your record on the force should speak for itself. And we'll emphasize that you had been under quite a great deal of stress before the assault. So you weren't thinking clearly. And we'll show that your intent was not attempted murder or to seriously harm. Then there's the fact that you've quit drinking and cleaned up your act all by yourself. Judges like to hear that people have repented, turned over a new leaf, that kind of thing."

"What about how it was a mistake and I roughed up the wrong person?"

"No, we'll steer clear from that one. It doesn't matter if your intended victim was really a criminal and not a musician. The law doesn't take kindly to you assaulting either of them. Especially right now, with this publicity about police shooting people needlessly and kicking them while they're down."

"It figures," said Bolan. "Nobody ever looks at our side of the story. All the guys on the force are pissed off. Morale is at an all-time low. We ask for semi-automatic pistols — and finally they say yes, but with budget cuts it will take ten years before everybody gets one. Even though the assholes on the street are coming at us with nine millimeter guns and dum-dum bullets that make your head explode. They're better equipped than we are — and we're the cops."

Brodsky nodded in agreement. "I understand where you're coming from, Chuck...but let's not forget about what people see as an abuse of power. Your beating that musician is just one example."

"That was a mistake. Shouldn't have happened. What I'm talking about is the politicians and media being so worried about police violence and racism on the force that they're forgetting one thing: how dangerous it is to keep this city safe nowadays."

"I'm sure that's the way it is but politicians are only swayed by public opinion — not the truth."

"The trouble is that everything they ever learned came from books...not on the street, that's for sure. Look at the yahoos on the Police Commission, telling us how to do our jobs — and not to ever make mistakes. Calling us racists because some scummy dealer gets shot...and he happens to be black. I'd like to see one of them do our job, run up the back stairs of some shithole and break into a crack den full of wired-up weirdos with sawed-off shotguns."

"Okay, okay," said Brodsky, raising his hands for emphasis, "your point's made. But the fact of the matter is that you beat an innocent person — who just happened to be well known, to make matters worse. And whether it was a mistake or not, you're charged with aggravated assault with intent to murder."

Bolan stiffened at those words, as he did every time he read or heard the charges against him. "So what are we looking at here? Are you going to be able to get me off?"

"I honestly can't say."

"What's that supposed to mean?"

Brodsky looked him straight in the eyes. "The judge may see things our way and agree that the charges don't fit the crime, that you fucked up and you're sorry. On the other hand there were plenty of witnesses who watched you hurt the musician — including his wife. So the judge may want to make an example of you…to keep the rest of the force in line."

"And if that happens?"

"If you're found guilty, then you'll probably end up being sentenced to a prison term — but not more than a year or eighteen months. With parole for good behavior you might only serve four or five months…certainly not the end of the world."

Not the end of the world! Bolan's heart dropped. Who was he trying to kid? Going to jail would spell the end of the life he'd lived so far. With a record, he could never be a law-enforcement officer again — and that was all he knew how to do. He tried to imagine himself serving time in an institution where he'd placed a number of inmates over the years. They wouldn't be very happy to see him. The thought sent chills through him.

***

Katherine Bontempo was standing at the entrance to the Robarts Library, fidgeting with a paper clip as she waited, her long skinny fingers twisting it into grotesque shapes until finally it snapped. A normally hyper, impatient person, she was bothered that Adrian Lee was already twenty minutes late — and worried he might not show at all, that maybe one of them had gotten the date or time wrong. Only those attending the University of Toronto had access to the large research library; some of the floors were restricted to graduate students. Without her, Adrian would be denied entry. She decided to give him another ten minutes.

Now a senior librarian, Katherine had known Adrian since he first started going out with Jennifer. She and Jennifer had been classmates at university, both of them enrolled in Bachelor of Arts programs with some common courses. Later, after graduation, Katherine branched out into library sciences and eventually earned her Master's degree. Although the pair weren't as close as they'd once been as students, they still had lunch together every couple of months and dinner three or four times a year. Conservative in appearance, Katherine Bontempo had dark brown hair that was always cut quite plainly, lopped off bluntly just before it reached her shoulders, which wasn't particularly flattering since she had a finely chiseled, angular face and expressive brown eyes. Her outfits were middle of the road too, never daring or too boldly colored. Although she was warm and considerate, her taste in men seemed to run in a distinctly opposite direction: tough, mean-spirited, flawed individuals who often victimized her. The most recent relationship — a year-long affair — had just ended a couple of months before; he worked in a parking garage, had a drug problem and sometimes struck her when he was stoned or drinking too much. Now Katherine Bontempo was living alone again in her small suburban townhouse.

She spotted him walking toward the modern grey-slab library building, which seemed so out of place among the brownstones that comprised most of the downtown campus. Adrian sauntered up the steps and held open one of the large glass doors for two young women who were burdened down by briefcases and books. In black jeans, black cowboy boots and a black leather motorcycle jacket, he cut a shadowy figure against the piles of slushy melting snow that remained from a heavy downfall two days before. This day had been absolutely balmy though, with spring-like warmth that was unusual for mid-January.

He smiled at Katherine and greeted her with a peck on the cheek. "Sorry to be so late," he said, "but it took a lot longer at the doctor than I thought it would."

"Oh, is something wrong?" she inquired.

"No, no, it's just the sports doctor I go to. Maybe this arm hasn't healed right since it was broken. I'm having some trouble with it, especially pushing weights and in karate. Even when I play drums there's a little pain."

"It sounds serious."

Adrian shook his head. "The doctor doesn't think so. He says I'm overdoing it with the workouts. So I guess I'd better slow down a little." He unzipped the jacket to reveal silver buttons that jumped off his dark shirt. A number of people glanced over at him as they went about their business, but even those who recognized him didn't intrude.

"Well, let's go then." Katherine turned and motioned to a security guard. "He's with me," she said smiling.

They took an elevator up two floors and emerged into a strangely silent environment. This was truly foreign terrain for Adrian; walking along endless narrow aisles between ten-foot-high crammed bookshelves made him feel a little claustrophobic. Finally the two of them entered an open area near the rear of the building and went to Katherine's tidy metal desk. She took her place behind it while he pulled up a stiff-backed chair.

"So...have you got something for me?" he asked.

"Of course. After you called on Monday I got right on it. Your friend in Cuba said the article was in the late forties, right? Well, he was close. It was in the Southwestern Journal of Anthropology in 1950. The information for the piece was from a speech that William Bascom gave here in Toronto in 1948."

"So Bascom was well known, eh?"

"Yes, quite. A top anthropologist and professor at UCLA."

"I'm glad you had the journal handy."

"As a matter of fact, we didn't have it going back that far. So we phoned UCLA, and they faxed us a copy of the article. They're sending a photocopy by mail too."

"Good stuff."

"Your friend was right about something else: there's very little on Santeria in English. I went through our whole microfich indexing system but could only come up with these." She opened a drawer and took out four books, which she pushed across the desk to him. "The one with the verses is in Spanish," she pointed out. Then she passed him five loose pages held together by a paper clip, the ones that had been sent by fax.

Adrian opened one of the books, a thick old volume called The Golden Bough by someone named James G. Frazer. He flipped through hundreds of well-thumbed pages, feeling a little downhearted as he noticed all the words, suddenly realizing how much work there was to researching. No wonder he preferred songwriting.

"That's one of the best books on contagious magic," explained Katherine, enthusiasm bubbling up in her. "It's from 1911 and has a whole section on how things that were once in contact can continue to act on each other without any physical proximity. They call it sympathetic magic."

"Sounds like you've read it already," Adrian remarked, glancing up from the pages.

"Hardly. I just checked to make sure it was something like you asked for. And then there are these two books about the Yoruba of Nigeria and their rituals. There's lots of stuff here."

"Great. I'm on my way to becoming an expert on primitive religions."

The librarian laughed. "You mentioned the ritual in Cuba and the psychiatrist…but I still don't get it. How come all this interest?"

"I thought I'd write a thriller about it."

"Seriously?"

Even after all these years, Adrian thought, she didn't know when he was putting her on. "Can you imagine me writing a novel about Santeria? No way. I'm just fascinated with this stuff after being so close to it in Cuba, that's all. And that guy I told you about–Ricardo Sosa–was an excellent teacher. He really got me going. Who knows though…I may get a song or two out of all this." He patted the stack of books to emphasize his point.

"I'm surprised you don't have Jenny on the trail helping you dig up information."

"Nah, this is my hobby. In fact, when we were in Cuba, I think she was a little pissed off at me for getting so involved."

Katherine looked at him quizzically. "That's odd. I thought Jenny would really be into this."

Adrian shrugged. "Maybe she's just giving me some space to do my own thing." There was a pause. "Anyway…I guess I'd better let you get back to work." He stood up and gathered together the papers and weighty hardcover volumes.

"I should have a picture of this," she laughed. "Never in a million years did I think I'd see you in this place with a stack of reference books under your arm."

"Well, I do read, you know."

"I know. I'm just kidding you for a change." She came around from behind the desk. "I'll have to let you out or somebody will squawk…especially when you're carrying books."

They walked back along the same cramped aisles, occasionally squeezing by someone who was intently scanning the packed shelves. Downstairs in the checkout area near the exit she stopped by the main desk and nodded to the security guard to let him through. A couple of male students on their way in hesitated for a few moments and stared at Adrian, obviously aware of whom he was.

He ignored them and turned to Katherine. "Thanks a lot. I owe you one for this."

"No problem, gorgeous. This is what I do every day."

"I really do appreciate the trouble you've gone to."

"Well, it's great to see you. You're looking good too. Jenny told me a few weeks ago how miserable you were after that…that…trouble." Her voice trailed off.

Adrian stiffened. He could tell right away Jennifer had probably confided in Katherine about everything — his writer's block, perhaps even his impotence.

Chapter Seventeen

Since the evening before, more than fifteen inches of heavy, moist snow had devoured the landscape, dropping from a cheerless sky almost the hue of gunmetal. This morning was a little brighter at least — an oyster grey that was benign-looking but stripped the world of color — and the snow had been reduced to a trickle of flurries. By this time just after rush hour, salt and dirt had only been spread on main streets, so much of the city had slowed to a crawl as people dug out of their driveways and navigated slippery streets on their way to work.

The orange and black Diamond cab pulled over toward the curb through a mountain of brown slush. The driver, who looked and smelled as though he'd just crawled out of a hole, slapped the flag down to halt the meter. A little packet of coconut-scented air freshener bobbed from the rearview mirror — but it was no match for the overpowering body odor and smell of stale tobacco that clung to the cabbie. Glad to be getting out, Adrian filled in the taxi voucher, glancing at his watch for the time and date: nine-thirty on the eighteenth. As he scrawled his signature and handed the piece of paper to the driver it occurred to him that February was more than half over and he'd spent all of it except weekends in court every day. For almost three weeks he'd had to endure life as a three-ring circus, where he was the star attraction.

Each morning a media horde would descend upon him like a pack of jackals, scavenging for whatever small juicy morsels might be available. Of course, the Crown prosecutor had already warned him about speaking to reporters — not that he would've anyway with a case before the courts. Still, on his way in day after day they fired the same questions at him, shoved microphones into his face and shot video footage and dozens of still photos. Over the years he'd given more interviews than he cared to remember, but always to fawning music journalists who hung onto every word he spoke. What a different breed these people were. Without any statements from him, they took to describing what he was wearing that day, and how Jennifer was dressed if she were accompanying him. Since cameras aren't allowed in any courthouse, they covered all the entrances, lying in wait, hoping to snap some new shots. Every night on the TV news, there he was walking up the steps into court. Then the same kind of shot in the next morning's newspapers. After a week or so there was file footage of him, used over and over on television; he was a one-man rerun.

Stepping out of the cab, Adrian hopped gingerly over some foot-high globs of slush at the roadside, trying to avoid the rust-colored icy mess. He knew his shoes would be soaked before the two-block walk to court. After all these years he'd never been able to accept the idea of galoshes or rubbers because they just weren't cool; it was a throwback to high school, and unfortunately for his footwear the attitude had stuck. His sleek black Italian oxfords weren't made for this kind of winter lashing.

Most other mornings though — when the sidewalks were clear of snow — he enjoyed the little trek to the courthouse. It was rather like a game. Each day he had the taxi drop him off at a different spot so his arrival wouldn't be obvious to the press corps. He could survey the scene before deciding which entrance was the least populated by media people and afforded the easiest access. Adrian had learned all this the hard way. The first day in court, he and Jennifer arrived in a chauffeur-driven limousine that the band's manager, Reg Howarth, had arranged for them. The sheer conspicuousness attracted not only the media but dozens of fans who had nothing better to do than wait around for a glimpse of him. To add to the confusion there were also a number of placard-carrying protestors screaming out slogans about police brutality.

Driving his own car downtown wasn't much better. He'd park at a nearby underground lot but was always discovered by a photographer or video cameraman as he climbed the stairs to the exit. So he got Reg to start a cab account, and was picked up at his house each morning and dropped off nearby his destination, where he could begin the little subterfuge.

Rounding a corner onto Bay Street, in the heart of the city's financial district, he had the Old City Hall looming straight ahead, a century-old stately structure that now housed courtrooms. Built of pinkish sandstone blocks and with a chameleon-like roof of copper that had oxidized to light green, it sported a massive belfry with an ornate clock on each of the tower's four sides. As he drew closer to the intersection of Bay and Queen, Adrian noticed the main entrance seemed to be unusually quiet, without the throng of reporters and photographers who normally accosted him. Maybe they were covering the side and back entrances, since he hadn't gone through the front door for two weeks.

At the stoplights he lifted the collar of his camel overcoat up around his neck, covering his long but neatly trimmed hair, in an attempt to disguise himself somewhat. Hands jammed into the coat pockets and his head facing down to the road, Adrian rushed across the intersection and toward the steps of Old City Hall. The bells from a clattering old streetcar startled him for a second. Downtown sounds–cars slurping through the snow, horns honking, trucks rattling–assaulted his ears. The moist air seemed to intensify smells too, from car exhaust and diesel fumes. His feet were wet and cold now. With the temperature hovering around the freezing point, there was a dampness that cut to the bone, worse than any really cold day when the air was dry. He was halfway up the stairs toward the warmth inside when–

"–Mr. Lee." A loud nasal voice to his left summoned him. It was Curt Makit, court reporter for the Globe and Mail, a tall man with a perpetually red runny nose. "Mr. Lee, how about it? The trial's probably finished today. How do you feel about the outcome?" He stepped out in front of Adrian.

"Excuse me," came another voice, a woman's.

Adrian stopped and turned. It was Jan Fletcher from one of the TV stations; he couldn't remember which at the moment. An obese cameraman's camcorder hummed away, catching the musician's look of disgust on video.

"Do you have any comments? Is he going to get off?" she asked.

"I have nothing to say." Adrian spat out the words and stepped around the Globe reporter, only to be confronted by another journalist coming out of the building. The musician pushed between them and aggressively barged his way through one of the large wooden doors.

At least there were no cameras inside. But print and radio reporters trailed him doggedly, a little quieter and more restrained, but just as bothersome nonetheless. During the first days of the case, even while being pestered by the media on his way in, Adrian had marveled at the architecture of Old City Hall, which he'd never been in before, even though he had lived all his life in the city. From the patterned mosaic tiles on the floor to the cream-colored marble walls and well-worn mahogany benches, this environment was steeped in colonial British tradition. Only the trains of sterile fluorescent lights and ubiquitous "No Smoking" signs were from the present; everything else dated back to the turn of the century, when they still built palaces like this that reinforced the public's reverence for authority. A stained-glass window three storey's high dominated the foyer, greeting visitors with its images of WASP males, subservient aboriginal people, a Union Jack flying high and the city hall being built in the background. All this under the words: "Industry, Integrity, Intelligence."

But today as he strode up the stairs in front of the colorful cut glass, Adrian wasn't dwelling on architecture. As the court case had unraveled now to a logical conclusion, he was distinctly aware of the possibility that detective Charles Bolan was going to walk away from these criminal charges free and clear. That unsettling thought had been troubling him since the third day of the trial; the doubts had been growing inside ever since, like a trickle of bile that's turned into a flood. He could almost taste the anger lodged in the pit of his stomach.

Immersed in thought, he ceased to be aware even of the reporters pacing him as he marched along the second-floor hall to Courtroom 121. It was one of the largest of the thirty-two courtrooms spread out on three floors of the building, along with bail rooms and offices for the prosecutors. There was a fourth floor too, with rooms for the media to file stories from and congregate in between sessions.

"Good morning," came the usual unemotional, businesslike greeting of Barbara Poynton, the Crown prosecutor. She was a tall wiry woman, and the black robes she wore emphasized these features. A sprinkling of grey in her otherwise dark hair added some much-needed mature looks to her young visage.

Adrian swung around to face her. Reporters had encircled both of them, eagerly anticipating a slip of the tongue that might result in headlines.

"How are you?" he asked, equally formal, unbuttoning his overcoat and straightening the conservative tie that went with an unobtrusive double-breasted suit.

"Fine," she replied. "We still have twenty minutes. I wonder if I could speak to you inside the courtroom."

"Sure."

"Thank you."

She walked over to the door and tapped loudly a few times on the frosted-glass window. Opening it just a crack, a security guard scrutinized her for an instant, nodded hello and beckoned them in, closing the door behind.

Courtroom 121 was an imposing place, full of dark stained wood: the ceiling arches, balconies, benches and, most of all, the heavily ornamented judge's bench. It was throne-like, with a frame and peaked roof, and large globular lamps on each side of the structure, resembling something right out of a Dickens novel.

Inside — and well away from the reporters' earshot — Barbara Poynton became a little more animated, forcing a weak smile. Yet tension still showed in her features. This was her first high-profile case as a prosecutor. Adrian could see from the circles under her eyes that she hadn't been sleeping much since the trial had begun. While he sat down on one of the benches, she stood there rather ill at ease, bulging briefcase in hand, hovering over him like a schoolteacher during test time.

"Your wife isn't with you today?"

"She'll probably be here in a couple of hours," he answered. "There's something with her volunteer work — you know, CANFAR, the AIDS group."

The woman nodded. Then there was an awkward silence.

"As you're aware," she began finally, "today the defense counsel and I were supposed to address the judge with our final summations. Well, there's been a little twist. Remember Reg Howarth's testimony last week? Now there's been a motion to recall you this morning for a cross-examination relating to what he said."

Adrian sighed out loud. "Yeah…great. I thought we'd just about wrapped this thing up."

"To tell you the truth, I'm as surprised as you are."

"What do you think Reg said that they picked up on?"

Barbara Poynton shrugged and forced a tight-lipped little smile. "I was going to ask you the same thing."

"Well…nothing comes to mind right now. Shit, I can't even remember what he was talking about; there's been so many witnesses."

"You never know — it might be a ploy, a last-ditch attempt to discredit you."

"Why?"

"Because then your testimony would be the final thing the judge remembers before our summations. It might stand out in his mind. Especially if they can make you look bad — which of course they can't."

"My lucky day," said Adrian dejectedly, not buying her attempt at ending on a positive note. "Five hours on the stand wasn't good enough before. Now they want blood."

"Don't worry. You'll do just fine. And I'm sure you won't be up there very long either. Just think of it as an opportunity; you're going to have the last word."

"Thanks for the motivational speech, but there's no way I see this as an opportunity. No way."

"Well, keep your chin up…and don't give an inch."

The door was opened again, this time for the assistant Crown attorney, Gim Wong, a pudgy young Asian man with an easygoing manner. He carried a shiny, new-looking briefcase that was even fatter than Poynton's, absolutely stuffed to the brim with file folders and stacks of papers. He smiled and nodded to each of them.

"Excuse me," said Poynton, "but I think we'd better get ready now." She left the row of bench seats and joined her assistant at their table up front in the courtroom.

Adrian watched as the two of them spread out papers and conferred, their voices never more than a whisper. He noticed Wong was as bleary-eyed as his boss, probably from putting in the same kind of hours on this case as she had.

While he did appreciate their tremendous efforts, Adrian had never felt any degree of confidence in these prosecutors. They seemed too inexperienced and mild-mannered, not aggressive enough to stand up to the defense. Of course, it would take a special kind of person indeed not only to lock horns — but come out a victor — against Charles Bolan's lawyer.

At that instant, just when Adrian was thinking about him, Barry Brodsky entered the courtroom with his client, the police detective. They both went to the front and sat down at their table. The defense lawyer, attired in black robes like the prosecutor, unlocked his maroon briefcase with a tiny key that he kept in the pocket of his pants. He glanced over at the prosecutors' table and nodded curtly to them as he meticulously laid sheaves of papers down in a particular order known only to him.

Before he'd ever laid eyes on the lawyer, Adrian had been told about him by Barbara Poynton, how he was nicknamed "the Beast," and how his style was pointed and lacking in subtlety, going for the jugular without hesitation. If he were a chess player, she'd explained figuratively, he would force considerable blood-letting at the beginning of a match, sacrificing players on both sides without mercy in his attempt to win. Adrian had been keenly aware of Brodsky's bulldozing strategy right from the start of the trial when he'd been called up on the stand as the main witness for the prosecution. After being examined in chief by Poynton, he spent the rest of the day under brutal cross-examination by the Beast, who wasn't above using any method at his disposal to disparage Adrian's testimony. That was his job — and he did it well.

A few minutes later the door to Courtroom 121 was opened to the public, and in they streamed, each of them given a once-over by the security guard. During the first days of the proceedings they queued up to ensure getting a seat. Although there weren't lineups anymore, the room was still full every day with reporters, two or three illustrators hired by the newspapers and television stations, a formation of police officers lending support to the accused, friends, relatives, fans of the band, witnesses and curious onlookers — right up to the fourth and last row in the balcony. At this time the courtroom's usual silence was shattered by the hubbub of people shuffling down aisles, their feet sometimes banging the wooden legs of the benches, voices loud and reverberating off all the hard surfaces.

Of course, Brodsky had elected trial by judge alone rather than judge and jury. No defense lawyer who was sound of mind would ever risk the potential bad feelings that members of the public might harbor toward police — especially in light of the continual media coverage of brutality by law enforcers over the years.

As the courtroom filled, the defense lawyer was in a huddle with his client, arm around the big policeman's shoulders, speaking in a hushed voice. Bolan nodded occasionally but otherwise his face was impassive, showing no emotion, giving no clue as to what instructions he was taking. Adrian watched the two men intently for a few moments, noticing how the detective's late seventies suit, with extra wide lapels and flared pants, pulled across his back, causing a row of wrinkles in the fabric. The collar of his white shirt was obviously uncomfortably tight because the top button was undone — just as it had been on all the shirts he'd worn to court — so the unstylish red and blue tie hung crookedly at the knot. Three weeks before, Adrian had had his first look at Bolan since the beating; recollections of the incident came flooding back to him, along with feelings of anger and contempt. Throughout that day — even while he was on the stand testifying — he couldn't take his eyes off the detective, casting disdainful glances and at times peering right into the big man's face. After the cross-examination and back in his seat beside Jennifer, he'd continued to focus on Bolan, unable to hide the way he despised the cop but perversely curious in his desire to stare, to the point where Jennifer had lightly nudged him in the ribs with her elbow and motioned for him to stop. Now, as he watched the policeman, Adrian was less obvious about his feelings after so many appearances in court; yet there still lurked in him a good measure of seething animosity — it was just more hidden.

The lawyer continued to coach his client in hushed tones. It was funny, Adrian thought, how the Beast aptly described Brodsky physically as well as his courtroom demeanor. From his widow's peak downward, the lawyer was incredibly hirsute, with thatches of course black hair sprouting everywhere that wasn't clothed: just under the adam's apple where his razor finished taming a tough blue beard; on the tops of his hands and on his wrists when they protruded beyond the starched white shirt cuffs; and in particularly long and bushy eyebrows that were perilously close to the widow's peak. Adrian imagined the man unclothed, looking more like a gorilla than a homo sapien. Another thing he noticed were the patches of psoriasis — silvery flaky skin plaques — that were sometimes visible on his wrists and in front of his temples and ears.

It was almost as though Brodsky's burly animal-like looks had been tailor-made for his courtroom style — an unbeatable combination to strike fear in the hearts of prosecutors everywhere. On more than one occasion, his cross-examinations had made mincemeat of Barbara Poynton's witnesses. The defense strategy was straightforward and proving very effective: no mens rea. That is, there was no deliberate criminal intent; instead, given Bolan's state of mind at the time, he was not in control of his emotions or common sense and gave in to an irresistible impulse, which had been building in him as he searched for the criminals who'd run him over and beaten the other detectives.

After Bolan had been formally charged with aggravated assault with intent to murder, Brodsky had attempted a plea bargain to the lesser charge of common assault. But Poynton would have none of it. So like a cornered cat, the Beast decided to lash out at the prosecution's case, to break down witnesses unmercifully in every way he knew how — plus call an inordinately large number of people to testify for the defense.

To Adrian, the proceedings had become a marathon of tedium after a few days. After he and Jennifer had both been on the stand — and viciously cross-examined — the Crown had endless testimony from the ambulance driver and paramedic who were on the scene immediately after the beating, to describe the musician's physical state and exactly what he looked like. Then there were two hours of testimony with the doctor who'd treated him at the hospital, going into intricate detail concerning each and every blow to the body. The physician's evidence was used to corroborate Jennifer's testimony about the severity of the assault. After the prosecuting attorney had finished, Brodsky grilled the fatigued-looking doctor for four more hours, tying him in knots of contradiction toward the end.

But the Crown's line-up was nothing compared to what the defense had in store. The parade began with Bolan's partner, Rita Barrett, and continued with the accused's wife, three associates on the police force, the doctor who had treated him and prescribed medication after he'd been slammed by the Porsche, a psychiatrist offering opinions on his mental state at the time, the head of the kids' hockey league where Bolan was coaching — even a minister from the neighborhood church, testifying to his good character, though it came out later during cross-examination by prosecutor Poynton that Bolan hadn't worshipped in years. Throughout their testimony and the clever questioning by Brodsky, Adrian's heart sank as he watched the Crown's case crumbling in an orderly fashion, the way buildings go down when a wrecking crew dismantles them piece by piece. Most of Poynton's cross-examinations seemed lackluster and without any sharp edge, not that there was much evidence from these witnesses she could really drive a wedge into or discredit. So now it all came down to a final day of summations before the judge would make his decision.

The court clerk, a tall young black man, entered. "Oh, yea, oh yea," he bellowed, "this court is now in session." The crowd rose to their feet. "Justice Tupper R. Briggs presiding."

As he made his way in, the small balding man with wire-rimmed glasses was dwarfed by his enormous bench. He sat down quickly, motioning with his hand for those in the courtroom to do the same.

After a pause and clearing his throat the clerk resumed. "Criminal Case number 89-728. The Crown versus Charles Arthur Bolan."

The judge glanced at a sheet of paper for a moment and then looked up. "Defense counsel has motioned to recall witness Adrian Lee for further cross-examination, relative to testimony already given by a business associate of the witness, Reginald Howarth. Mr. Brodsky, as I told you and Ms. Poynton in my chambers, I have no objection as long as the line of questioning is pertinent. So let's get on with it."

Adrian's name was called and, after being sworn in, found himself up on the stand facing the Beast once more.

"Mr. Lee," said Brodsky, hesitating for an instant as he trained his dark, deeply recessed eyes on Adrian's, "you're absolutely convinced that the accused intended to kill you…and indeed perpetrated a willful act of aggravated assault upon your person?"

"I have no doubts about that."

"I see. Of course, according to testimony given to this court by a paramedic on the scene, as well as a physician who treated you at the hospital, there's no concrete evidence to prove that the accused would have–or could have, for that matter–killed you. And–"

"–Objection, my Lord," said Crown Attorney Poynton loudly as she sprang to her feet. "First of all, this court is aware the witness suffered serious injuries at the hands of the accused. Secondly, what do these remarks have to do with the previous testimony of Reginald Howarth?"

"Sustained. Just what are you driving at, Mr. Brodsky?"

"My Lord, my next question will clarify the matter."

"Well then, as I said before, let's get on with it and not test the patience of the court any further."

Brodsky swung around to face Adrian again, a vision in blackness, his pants, robes and hair all dissolving into one dark blur. "Mr. Lee, a week ago yesterday in this courtroom your business manager, Reginald Howarth, described your condition as severe and long-lasting after the mishap with the accused on September sixteenth. Is this true?"

"Yes, if I remember correctly, it is."

"Mr. Howarth told the court that even after your right arm had healed, you were still incapacitated to the degree that your new recording had to be postponed, as well as a concert tour."

"That's right."

"He said the injuries had an effect upon your mental state, to the point that you could not work. Is this true also?"

"Yes."

"Mr. Lee, you're a professional musician, a drummer. Did you play your instrument at all while your arm was in a cast?"

Adrian looked at the Beast quizzically. "Yes, I did, so my other three limbs wouldn't get out of practice."

Brodsky nodded. "I see. What about exercise? The court has heard that you're somewhat of an active person, one who likes to work out. Less than two months after the mishap, isn't it true that you were running, lifting weights and practicing high-level karate?"

"Objection, my Lord." Poynton was up again. "Where is the defense leading us with this line of questioning?"

"Overruled."

Brodsky nodded his thanks to the judge. "Well, is it true, Mr. Lee?"

Adrian's back was up. "Yeah, I was getting in shape. So what?"

"Let me ask you this: over the Christmas period, your injuries didn't prevent you from vacationing out of the country, did they?"

"My wife and I went on holiday to Cuba."

"I see." The defense counsel paused to turn around, survey the faces in the crowd and then slowly fix his eyes on Adrian again. He stuffed his thick hairy hands up under his robes into his pants pockets and leaned over. "Were you active while vacationing?"

"A little."

"Did you swim?"

"Yes."

"Did you walk considerable distances…say a mile or more?"

"Yes."

"Were you jogging or running at all?"

"Yes, a few times."

"Working out?"

"Not really, just doing a few karate exercises on the beach."

"Did you play any sports?"

"Yes. I played some squash."

"Squash. That's a vigorous game. Let's see now — swimming, running, karate and squash. You must've been feeling pretty good by then."

"I was on the mend."

"On the mend? You did more in two weeks than I've done in ten years."

Chuckles could be heard throughout the courtroom. The Crown attorney leapt to her feet. "Objection, objection!" she yelled over the noise.

"Sustained. Keep your comments to yourself, Mr. Brodsky," admonished Judge Briggs.

"My apologies to the court, my Lord." He stepped back and absent-mindedly scratched a patch of red and silver scaly skin under his left ear. "Mr. Lee, you consider yourself an artist, don't you?"

"To a degree, yes."

"Artists can be somewhat temperamental at times, can't they?"

"I'm quite professional when it comes to my career." Adrian glared at the other man. Then he glanced over at Bolan, who might as well as have been a mannequin, hadn't seemed to have moved at all — back straight, hands still together on the table in front of him, eyes glued to him but without any hint of emotion.

Brodsky continued. "Your business manager, Reginald Howarth, told the court you were unable to complete songs for your new recording after the mishap with the accused. Have you finished them now?"

"Yes."

"How long did it take to accomplish this task?"

"I was faster than usual this time."

Brodsky moved in closer. "How long?"

"Two weeks or so."

"Despite the alleged severity of your condition, this mental anguish simply disappeared all of a sudden…and you became a faster composer than before."

"Objection, my Lord."

"Overruled."

The defense lawyer turned to the judge. "I submit, my Lord, that Mr. Howarth's testimony has been conjecture — pure and simple. There isn't a shred of evidence to prove that Mr. Lee's unfortunate case of mistaken identity by the accused resulted in a long-lasting, damaging situation. Despite the charge against the accused of aggravated assault with intent to murder, Mr. Lee's life was very much back to normal just over a month later. Certainly this business about being unable to compose songs could be attributed to a temperamental artist running up against a blank wall…rather than the aftereffects of his mishap with my client, the accused." Grandstanding now, Brodsky turned around to face the entire courtroom. "I also submit, through cogent evidence heard this past week, that the accused was in no condition to have any conscious intent to murder or assault. First of all, he was still in considerable pain from a grievous attack upon his person in the line of duty a few days before. His senses were dulled by a potent mixture of painkillers, tranquilizers and excessive alcohol consumption. In addition, as was pointed out by a number of his fellow officers and his wife, Mr. Bolan was undergoing serious mental stress and depression. And just minutes before his contact with Mr. Lee, he'd been at the scene of a policewoman's murder. When taken together, all of these factors had rendered the accused incapable of not only intent to murder but indeed to even hurt — "

" — Objection, my Lord, objection!" Poynton's face was showing more emotion now than at any time during the trial, her dark eyes ablaze with anger, blood rushing to her cheeks. "What is going on here? Defense counsel sounds like he's rehearsing his summation before the court."

"Sustained."

The Beast turned to the Crown attorney and smiled at her. "I have no further questions."

***

The next morning, there was a nerve-twisting stillness in the packed courtroom, as everyone waited anxiously to hear Justice Tupper R. Briggs' verdict. Now it all hinged on his one- or two-word pronouncement: guilty or not guilty. Months of preparation, weeks of trial, the consumption of dozens of people's time — and in some cases, their lives. At this moment, the man with the final say sat on his throne above the throng reading a sheet of paper, perhaps his notes, and not once did he so much as glance up, seemingly oblivious to the ardent apprehension around him.

Jennifer was next to Adrian, clasping his hand so firmly her knuckles were white. He didn't notice though as he looked over at Bolan's massive frame squeezed in behind the table, back rigid as a fencepost, eyes straight ahead focused on Justice Briggs, his feelings well and truly submerged except for one giveaway: he kept licking his lips — a key to the tension that was as real in him as it would be to anyone under the same circumstances, even if he did attempt to disguise it. The body language of Barry "the Beast" Brodsky, on the other hand, spoke of self-confidence, great stores of it; he slouched in his chair, elbow behind him slung over the back, one leg crossed over the other knee, like he was watching a football game on television, not awaiting a verdict in court.

Next Adrian surveyed the Crown's table, where Poynton and Wong sat together, wordless and uninspired-looking, each of them glancing down occasionally, to where some file folders were closed and piled neatly, because no matter what startling revelations might have been inside them, the time had run out for presenting information. In her forty-five-minute summation the afternoon before, the Crown attorney had depleted her arsenal by referring briefly to testimony by all of the witnesses for the prosecution, painting a picture of Bolan as a rational individual who badly abused the responsibility vested in him, who was used to having things his own way as a policeman — and was quite in control of his faculties despite the mistaken identity of the man he assaulted so seriously. It was rather a stirring and well-rehearsed speech, Adrian had to admit.

But then Brodsky got up and delivered lines that would've done Winston Churchill proud. After three weeks of behaving like a Tasmanian devil during cross-examinations, the Beast became a study in eloquence, a master storyteller recounting the unfortunate plight of a good man caught up in circumstances beyond his control, a dedicated public servant for a quarter-century on the verge of a breakdown. Yes, Charles Bolan was a victim himself who had inadvertently made a grave mistake, and had since recanted and felt great remorse at the unexpectedly tragic turn of events. Certainly harm had been done but there had never been a conscious intent to inflict pain and inconvenience upon an innocent person. What damage had been done though — completely by happenstance — definitely did not qualify as aggravated assault with intent to murder.

So after weighing the evidence overnight, Justice Briggs had come to a decision. He peered up above his round spectacles at the assemblage in Courtroom 121. Brodsky straightened up in his chair. Journalists stopped whispering. Every eye was fixed on the diminutive man with the bald pate, which shone under the glare of the large spherical lamps on each side of him.

"I believe upon consideration," he began in a monotonous voice, "that why this unfortunate turn of events happened is just as important as what happened. I have heard testimony from witnesses describing in detail the circumstances surrounding the conduct of the accused, Charles Bolan, last September sixteenth. Other witnesses — from the medical profession — have provided evidence of the extent to which Adrian Lee was injured in this assault. The lawyer for the defense, Mr. Brodsky, has also presented opinions from experts concerning the emotional and physical state of the accused during the period in question."

Adrian sat there biting his bottom lip, grimly listening to the judge's address. He knew exactly what was going to happen, just as he'd sensed it almost from the beginning of the trial. Anger still inhabited him, pent up and unabated; he could feel it in the pit of his stomach, dull and heavy, like a lump of lead.

"In a fair and free society," Justice Briggs continued, "there is of course no excuse for excessive force or brutality among our keepers of the peace, those who uphold the laws of the land. To overstep this dictate is to chip away at the liberty we all cherish, as well as our fundamental rights under the constitution."

Sitting perfectly still beside his lawyer, Bolan was staring down into the depths of the mahogany tabletop. Adrian watched him for a moment, trying to decide whether the detective was even listening to the judge's words or was off somewhere else. He turned around behind him and looked at the team of policemen and Bolan's partner, the black woman. Adrian could spot the cops right away — even though they were scattered throughout the crowd like nickels in a handful of change. Dressed in their Sunday best, these were big white men with expansive shoulders and thickset necks. Their haircuts always gave them away: closely cropped around the ears, almost military style. A couple of them sported moustaches that were neatly trimmed, never extending past the width of their mouths. It was a courtroom clique, Adrian thought, to provide strength in numbers for a fallen comrade, with a loyalty so strong they'd give up a vacation day to be here.

Suddenly he felt quite alone and unprotected; as he turned to the judge the feeling grew stronger. Now Justice Briggs was dwelling on the accused's state of mind while under duress at the time of the assault, and how this might have contributed to an act that was entirely out of character for the man.

He's really pouring it on, Adrian thought. Sounds more like the defense lawyer than a judge. He glanced over at Poynton, and could tell by her face that the case was sliding headlong toward an unfavorable conclusion. Jennifer squeezed his hand even more tightly and turned to him, silent, but the expression on her face and raised eyebrows told him she knew too. He shrugged and smiled weakly.

"Will the accused please rise?" asked Justice Briggs, pushing his glasses farther up the bridge of his nose and scratching where they had been. There was a shuffling as Bolan stood up, the clatter of his chair sliding across the wooden floor, and it had about the same impact that an explosion might have in this silent courtroom. Then Brodsky got up and stood beside him. The judge continued, "After examining all of the testimony given during this trial, I should indicate that the verdict has not been easy to reach. Nothing is clear-cut about the case; there are many grey areas. However, in terms of whether this was indeed purposeful aggravated assault with intent to murder, only one reasonable course of action is left open to me. Charles Arthur Bolan, I find you not guilty."

Among the crowd there was an immediate stirring, some sibilant whispers and even some restrained cheering. "Quiet in my court!" Justice Briggs ordered. "I'm not finished...and I'll have no disruptions." Once again a hush fell over the assembly.

"My advice to you, Mister Bolan, is to receive regular psychiatric or psychological counseling until it is deemed by the practitioner that you are not susceptible to breakdowns of this sort again. While by the letter of the law I cannot convict you of the charges laid, it is clear that Mr. Lee was without question the victim of an unprovoked hostile act of violence against his person. On lesser charges it is possible that you would have been convicted." There was a pause while the judge looked down for an instant and scribbled something onto a piece of paper. Then he looked up. "Court is adjourned."

Bolan was mobbed by his wife, three children and friends on the force. He took it quite calmly, smiling and nodding his head, keeping his cool even when Rita Barrett threw her arms up around his shoulders and hugged him for almost a minute. Barry Brodsky waited outside the circle until the others had all finished their congratulations, and then simply shook his client's hand. Uncharacteristically emotional all of a sudden, Bolan slapped the other man's back and tousled his hair, the way jocks do after they've won the cup.

Adrian approached Barbara Poynton, who stood with her assistant placing file folders in briefcases. She flashed him an exasperated win-some-lose-some smile. He appeared in shock as he spoke. "What's going to happen to him now?"

The Crown attorney put down the papers. "Chances are he'll be nicked twenty days' pay after he's reinstated," she replied. "There's always the possibility — but a really slim one — that they'll reduce his rank for six months. My bet is he'll lose the pay."

Jennifer walked up beside Adrian. "I just don't believe it," she said. "He actually beat my husband like that...and he gets off."

"There will still be a disciplinary hearing," explained Poynton. "The force always has them for charges against the Police Act. That's when he'll be fined."

"Big deal," blurted Adrian angrily now. "Twenty days' pay — and he almost killed me."

Wong, the assistant Crown attorney, was a little taken aback at the outburst. "It hasn't been easy on him, the uncertainty of these months, the publicity, going without pay, the legal bills. I think he's learned his lesson."

Adrian shook his head. "Lesson — what lesson? Once he's reinstated he gets back pay, doesn't he? It's like nothing even happened."

"Wait a minute," interjected Poynton, "there's still the civil suit to be settled. Your lawyer will go after him for damages done to you physically and mentally...as well as the financial disruption to you and the band."

"That's bullshit — "

" — Adrian, keep your voice down," chided Jennifer, grasping his arm.

"I don't care about money," he said, quieter and more controlled now. "What do I need money for? Anyway, even if I did, he goes into this lawsuit after being found not guilty of a criminal offense. He's already one up on me. And assuming we win, he wouldn't pay the shot, would he?"

Gim Wong shook his head and spoke up right away. "The force has insurance, or the Police Association might help him out."

Annoyance was evident on Barbara Poynton's face as she glared at her assistant for inflaming the situation even more by being so quick to volunteer information.

Adrian's voice rose again. "You call this justice!" he mocked. "Legalized brutality — that's more like it. What he did to me, people get arrested for doing to animals."

A number of reporters had moved up to the front of the courtroom, hoping for a statement from the musician, or at least a chance to eavesdrop on his conversation. Surveying them nervously, Poynton motioned to Adrian in an attempt to calm him down. "I know how you must be feeling," she started, "but this isn't the place — "

" — You don't know," interjected Adrian, cutting her off. "Think about what it's like to have the shit beaten out of you, your teeth broken, your ribs cracked, a fractured arm, going to hospital. That prick shouldn't be out on the streets again…let alone with a gun."

He glanced over at Brodsky, who was alone piling papers back into his briefcase. Adrian broke away from the others and marched over to the defense lawyer. Adrian leaned over the table, looking up at the other man. "How can you call yourself a lawyer?" he said, voice wavering. "You obviously have no conscience or sense of justice."

Brodsky seemed unfazed. "On the contrary, Mr. Lee, I believe justice has been served. A man who made a mistake — albeit a bad one — hasn't been found guilty of a charge that clearly would've ruined his career and sent him to jail."

"What goes around, comes around," hissed Adrian. "Just wait. You'll get what you deserve."

"Save the dramatics for the stage," said Brodsky with a steely smile.

Just then Bolan left his family and associates, coming right over to the table beside Adrian. His smile disappeared and he turned serious. "I guess you probably want my blood," he started, pausing to find the rights words. "Nothing I say is going to make you feel good about me, that's for sure. But…but I want you to know how sorry I am for everything. Although it was bad for you, this experience has changed my life — for the better."

Adrian laughed derisively. "You think I'm going to swallow that? I hope the both of you rot in hell."

Touching Adrian's shoulder from behind, Jennifer motioned for him to come with her. As they walked away Adrian could hear Brodsky tell Bolan, "Don't mind him. He's just a sore loser, a spoiled brat."

"I'm going to get them if it's the last thing I do," Adrian muttered, almost inaudibly.

***

Outside the doors to Old City Hall, there were dozens of people — many of them from the media — clustered and clamoring, struggling to be heard above the din of downtown traffic. As Adrian and Jennifer walked outside, flanked by two uniformed policemen and with a trail of reporters in tow, the crowd surged forward.

Standing nearby the entrance was Oxford Sibb, a black man of average build and average looks attired in a forest-green trench coat. Almost as many microphones were thrust into his face as Adrian's; the only difference was he enjoyed the publicity. As self-proclaimed head of the Black People's Protection League, he'd been decrying police mistreatment for the past decade — and had actually built up a large and vocal lobbying group.

At the instant Adrian was passing by him, he called out in a strong clear voice. "Mr. Lee. Oh, Mr. Lee. Let me say just how sorry I feel for you today."

Adrian stopped and turned. Jennifer tugged at his elbow to keep him moving through the chaos. Cameras clicked and camcorders whirred. "I feel sorry today too," said the musician loudly over the turmoil, "sorry at the miscarriage of justice."

"I'm from the Black People's Protection League," shouted the other man, spotting a golden public-relations opportunity. "And now you know firsthand what we've been up against for many years — except that unlike many of our brothers, you're still alive."

"I understand," Adrian blurted out. "It can and does happen here. The racism you've been talking about probably does exist on the police force. But the brutality doesn't end with minorities either — if I'm any indication. It doesn't matter; either way the police always get off."

Reporters were having a heyday with this exchange between the two men. Jennifer was trying to get her husband's attention, speaking right into his ear. "Adrian, stop it," she told him quietly. "Remember what the Crown attorney said. Don't give out any statements." He didn't pay any attention to her but instead walked over and stood beside the black leader.

"Join the struggle then," Sibb insisted, "and speak out against this injustice. Don't let it fade from memory."

"Don't worry," responded Adrian, "it won't. I will never forget. I never will as long as I live." His voice sounded different, unusually harsh.

Chapter Eighteen

He wanted more of it. Ever since that night in Cuba two months before, Adrian had been reliving the experience in his mind: the incredible adrenaline rush and accompanying sensation of power and strength, as well as the amazingly heightened feelings during lovemaking. It was as though a powerful drug — a highly addictive one, at that — had snaked through his system and altered his consciousness in a way that would forever be etched in his soul. Yet he hadn't taken anything; the magic must've worked on him. What else could it have been? Of this he was certain: there was no chemical high even remotely like it. And why, from that point, had a sudden and quite dramatic change come over him? He'd puzzled over the episode many times, unable to come up with any pat answer that could logically account for the change in his behavior.

The effects lingered for days afterward, contributing to his prolific songwriting and overall sense of self-esteem. And there was something else too that didn't go away for a while — the charge on his sexuality. Over the years he'd noticed how some good hash or a few snorts of fairly pure cocaine could extend the apex of eroticism. But that was so insignificant compared to this. Jennifer had remarked on it too, aware of a difference in him, the way he made love, saying he was strangely rough and animalistic, unable to put her finger on it precisely — just that he was different, that's all. Until the overall sensation wore off, his sex drive had been skyrocketing; when he couldn't be with Jennifer, he released himself, sometimes five or six times a day. A week after they'd returned home, the feeling had pretty well diminished and he was almost back to normal.

But was it really the aftereffects of the Santeria ritual that had been responsible for what he'd experienced, this newly discovered explosive strength? Or was it simply his own state of mind? Over the years, of course, there had been more than a few premonitions buried in his dreams. Was this a contributing factor? Maybe he had some gift. He had to find out for sure. Something had put a spark in his soul — and he wanted another taste, to feel that rush of omnipotence again.

He'd read everything, all the books from the university library, and taken copious notes. In addition, he'd struggled through the orichas, using a Spanish/English dictionary to translate the words so he knew what they meant. Then he'd memorized one specific chant until he could recite it easily in Spanish. It was the easiest one he found, to a deity called Ogun, the god of vengeance and retribution.

Of course, what he was doing now seemed absolutely ludicrous. Adrian had felt giddy about it earlier that morning too, while he was driving around downtown searching through a number of health-food stores and plant shops. He'd managed to get potted living plants of all the herbs: cumin, fenugreek, nasturtium and cilantro. And now there he was, in his basement recording studio surrounded by the sparkling set of Gretsch drums and shiny Zildjian cymbals — with two incongruous additions. On the gleaming chrome rack next to six claret-colored tom-toms of various sizes were the sacred drums, which had been mounted by the band's percussion technician.

Adrian walked across the room carrying his latest possession and stood it behind the kit next to the snare drum. He'd commissioned an antique dealer to find it for him: an honest-to-God altar. This one was made of pine, very rustic, and had probably served its purpose in a small country church for a century. Onto this altar he placed the cloth sack, fresh leaves from the plants and a wooden bowl half-filled with distilled water. He glanced down at his snare drum, where two pages of scribbled notes lay on the head. These were his safety valve, so he could check to make sure everything was correct, that the herbs were right for this particular saint, that the words to the oricha were close at hand. It was imperative that details not be left out. Then Adrian realized one item was missing — although technically it really wasn't integral to the ritual.

Sliding out from behind the drums and careful not to bump the altar, he dashed out of the practice studio and through his gymnasium, bounded up the stairs two at a time into the hallway and up another flight to the library. After a little rummaging through the second drawer of the desk, he found what he was looking for. It took him a moment to hook the tiny latch on the string of beads and snap it around his neck. In his memory were thoughts of Maria, with her thickly accented English: "You will need, music man. Keep resguardo on." It couldn't hurt to wear the beads, he figured, not that anything was really going to happen. And they were no more ridiculous than the other elements in the ritual. If he were going to get to the bottom of this mystery and find out if Santeria had truly affected him — and even influenced his dreams — then he might as well do things right. Probably nothing would come of it; but at least he would know for sure and not have this craving for more. Perhaps the whole idea was as idiotic and irrational as it appeared, and that he'd tipped over the edge.

He went back down to the basement. About six feet from his drums was a tripod with a video camera on it. He started the tape rolling, and then seated himself behind the kit. For a few moments there was no sound or movement as he tried to get into the right frame of mind, to meditate on images from that night in Cuba. Afterward he moved his notes out of the way and took a deep breath. "Here it goes," he muttered, picking up a stick in each hand and tapping lightly on the sacred drums, instantly aware of how the hickory sunk into the goat-skin heads; there was far less bounce than he was used to with plastic heads. For such crude instruments the bongos actually had good resonance — almost as good as his own drums. The seven-stroke beat snapped crisply and quickly and then was lost in the sound baffles of the studio without the slightest hint of an echo. Never varying it, Adrian kept the beat going over and over, bringing up the volume ever so slightly every sixteen repetitions: boom ba-boom ba-boom boom boom. Soon it was mesmerizing as his mind danced with images from the ceremony that electric night — the heat, the crowd and, above all, the pulse. He kept at it, raising his sticks higher and hitting more forcefully, filling the small room with sound, over and over as the minutes ticked by, trying to focus only on the beat. His heart seemed to be racing, and his breathing growing heavier.

Something was beginning to happen now, unless of course he was just hyperventilating. Only the throbbing of the sacred drums seemed to be coming through as he lost touch with the surroundings; between flashes of the ritual in Cuba he saw blackness, growing around him, swallowing him. His eyes felt glazed over but he could make out the altar a foot away with the cloth sack on it, stained and filthy-looking. Despite the darkness overtaking him and numbness he felt spreading, from somewhere in the depths of his brain came an order: take the stones.

The sticks dropped out of his limp hands and onto the carpeted floor. Suddenly Cuba dissolved and the room materialized around him: his drum kit, the acoustic tiles on the walls and ceiling; cramped control booth across the room. The video camera's eye was still aimed right at him and humming away.

He waited until his breathing had returned to near normal and then leaned over the altar. In a whisper he began saying the words to the oricha. After carefully scooping up the herbs, he swished them around in the water, rubbing them between thumb and forefinger, all the while continuing to chant. His heart was starting to beat faster. Untying the drawstring on the sack, he let the stones tumble out two and three at a time, staring at them, noticing the ruddy-colored bits that flaked off as they were disturbed from their resting place. One by one he submerged them in the bowl until all thirteen were lying on the bottom. In a few seconds the water's clarity was spoiled by a murky brown film. Without missing a word Adrian massaged each stone, turning it in his hand and pressing the herbal mash over it. He repeated the words to the oricha without a break, chanting them in a monotonous voice.

Something was definitely happening. Every few seconds a rush would envelop him; he started to lose track of the chant and his surroundings, falling into a black void where there were just the stones and nothing else. He could feel his body wavering, giving in to the overwhelming sensation, powerless to turn back, his breathing heavier and louder, an absolute roar in his ears. No longer speaking he sat there with his hands submerged in the water, eyes riveted to the stones, blackness everywhere else.

Then it hit, like walking into a door but without the pain — an incredible jolt. He gasped.

Brodsky's face! Right there in front of him. Thick stock of black hair. His body materialized next, the white shirt, tie and then the fancy wooden lawyer's desk he was sitting behind. Looked like he was reading. He glanced up, as though someone had disturbed him. Then, like Adrian was watching a split-screen TV, there was Bolan's face. He could see it in front of him, a shocked expression but talking, the mouth moving without any sound; then the rest of him was visible too, the massive body and enormous hands. Doing up a green nylon jacket, he seemed to be walking toward Adrian. All around Bolan there was movement, a blur of objects speeding past, but he was in focus, every detail of his likeness. Brodsky was still looking up, mouthing words with no sound. Next they were all jetting through a dark grey tunnel, traveling so fast it was shaped like a funnel. Now the detective's image began to distort, flattening and getting wider. So did Brodsky's. From behind him in the vortex, Adrian heard it: You bastards! Who's stronger now?

It was his own voice but seemed disconnected from his body. Both Brodsky's and Bolan's images continued to stretch and become abstract. Then —

— A crash. The bottom fell out of the earth, or at least his dream. Consciousness flooded him, along with something cold and wet. All of his senses were assaulted. He moaned. Where was he? Stool under his left arm. Snare drum on top of him, and a painful throb where he had smacked his head on the way down. He was practically flat on his back, legs stretched out against the drum kit. The bowl had tipped, sending its leafy liquid down all over him. Pushing himself to his knees, Adrian immediately checked the top of the altar for the whereabouts of his stones. All of them were there, wet and shiny, next to the overturned bowl.

"My God," he gasped, standing up and surveying the mess. "Oh fuck, it works! I don't believe it."

***

The unassuming-looking town hall in the drowsy little community of Caledon had never been rocked to the rafters like this before, as though a prolonged earthquake were in progress. Extended notes from the bass guitar would cause all the aged windowpanes to vibrate, loosening the cracked putty around them even more and creating a hum that accompanied the music. In another room near the back of the building, row upon row of dishes — stacked neatly in roughly fashioned plywood cupboards and awaiting the next wedding or little-league banquet — shook, rattled and rolled whenever the two kick drums were thumped in quick succession.

This was the fourth day of rehearsal for Tangent in the town fifty miles north of the city, and the songs were coming together very tightly. A couple of weeks before hitting the recording studio, the band members always practiced their new material live at full volume, fine-tuning a little and breaking it in. That way they could capture some of the same flavor in the studio — and also know how to duplicate the sound in front of an audience. Older songs — some played literally a thousand times over the years — were rearranged and often integrated into a medley to freshen them up; no matter how boring they were to perform now, there was just no leaving them off the tour's play list because of their popularity. People always wanted to hear the old hits.

Inside the hall it was almost empty: just the three musicians, their manager, the synthesizer technician and two sound men from the road crew. Without a full house the music bounced all over the hard surfaces of the room, rebounding like a hockey puck and creating a steady echo. But onstage the tiny transistorized earplugs worn by each of the musicians provided a fairly clean version of the song direct from the source and minus the harsh dynamics of the room. Near the back, however, where a long-haired, lanky technician named Gil sat at the mixing board, a decibel meter read one hundred and twenty-four — about the same volume as a jet aircraft taking off — and it was difficult to pick out nuances in the music because of distortion.

The band was wrapping up one of their new songs, "Promises, Promises," which had a sixteen-bar guitar break as a finale. Cam Goodman's fingers stretched the notes to produce an almost plaintive wail from his instrument, augmented by reverb that he controlled from a foot console filled with buttons. While he played his lead, Adrian and bassist Denny Yorke worked out a series of complex polyrhythms; at times it was as if the two of them were dueling, each trying to outdo the other and throw Cam off the path. Denny was facing the immense drum kit, finger-picking his bass guitar and jerking its neck up and down to emphasize the accents. Adrian smiled at him and unleashed a barrage of short, perfectly controlled rolls around all of his tom-toms, filled in by intricate foot work on the double bass drums. As he approached the sixteenth bar, Cam's careening guitar lead took off in another direction, using the song as a matrix from which to build something completely original and improvisational. The other two felt it coming and flew with him, altering the tempo accordingly and continuing their game of one-upmanship.

Adrian had never felt stronger and more secure in his playing — powerful and precise without straining or tiring. Right now his four limbs were working completely independent of each other, setting the pace, laying down a thundering foundation for his fellow musicians to rise up from. And he couldn't believe his ears as Cam's finger work became more incredible by the bar, strangely imaginative, with subtle transitions as the music changed gradually from a lament into a driver, and then headed off into a maze of thirty-second notes. Adrian wondered how the guitarist would ever come out of it and find his way back into the song — unless of course he'd cop out and end it here, which was the easy route to take. No, Cam never did that; he always challenged himself. The tempo had picked up to an almost frantic point. Then without warning Cam motioned to Denny and Adrian with a raised elbow and gesturing eyes, telling the drummer to take the reins. The guitar and bass finished off with a roar; Adrian erupted into the solo fiercely, lightning strokes glancing off every percussion piece, faster and faster for ninety-six beats, as though a demon possessed him and — bang — he resumed the song's original tempo. With a swing of his head he invited the others to jump back in.

After six straight hours of rehearsal Tangent wasn't just smoking, they were on fire; the only thing missing was the enthusiasm of a crowd driving them even farther into the music. They were right in the pocket, just this side of exhaustion but feeling each other's every move and riding the groove as long as they could, bringing the song back around. Cam's skill was obvious as he slid back into the original tempo and picked up the melody again. Then he turned his head and nodded curtly, a signal he would finish on cue. Suddenly they stopped, all together, not even a fraction of a second apart on a tricky drop-dead ending.

There was silence for a few seconds. Then the applause from Reg Howarth and the roadies at the back of the room.

"Wow!" gasped Cam, noisily catching his breath and shaking his head. "I've just landed…from outer fuckin' space."

Adrian wiped stinging sweat from his eyes and used a towel to push back drenched matted hair. Not in memory had he been capable of this kind of playing, the best command he'd ever had over his instrument. Right now, he thought, there wasn't a drummer alive who could keep up with him.

"Never, never before," yelled Reg as he ambled toward the stage, "have I ever seen you guys put on a show like you did today. You were tighter than a nun's you-know-what."

Denny had collapsed onto the floor in a heap and was half-lying, half-sitting against one of the Marshall speaker cabinets. "Christ," he said weakly, "if we put on a show like that every night I'd be dead in a month."

Oddly, despite his exhaustion, Adrian felt energized, as though he could push himself even farther, because he hadn't quite reached the limit yet.

Reg climbed the five stairs onto the small stage, where there was barely room to move because of the equipment. "These new songs are gonna sound fantastic on record," he raved. "I can't wait until you guys hit the studio."

"Well, don't rush it," said Denny. "I'm still tripping over the words here and there. Like that line in "Promises, Promises"…about politicians being like geisha whores. What a mouthful."

Adrian was somewhat defensive. "My songs have always challenged your enunciation."

"True enough," laughed the bassist, "but this time you really outdid yourself. In "Judge the Judges" I'm using the word "Machievellian" in one of the verses. Another time, in "Out of the Ashes," I'm singing: "Nietzsche's right and I'm no violence monger…but everything that doesn't kill you does make you stronger." Who's going to figure that out?"

"The Hitler Youth," piped up Cam, who had started packing his guitars into cases.

Everyone laughed except Adrian. "You just don't get it, do you?" he said derisively. "All the songs are about the triumph of will over adversity, about the strength of the spirit."

"Sounds like you just came back from a war," commented Denny sarcastically.

"In a way, I did. You guys don't understand what I had to overcome."

Cam shook his head. "Like, oh m'god, not this again."

"Ah, don't waste your time thinking about that cop anymore," offered Reg. "He's a loser…couldn't make it in a women's prison with a pardon in each hand."

Exasperated, Adrian shook his head. "Thanks for the sensitive observation, but you're missing the point. My songs aren't about the cop. He's only a manifestation of what I've written about: overall injustice and abuse of power at all levels — no matter what society you live in. It's part and parcel of civilization."

"Could be you have a chip on your shoulder now," said Denny. "Like you want to get even with somebody. Is that it?"

"That's bogus," replied Adrian, starting to lose his temper. "Absolute bullshit. Why don't you stick to singing the lyrics instead of trying to figure them out?"

"Well, your stuff's a hell of a lot better than those shitty rap songs," grumbled Reg, as he undid his top shirt button and loosened a loud-patterned tie. "Guys with names like Ice Turd or Doggy Dog Turd. You know: 'Hey, baby, I got me an itch. Bend over the table and I'll fuck you, bitch.' What kind of crap are kids listening to anyway?"

Adrian managed a smile at the way Reg could trivialize any conversation. If you can't beat 'em, join 'em. "I'm sure it was no different when you were young. Parents were probably just as pissed at Little Richard or Elvis."

"But this rap stuff is different…it's subversive…killing cops, rioting, get the whitey."

"Yeah, right," Cam chortled, "it's subversive. And look at you — not exactly a prince. What's your excuse, doofus? There was no rap back then to be a bad influence on you."

"This is different though. Anyway, it probably won't last into the nineties."

Adrian laughed. "Bad call, Reg. You seem to forget that we're the dinosaurs here. I'll betcha there'll be more rap acts in the nineties than power trios like Tangent. It's going to take over, you'll see."

Denny had gotten up and was already putting on his ankle-length leather duster, in a shade of grey that perfectly matched the cowboy boots he wore. "C'mon, let's get out of here before a crowd of kids arrives again."

The day before, their rehearsal had drifted into early evening, after school had gotten out. Since the sound coming from the eighty-five-year-old building could be heard at least four blocks away, naturally all of the high schoolers who had just been bused home congregated on the main street outside the doors to the town hall, listening to the music and waiting to see rock stars almost the age of their parents — probably where they'd heard Tangent songs in the first place, or else when they switched the dial to some classic rock radio station. As they were leaving, the members of band obliged with autographs and chitchat for half an hour.

It was obvious Denny was too tired and irritable to repeat the experience today. He walked briskly from the stage and over to the roadies. Adrian watched them as he pulled on his coat. Lately his relationship with Denny had been a little strained, which was probably due to a mild case of jealousy. Denny had always been the band's front man, their unofficial spokesperson. But the finale to Adrian's court case had resulted in some unintentional image building. Due to the shock and anger he felt after the "not guilty" verdict, Adrian became an unwitting spokesperson on police brutality. He was in the papers and on the news even more than Oxford Sibb of the Black People's Protection League. An opinion piece he wrote for the op-ed page of the Globe and Mail had been syndicated and appeared in dozens of U.S. newspapers. MTV wanted him to come down and tell the story live to their teenage viewers. Reg had to field more than a hundred calls for speaking engagements.

Not content to simply recount his firsthand experience, Adrian had enlisted Kartherine Bontempo's help at the Robarts Library and had gorged himself on media reports of police brutality in two dozen countries, as well as numerous books on the subject. Not surprisingly he turned out to be an articulate and impassioned purveyor of information, always good for a thirty-second clip on the news.

Adrian walked with Reg and Cam to the door of the town hall, while Denny followed up. It was three o'clock, and the security guard had just arrived to watch over the equipment. Another guard would relieve him at midnight, so there wasn't a single hour when the building was vacant.

Outside, a few flurries blew in the stiff damp breeze. "Do you believe it!" exclaimed Cam. "We're getting snow on the first day of spring. Is this damned country ever going to warm up?"

The roadies were heading back to the city in Gil's car. Reg and the band members climbed into Cam's Range Rover for the fifteen-minute drive north to the guitarist's home. Staying there proved to be particularly convenient because they could continue to discuss the upcoming recording session after dinner and listen to the playback of the day's rehearsal. This was the way their songs evolved, by continually going over them, editing, adding and changing until they felt just right. The first evening, Jennifer and Denny's wife, Danielle, and their three kids had come for dinner. But since then it was just business. Even Cam's family kept a low profile in another part of the house while they worked.

As the Range Rover left the town behind and took to the highway, Adrian looked out at rolling hillsides, with snowy sections next to bare grass, like patchwork on a giant brown and white quilt. There were no buds on the trees yet, just spindly branches that barely moved as the wind blew through them; and everywhere the snow had melted on soil were great gobs of dark mud. The landscape was rather bleak at this time of year, but to Adrian there was an ascetic beauty all its own, predestining spring's rich cascade of color.

His appreciation of the pastoral splendor was interrupted by Denny complaining about eye strain. The bassist was always fussing with his glasses, taking them off and putting them on. Often he'd go without — as he had today — for a few hours while he played.

"Oh, I don't know why my eyes are bugging me," he said to Cam from the back seat, right beside Adrian. "But they're killing me. Maybe it's the dry air."

Cam nodded and kept his eyes on the road. "Funny," he remarked, "but my contact lenses aren't bugging me at all — and they've been in the whole day."

Reg had no opinion for once because he was collecting his thoughts, ready to pursue another matter. He'd arranged a sponsorship from an American beer company for Tangent's next world tour. Denny and Cam were both game but Adrian had kyboshed the idea right from the start. He was gearing up for a little more pressure.

There was silence during the rest of the trip. Cam turned off a side road into his driveway, which was lined on both sides with pine trees. The house was set back a couple hundred yards from the road, on the other side of a hill overlooking a river. Custom-built, it was a rambling two-storey brick home with ten thousand square feet of living space — not including the finished basement with party room and recording studio. Also on the twenty-five-acre estate was a small cottage for the live-in couple who took care of the grounds and housekeeping. He drove up to the front doors and parked there instead of using the attached four-car garage.

They all got out and proceeded inside except for Adrian, who stayed behind for a few minutes, breathed in the fresh earth-scented air and strolled down to the river, listening to it burbling over the rocks — a peaceful contrast after a day of ear-damaging amplified sounds. It was only a degree or two above freezing and the sun was buried under layers of ashen cloud, but he felt warm enough to sit down on a stump. He never seemed to get cold lately, as though his metabolism had been permanently kick-started.

Indoors, he knew there would be pandemonium at this moment, just as there had been the previous three evenings. The children and two dogs would be jumping all over Cam. Annie would be yelling to get things under control. Denny would be off to the telephone for half an hour talking to Danielle and their kids. After a sauna and shower, Cam would make drinks for everybody prior to sitting down to dinner and champagne. Once the kids were in bed, the three of them and Reg would listen to rehearsal tapes.

Adrian sighed. He was in no rush to join the others. In fact, he felt himself becoming more and more isolated. It was odd, he mused, how his playing could be so in tune with Cam and Denny — never tighter — yet he seemed to be distancing himself from them spiritually. The same thing was happening to him and Jennifer too. What the hell was happening to him? All systems were going: songwriting, playing, sexual prowess, physical shape. His problems should have been over. How could he feel so strong and alive but allow the most important person in his life to drift away from him? Jennifer kept saying she didn't feel close to him anymore; sometimes she said he even frightened her lately. What was that supposed to mean?

Getting up off the stump, he wandered over to the bank, staring into the riverbed at the rocks blanketed with moss and rushing water the color of copper. The effect was almost hypnotic. He shrugged it off. He couldn't shrug off another sensation though. Always there, deep inside at first, but growing a little at a time and gnawing at him. It was like a hunger of sorts. Or perhaps more like an addiction. His whole being had been nourished by that ritual; he'd felt the incredible power surge again, just the way he had after the experience in Cuba. And the feeling stayed with him for several days, although he could sense it diminishing gradually, just like a heavy drug wearing off. So a few days before the rehearsals began he tried it again, chanting the same oricha. Once more he saw Brodsky and Bolan, as though it were a vivid recurring dream.

Other things happened. His karate teacher couldn't believe the strength and agility he displayed during a lesson. During a workout in the gym, he pushed more iron than he ever had in his life — and hadn't felt exhausted afterward. All of his senses were more intense, like open nerves.

But now as he stood on the riverbank, craving another "fix," he wondered where it was going to lead — and whether it was worth it.

Chapter Nineteen

"I thought you weren't going to be a grumpy old bear anymore." Rita stood over Chuck Bolan, who was sitting at his desk in the Firearms Office amid the constant daytime din of telephones, noisy people and the intercom's incessant interruptions.

"Sorry, but I'm getting impatient, that's all. It's been almost a week since I got reinstated, and those asshole bureaucrats still haven't given me the okay to work on any projects…or with you."

"Don't sweat it," she said, pulling up a chair and sitting beside him. "You know how long it takes to do things around here — even getting a few new pens. They know you want your old assignment back…and they know that I want to team up with you again. So there shouldn't be any problem. Just keep your cool."

Bolan sat back and put his feet up on the desk. His brown eyes looked clearer than they had for years, and his paunch was a lot smaller now too. "Yeah, you're right. I just want to get back into it."

"That's what I came over to tell you. There's lots going on."

"Whaddya mean?"

Rita leaned over. "Our little friend who wants that plea bargain keeps talking. He gave me a tip about a chop shop where they were taking apart expensive cars. Good chance Richardson owns a piece of the action. I'm talking big time here, maybe ten or fifteen cars a day. Strip them and resell the parts separately. So we staked out for a few days. Then a big transport truck with American plates arrives. Before they put the car parts on, they unload two dozen boxes. And guess what?"

"Guns inside the boxes."

"Bingo."

"Any of the guys there cough up?" asked Bolan, who'd straightened up in his seat and was staring intently at her.

"Not yet."

"Gonna be a bitch to bust Richardson's ass. His word as a big businessman against the punks in the chop shop. And there's probably ten guys in between who do all the dealing."

"This is true," agreed Rita, "but I've been doing some homework, going through the files on this fella. Not exactly Mister Nice Guy. Big gambler. Big spender. Substance abuser. Pictures of him toadying up to Frank D'Antonio and other mob bosses. Caught in a room a few years back with a bunch of coke on the table."

"He get busted?"

"Nope. Someone else took the rap. He's clean. No record of any kind. Even got off a rape charge three years ago when the Crown dropped the case for lack of evidence — or maybe because the woman was paid off or threatened."

"Well, somehow we're going to nail Richardson's balls to the wall."

Rita nodded. "Got a good start though."

"Hey, you've done great work to get this far," Bolan added quickly, not wanting to diminish her accomplishment. "Now, let's figure out a way to get that bastard. Why don't we check out known dealers? If Richardson likes to put flake up his nose, then somebody has to supply him."

"Chuck."

"Yeah?"

"I'm glad you're back."

Bolan grinned. "Same here. We make a good team."

Straightening her purple knee-length skirt, Rita got up and stretched. "I'd better be going," she said, stifling a yawn, and then looking down at Bolan. "You relax and take it easy…even if you are bored."

"I'll try." Bolan grabbed his newspaper off the desk and held it out to start reading.

"If you want," she chuckled, "I can pin your paper to the bulletin board across the room."

"You're a riot. But for your information, I'm having my eyes checked next week. Who knows, I might even invest in a pair of reading glasses."

After she'd gone, he flipped through the first section of the Star, his reading interrupted occasionally to make small talk whenever someone he knew passed by. On page ten, he glanced over all the headlines — and jumped back to one in particular and the accompanying story:

Prominent criminal lawyer fights flesh-eating bacteria

Well-known Toronto criminal lawyer Barry Brodsky was listed in serious condition last night after an operation to amputate both of his legs. Mr. Brodsky is suffering from a virulent bacterial infection that

> devours human tissue at a rate of as much as an inch of flesh an hour. The disease, which is called necrotizing fasciitis, is rare and affects about one person in a million.

Bolan read the rest of the story. He couldn't believe it. How doctors didn't know why he contracted the streptococcus infection, since he hadn't been run down or suffering from any colds or flu. How the skin was coming off his legs in thick chunks. How the disease attacks so quickly that there's no time for massive doses of antibiotics to kick in.

Shock waves ran through Bolan's body. He'd just seen Brodsky three days earlier to settle his bill, and the lawyer seemed fine, in perfect shape, bright, cheerful, not the least bit sick. Now he was in a battle for his life, unconscious, and unaware that his legs had been removed. Bolan owed his freedom to this man and wished there was something he could do for him.

"Chuck."

Bolan reacted with a start. "What? What?"

It was Steve Polonski, a detective from homicide who was slightly built and always wore double-breasted suits and shined shoes to work. "Christ," he said, "you just see a ghost or something?"

"Just caught up in a thought," mumbled Bolan. "What's up?"

"C'mon down to the small meeting room. There's something you might find interesting." Polonski smiled at him, a salesman's smile with two rows of perfect gleaming teeth. His silver hair seemed to shine too, adding to the overall brightness of the man.

"Give me two minutes and I'll be there."

Grabbing scissors from the top drawer of his desk, Bolan cut out the article about Brodksy. He put it in the drawer for safekeeping, then grabbed his rumpled sport jacket and put it on while he walked down the hall.

Inside the meeting room, Polonski was talking into the speaker phone on the boardroom table. "I'm in the room with Detective Eugenio Rodriguez from Havana," said a voice on the other end of the line. "His English is limited, so I'm here with him to be of assistance."

Bolan sat down and looked over at Polonski questioningly.

"I've just asked Detective Chuck Bolan to sit in with me here. He might be able to shed some light."

"Hello, Detective Bolan. My name is Doctor Ricardo Sosa."

***

"We discovered her body part way down the side of a cliff," Sosa explained. "In a tangle of trees, scrub brush and thorns. Impossible to see from the air."

"What tipped you off then?" asked Polonski, looking straight down at the telephone.

On the other end, Sosa conferred with Rodriguez for a moment, both of them speaking Spanish in low voices. "Actually," he began, "schoolchildren from the town below noticed quite a number of turkey buzzards congregating at one place on the cliff. They mentioned it to their parents. Of course, everyone knew that we had been searching for the girl. One thing led to another."

Bolan shuffled in his seat. "So what's this got to do with me?"

"You're not gonna believe it," said Polonski. "Continue, Doctor Sosa."

"The last person to see Maria Cuevas alive was a musician — a drummer — named Adrian Lee."

Bolan gasped.

Polonski smacked the table with the palm of his hand. "Do you believe it, Chuck? This guy Lee was down there over Christmas for a couple of weeks. He and his wife stayed in a resort that Ricardo here manages."

"So what was he doing with this Maria woman?" Bolan asked.

Sosa's voice came through hesitantly. "We…we…had all been at a ritual near the town."

"A ritual?"

"Yes, something called Santeria, a primitive religion in Cuba. Adrian had taken an interest in it. So he and I rode a bicycle to where they were holding this…this event. During the ritual we were separated. I couldn't see him. There was a commotion, some witnesses say. Adrian roughed up two of the people there."

"What!" exclaimed Bolan.

"He kicked and punched them. I didn't see this but I've been told that's what happened. Maria escorted him out. A number of people saw them together at the back door. I searched all over town and up and down the roads but didn't see him again for about two hours. Finally I heard him calling me from behind as I rode. He was walking alone back toward the resort. When I asked where he had been, Adrian said, 'I was trying to find you.' Nothing out of the ordinary transpired after that. The next day he and his wife went back to Canada."

"What about Maria missing work?" asked Polonski. "Weren't you concerned the morning after?"

"Not really," Sosa replied. "Maria had the week off."

"Wouldn't she come back to sleep though?" piped in Bolan.

"Not necessarily. How do I put this?" Sosa chose his words carefully. He was still mortified over her death — but didn't want any nosy police delving into the personal relationship he'd had with her. "Maria was a very independent young woman; she had a mind of her own. It was not unusual for her to spend time off with somebody."

Polonski fired another question. "Was she raped?"

After repeating it to Rodriguez, Sosa listened as the Cuban detective told him what to say. "You have to understand," he said slowly, translating as Rodriguez spoke, "that the body had decomposed badly in the heat …and…and had been ravaged by buzzards for almost a month. The report from the forensic lab in Havana said that…that…she had sex shortly before her death — although there was no trace of semen inside her."

"Any DNA findings," asked Bolan.

Sosa laughed out loud and repeated the question in Spanish to Rodriquez, who also burst out laughing. "This is 1989. DNA fingerprinting is barely four years old. Cuba will be lucky to have it by the next century — or the end of the next century."

Rodriguez began to speak, halting every few moments for Sosa to translate.

"He says this is a very difficult case," Sosa explained. "No one saw the two of them together later on — just at the door. And even though there was a moon that night, it's still very dark and dangerous next to the cliffs. Maybe she tripped. Or jumped. Or was thrown. There is not a lot for the police to go on."

"Shit, no," mumbled Polonski. "What do you need from us?"

"You check Adrian Lee," said Rodriguez, his words thickly accented.

"But there's nothing really to check into with Adrian Lee. He's clean. Got beat up by mistake and made a big stink in the media. Doesn't have a record — except the musical kind. Nothing out of the ordinary in his past — except that he's got a lot more money than all of us put together." His teeth sparkling, Polonski laughed at this attempt at humor. No one else joined him.

Sosa's voice came on the line again. "What about an opportunity for all of us to ask Adrian some questions? A conference call like this."

"I'll tell you something right now," said Bolan. "This guy Lee is not going to answer any questions from the police. He hates us."

All of sudden it hit Sosa. This was the police officer Adrian had spoken of, the one who had beaten him so badly. The Cuban remembered how close he'd gotten to Adrian, how they'd formed such a friendship. It seemed nonsensical to him that he couldn't just go to see the musician on his own and ask a few questions. Probably Adrian knew nothing at all about Maria's death. In the worst case, she might have tripped while they were together, and he had been afraid to say anything ever since — although he hadn't looked shaken or troubled that night and the next morning.

"Chuck's right, you know," Polonski said. "He won't talk to us. And you don't have enough of a case for us to bring him in on suspicion of any crime. This isn't Cuba, you know. We can't just haul him in for questioning and toss him in jail the way you guys probably do."

"We are not that naïve," pointed out Sosa, taking exception to the Canadian's comment. "However, we thought that he might be cooperative and agree to a short telephone call."

Bolan chortled. "Good luck! He's not going to agree to anything — just squawk to the press and sic his lawyers on us."

Sosa repeated that to Rodriguez, and they both spoke for a moment. "He wants to know if we can use the assault on two men at the ritual as grounds for any investigation."

"Common assault isn't an extraditable offense," answered Polonski. "But it might work as an excuse to talk to him — once there's confirmation that he was the one who actually did the punching and kicking."

There was another huddle as Sosa and Rodriguez spoke in low voices. Sosa knew they were getting nowhere. "I'm going to leave you telephone numbers where both of us can be reached. You should know too that a couple of months from now I will be in your country for a medical conference. It takes place in Montreal, which I believe is close by, is it not?"

Bolan nodded at the telephone. "Less than an hour by jet."

"Excellent," responded Sosa. "Then if there is any progress in this matter, I could come by to see you." In the background, the other Cuban spoke. "Detective Rodriguez says that he'll get a sworn statement and positive identification from the two men at the ritual. However, he wonders if you have any good photographs of Adrian Lee."

"Christ, we've got a whole file on him — with a zillion pictures," offered Polonski. "Video frame grabs from the news, newspaper and magazine shots. There's a pile of them three inches thick. We can have some dupes made and send them to you by courier."

"Canada isn't Cuba, I know…as you were so quick to point out earlier. But police files on a man without any criminal record do remind me of my own country."

Polonski grinned. "Guess you got me there, Doc."

***

Jennifer was sweating heavily after an evening workout on a stationary bicycle and treadmill. She yanked off her hot running shoes and walked out of their home gym into the hall. Just as she passed the doorway to Adrian's recording studio, something was under foot.

"Ouch!" she said out loud, hopping a little and glancing down to find out what she'd stepped on. Grabbing it off the carpet, she couldn't believe her eyes: one of those stones that Adrian had in Cuba, still caked with centuries-old blood. But he told her that he'd thrown them away. She went into his studio and glanced around the room, looking for anything amiss. It looked the same as always. Then Jennifer peeked in the closet where he kept all his carrying cases for the drums. Inside was a piece of wooden furniture. At first she wasn't sure what it was. So she dragged it out for a closer inspection, the realization of its purpose sinking in. She ran her fingers over the water stains on the top boards before returning it to the closet.

Feeling betrayed, she marched upstairs to the kitchen and threw the sacred stone into a garbage can under the sink. What, she wondered, was Adrian doing? Perhaps this might explain his increasingly strange behavior. Jennifer opened the fridge, took out a bottle of spring water and gulped down a third of it. A thought crossed her mind. She raced up to the second floor and into the office, thinking it might hold further clues, or at least provide the reason why Adrian had been reading so much lately. On his desk was the usual clutter of papers. Turning around, she surveyed the bookshelves and found what she was hunting for immediately. Large unfamiliar-looking volumes were stacked on their sides in front of other books — a temporary arrangement, for sure. Once she'd perused them, her suspicions were confirmed. All of the books and photocopied research papers were from the Robarts Library.

"He's nuts," she mumbled to herself while dialing Katherine Bontempo's home number.

"Hello."

"It's me…hi."

"Jennifer, how are you?"

"Fine, I guess," she replied with a hint of doubt in her voice.

"What's up?"

"There's a bunch of old books here in our office…all about Santeria, sympathetic magic and other weird and wonderful stuff."

"Those are what I got for Adrian," Katherine said. "Didn't he show them to you?"

"Not really."

"As a matter of fact, I was going to call him again. I need to get everything back. He's had them since the end of January."

Jennifer shook her head and took another swig of water. "I'll bring them in for you in the next few days."

"Thanks. That'd be great. I'm sure he's finished with them now."

"I certainly hope so."

"Funny, I thought he would've mentioned…" She let the sentence fade.

"We haven't exactly been communicating lately."

After a few more minutes talking to her friend about other things, Jennifer hung up the phone and sat on the edge of the desk. What was she to do? Confront Adrian because he was playing a secret little game? Was he really taking this Santeria thing seriously? Was he right over the edge? She decided not to say anything, and when he noticed the books missing and came to her, then they'd talk. It was the strangest thing though: every time she thought about those muddy little stones and that altar, tingles went up and down her spine.

Chapter Twenty

It was the strangest thing: an overwhelming desire — really almost a command — to see the cop, to confront him. For a while Adrian denied the urge, which kept growing, hounding him, as though he weren't in charge of his own mind and body, following someone else's orders instead, no longer the master of his own will. He found himself telephoning the police station and asking for Bolan. They said the detective was due in around noon. Driving downtown he should've felt foolish but didn't. Nothing seemed bizarre to him anymore; everything was taken for granted. His fingernails and toenails were growing so fast he had to cut them four times a week. Why? There were periods when time disappeared, and he didn't know what he'd been doing and where he'd been for those hours, whether he'd blacked out or not. Why?

He wheeled the Jaguar into the parking lot behind Fifty-Two Division. Twenty minutes passed. Adrian got out and walked right up to the back entrance of the building, where police officers came and went when changing shifts. He watched them head toward different cars in the lot, often two or three piling into one vehicle. Then it happened. A cream-colored Oldsmobile turned in the driveway. Bolan drove past and into a vacant spot about fifty feet away. Adrian stared at the bulky man getting out and lumbering toward the door, stopping briefly to toss a cigarette onto the pavement and squash it.

Bolan caught sight of the musician and halted for an instant. The shock was evident on his face.

Adrian couldn't believe his eyes. His heart pounded like one of his bass drums. It's exactly the same, he thought. Identical to what I saw. But as startled as he was, Adrian wasn't the least bit frightened; on the contrary, he felt completely in control. Because it was cold and gusty Bolan was doing up his green jacket. Half a dozen hockey crests were stitched on to the nylon. It was precisely as Adrian had seen during his basement ritual.

"What are you doing here?" the detective asked, still twenty feet away.

"I wondered how you're feeling."

"Yeah, right. As if you care."

"Are you all right?" Adrian smiled, yet it wasn't a friendly gaze, more like a challenge, competitive with teeth clenched.

Bolan approached, a look of incredulity on his face. "What the fuck is going on!" His voice was raised.

"I told you before: I came to see how you're feeling."

"I want to know what you're up to," demanded Bolan, growing impatient. He stepped right up to the musician, just inches from him.

"I want to make sure you feel well."

Bolan shook his head, brow furrowed and eyes narrow. "I don't get it."

"You will." Adrian kept smiling for a few seconds, then turned and started back to his car.

The detective's first inclination had been to go after him, spin him around, slam him up against the wall and demand to know what was happening. But he fought the urge, figuring the guy was just trying to goad him, make him throw a punch so he could lay on more charges. Bolan watched as Adrian climbed into the Jaguar. It was all so stupid, the entire incident, yet he had this unsettling feeling — and couldn't figure out why. His rational mind told him not to worry about it. But that peculiar smile had him spooked. He thought about the conference call with the Cubans and the death of a young woman.

As Adrian fired the car engine and took off, he glanced sideways and noticed Bolan's face. There was definitely more than just apprehension showing — there was fear too.

Perfect.

***

"There's something weird goin' on."

"What's weird?" asked Rita, at her desk next to Bolan's. They had been working together again for two days now.

"I can't explain," he said. "The prick was asking me how I'm feeling, if I'm all right."

"Don't pay him any mind. He's just mad. Still bugged about the court case. Wants to make a big fuss."

"Nothing adds up. He was with that woman who was killed in Cuba…after assaulting a couple of guys."

"So what? Polonski says there's no case. She might've fallen over the cliff. And those two guys…who knows? Could've said something to piss him off. So he reacted with his fists. Big deal."

Bolan shook his head. "Nah, I don't buy that. He makes a special trip to see me in the parking lot just now? I wonder what he's up to."

"I'm up to a smoke," said Rita, reaching for her purse under the desk. "Want to join me outside in the cold?"

"Maybe later, thanks."

As she went down the aisle putting on her coat, Steve Polonski passed her, undoing his black trench coat as he walked. "Chuck," he called out.

Swiveling his chair around, Bolan faced him. "Whaddya up to?"

"Just listening to the radio in my car. Guess what?"

"I dunno. Some politician's caught with his finger up his ass?"

Polonski approached him. "Uh-uh. Your lawyer friend's dead. It was on the news."

"Shit." Bolan's mind raced.

A few minutes passed, and he was on the telephone to Baker, Thomson, asking for Barry Brodsky's secretary, the newspaper clipping in front of him on the desktop.

"Hello." Her voice sounded somber, close to tears even. She sniffled.

"This is Detective Bolan. Do you remember me?"

"Of course."

"I can't tell you how sorry I am to hear about…about Barry passing away."

"We're all in a state of shock here," she said, "even though it was kind of expected. He'd been in a coma for the past three days. Not much hope. Disease had eaten away too much of him before they could slow it down. Passed away in the middle of the night."

Bolan braced himself. "I know this isn't the time. But it's important — really important — for you to answer this as best you can…I mean…under the circumstances."

"Yes?"

"Do you remember Barry ever talking on the phone or having a meeting with Adrian Lee, that rock drummer…ya know…from my case?"

"I sure do." Her voice was more composed now. "He was at the reception desk. They buzzed me. Said he wanted to see Mr. Brodsky. Didn't have an appointment. Barry said to let him through anyway. So I went and got him…brought him into Barry's office."

"Did they meet for long?" Bolan could barely contain himself. He knew it. He just knew it.

"No. Only a couple of minutes, it seemed like. Then this Mister Lee came out. I think he was smiling or laughing. Walked right out. I didn't even take him back to reception."

"And Barry?"

"He came out a minute later and just stood in the doorway. Only said one thing."

"Do you remember it?"

"How could I forget it? He said: 'What an asshole!' That's all. Then went back into his office."

***

The dog would be the hardest part. It was running around the basement recreation room, tail wagging, panting, yelping excitedly and bumping into the sofa and coffee table. He was trying not to show any affection except when necessary to calm the animal down. Of course he wouldn't give it a name. No sense in compounding the issue. The trouble was, he found it difficult to resist petting the little beagle, to avoid running his fingers over the smooth coat of shiny black, white and tan fur. After jumping about so frantically, every five or six minutes it would fall down completely exhausted, round brown eyes closing, asleep or nodding off for a few moments. Then another burst of activity.

Adrian kept his eyes on the four-foot television screen. The video he'd made the day before was being replayed for about the tenth time. Fascinated, he watched himself swaying on the drum stool, eyes shut, lips moving inaudibly, repeating the words to an oricha. Then his head flopped back, eyes open now but just the whites visible like someone who's overdosed on sleeping pills. It was eerie seeing himself in a semi-conscious state. After a few moments the star of the video came to, a dazed look still on his face and hands immersed in the bowl with the sacred stones. He looked confused, nervous even, glancing around furtively trying to get his bearings and orient himself to the real world again.

Just then the dog leapt onto the sofa, giving him a start. Using the remote control, he switched off the TV set, receiver and video player, while the puppy playfully nipped at his fingers with tiny sharp teeth, growling every time Adrian yanked his arm back. Its little tail was wagging continually like a metronome.

Everything had gone smoothly. After Jennifer had left for work, he looked up pet stores in the Yellow Pages. Driving out to a suburban shopping mall, he arrived at ten o'clock, just when the stores opened but before the crowds gathered. It only took five minutes to make a suitable choice.

"Are you sure it's not more than three months old?" he'd asked the lanky balding man behind the counter as he peeled three one-hundred-dollar bills from a stack in his wallet.

"I told you before," the man had replied testily, "this puppy's only eight weeks old. You can tell by how much the teeth have grown. I know my business."

Getting the dog into the house had proved easy too. He took along a foam-lined black case in which he usually transported his snare drum. Although close to the street, their home still afforded a great degree of privacy, with mature trees — albeit bereft of leaves yet — and a tall wrought-iron fence. Adrian had scanned the sidewalk and neighbors' yards; no one appeared to be watching.

So now here he was for the third and last day in a row, culminating in the feeding of the stones. The stones must be fed.

In the next room — his studio — everything was arranged for the ceremony. But he just sat there, pushing the dog away every time it bounded over and jumped up to lick him. As the moment drew nearer it was difficult coming to terms with what he had to do. There was a hunger in him, an insatiable one that wouldn't let him be, gnawing at his psyche, pressing him on to renew the glorious presence and strength he felt. Once the sensation of power started to wane after a few days, a deep-seated urge took over, inviting him to recharge the battery. Why not? Lately Adrian had felt more in control of his life than ever before; he was capable of whatever he put his mind to, it seemed. Nothing was going to stand in his way — especially not the specter of helplessness he'd experienced in the face of a brutal attack and later in front of an impotent judicial system.

But what exactly was happening? Certainly his reading didn't qualify him as an expert on Santeria. Deep inside Adrian knew he was flirting with something ominous and dark, light years beyond his understanding. He knew it the first time he performed a ritual when the lawyer and detective appeared vividly in his mind. He was well aware of what contagious magic was when he confronted Brodsky in the office and Bolan in the parking lot. But it was almost like he wasn't there, that he was dreaming, and in his dream he did these things, that they were happening involuntarily, as though something else was guiding him. The lawyer and policeman became obstacles to overcome — like his writer's block — so the record could be set straight and life go on as it should. But on the other side of his consciousness, there was this nagging, a fear of getting in too deeply, way over his head.

He got up and started toward his workshop, the puppy right on his heels, occasionally tripping over its own oversized paws. There he took some twine and tied it around the dog's neck, leaving a couple of feet for a leash. Then he picked up the wriggling animal and went to the studio. Not being a hunter Adrian had never killed anything before. He ate meat but somehow that seemed irrelevant. One of the few things he remembered about high school was dissecting cats and rabbits in science class. That hadn't bothered him in the least. What he couldn't stand was the sickly pungent odor of formaldehyde from the pickling agent in the jars. He would never forget that smell because it was associated with death.

Two brand-new cotton sheets he'd bought were spread over some of his drums and on the floor underneath the altar. The bowl and handful of herbs sat on top of the wooden structure. There was no sound in the studio; even the dog was quiet for the moment. Adrian went over and switched on the video recorder. Then he climbed in behind the kit, carrying the beagle shoulder-height in his arms so it wouldn't knock anything over. He put down the dog and tied the leash tightly around one of the legs on his drum throne, leaving little rein.

Next he scanned his notes for a minute, double-checking the words to the oricha, which he knew by heart. His lips barely moving, he began repeating the chant to himself quietly. This ritual and the others he'd performed were directed toward Shango, god of war and retribution, the most savage and powerful of all the saints in Santeria. Adrian clasped the beads around his neck, making sure they were still on, as they had been for the ceremonies of the past two days.

Everything had to be exact. He remembered Ricardo Sosa's warnings. Nervously he glanced down at the pup, which was curled up at his feet now, eyes squeezed shut and a furry furrow on its brow. The prospect of what he must do daunted him. But all the details — right down to the age of the animal and mixture of herbs — would ensure that the stones' magic was enduring and strong.

Reaching for the remote control, he aimed it into the little recording studio. Immediately an audio tape began to roll, with the seven-stroke beat overdubbed three times, so it sounded like a team of drummers all playing the same thing. He took a few deep breaths and picked up the sticks, beginning to beat lightly on the hide heads of the sacred drums, keeping time with the tape recording. The dog jumped at their sound but Adrian took no notice of it straining on the leash, feet sliding as it pulled to get away. As he tapped the beat over and over he kept repeating the oricha to himself. After a while he spoke louder to keep up with the drums. The beat got stronger and sped up slightly. Adrian concentrated on the drums' pulse and nothing else, although he hadn't felt anything yet or altered his consciousness at all. He kept at it for another ten minutes, waiting for the rush that would spread from the pit of stomach right up to his head. It wasn't happening. He tried not to think about it. He just kept pounding with his sticks, harder and louder until the sound was deafening, letting it fill the room and his mind. On and on he drummed, forcing himself to think only of the beat.

Finally his patience was rewarded.

He could feel his breathing getting heavy, as though he were hyperventilating, and blackness mingled with distorted images in his brain. His eyes lost their focus; he ceased to see anything of his surroundings — only flashes of color in the darkness. He could hear his breathing over the pounding drums, heavier and heavier, pulling him deeper into a swoon. Then he distinctly heard something else — an order: take the stones.

His eyes opened; he was in the studio again; the puppy stared up at him, yelping a little. After putting down the drumsticks he wiped his forehead clear of sweat, something he hadn't expected since the basement was always quite cool. The tape recording of the drumbeat continued to blast from the studio monitors. Once his breathing subsided to normal he rose, repeating the chant in a low voice as he stood over the altar. The herbs felt dry in his clammy hands when he picked them up. Into the bowl of cold water he dropped them, rubbing his fingers through the leaves, mixing everything together. Still speaking the words of the oricha he removed his hands from the bowl and bent down in front of the altar, reaching around to the little shelf down the front. His fingers found the cloth sack and took it by the drawstring, carefully pulling it out of the altar with both hands, the way people in the movies take money out of a safe. After placing it beside the bowl he reached down again and grabbed hold of a carving knife purchased a few days before.

Grasping each stone separately Adrian washed them all in the herbs and water, sliding them carefully between his fingers. He felt light on his feet, the slightest bit dizzy, like he'd been drugged. And even though he'd been too warm just a few minutes earlier, now there was a chill running through him, making him shiver and drying the perspiration on his body, replacing it with dampness and stickiness. He kept chanting and washing the stones until they were all submerged, with the herbs lying around them in the bowl, like eggs in a nest. Then he held the knife over the bowl, splashing water all over the blade, caressing the wet steel with his fingers. After putting it back on the altar he removed the stones from the bowl one at a time, laying them beside the knife. A quiver ran up and down his body; it was all he could do to hold the bowl steady and not spill water as he lowered it to the floor.

Next, he picked up the dog, gripping it firmly just under the neck while the rest of its body rested on his arm, legs dangling over each side. The animal, its eyes wide open and watery, stared up at him but Adrian didn't notice. The more he glanced down at the stones, the more blackness threatened to engulf him.

Hurry up! said a voice inside his head. Before you pass out. Don't fuck it up. Do it! Do it! He raised the knife with his left hand, his breathing growing rapid, his heart racing. As loudly as he could manage, Adrian began to chant a variation of the first oricha, with some differences. The words were a cross between Cuban and some African dialect; he didn't worry about the pronunciation but spoke them the way he'd memorized them. Six times he repeated this chant. The dog's ears went back, and although it was just a puppy it seemed to know something was going to happen. He twisted his right wrist around, using it to clutch the back of the animal's neck, tugging at the soft fur, yanking the head backward so its wide, round eyes looked straight up at him. The beat continued to pulse from the speakers. Adrian started to wobble on his feet; the room was disappearing around him. Just the altar and the stones and the drums and the dog were there. That was all he could see. Then he did it.

Something went wrong. The puppy's feet were kicking and clawing wildly at his breast, struggling to get away from him. It was squealing, a low-pitched gurgling sound. But he'd already dug the knife in. Not far enough though. He slashed again, pushing with all his might, digging through stubborn tendons, trying to finish before he was swept away into the blackness that was everywhere now. The squealing stopped, yet the four legs continued to jerk spasmodically. After a final tug on the blade, its head flopped back and blood gushed out like from a hose, spilling over the altar, flooding the sacred stones. There was crimson all over him too, oozing down the front of his shirt and pants, dripping onto his shoes. The warm blood ran onto the sheet also. And it splattered all over his Cuban drums, leaving deep red blotches on the hides. He dropped the carcass and buried his hands in the stones-and-blood mixture. A voice in the back of his mind told him to taste it, to drink it. His cupped hands met his mouth, and he drank. He leaned over the altar for support as he did so, gasping for air, letting the feeling rush him blindly through darkness as it put an electric charge on his soul and penetrated every region of his body, from the depths of his bowels right up to his head. For an instant he glimpsed himself from far above, crouched over the wooden shrine, knees buckled, arms glowing red and — strangest of all — his eyes open and staring blankly upward. He looked down into his own eyes. Then the image dissolved into a swirling dark grey tunnel.

His voice — it was laughing from somewhere, from behind maybe. No, it wasn't his voice. It sounded a lot like it but wasn't quite right. It was that other voice inside him. Uproarious laughter. Now words. At first he couldn't make them out but they were growing louder. Beckoning him to look, to see. That's when he saw it in front of him. Bolan! He was dressed in white and was so pale he looked like an apparition. As the image came closer it distorted, flattened and got wider, like a mirror in a fun house, losing the three-dimensional aspects. But Adrian could make it out anyway: the detective's face wasn't just pale; it was yellow and so were the eyes. Then from behind came that voice like his own again. Screaming now. It's done! It's done! Just laughter after that, boisterous laughter, fading, going away. Then blackness.

Coughing. He was coughing, choking maybe. As his eyes focused on the room, Adrian brought his hand up to cover his mouth — and then recoiled instantly, but not before covering his lips and chin in tepid blood. The sight of gore up to his elbows turned his stomach. He had collapsed, lying partially on his side, upper torso propped against the base of the altar, legs splayed on the crimson-stained sheet. The drumbeat was still pounding away, filling the room.

"Oh, God, what did I do?" he gasped out loud.

Then he saw it, under his right leg, and the vomit welled up like a burning ball in his throat. The puppy. Most of its head was over his pant cuff; the rest of the body was underneath him. He cried out in disbelief, more horrified and sickened than he'd ever expected to be.

Get hold of yourself. Don't lose control. His face and clothes were caked with blood; they'd have to be washed or thrown out. Everything in the vicinity of the altar would have to be scrubbed. But he couldn't hold back any longer; he got up feebly and ran for the bathroom to be sick but only made it as far as their gymnasium when the retching began, among all the exercise benches and weights.

A few minutes later, without even washing off, he returned to the studio, switched off the recording of the drums and grabbed his camcorder from the tripod. Still weak and stinking of vomit and blood, he made his way into the entertainment center, flicked on the video player and punched the rewind button. He only went part way back.

There he was on screen, after the dog had been sacrificed. What he saw was utterly unbelievable.

He was bigger! There was no mistaking the fact. It was just as Ricardo Sosa had said, something about puffing up like a blowfish. Maybe the breathing caused it — hyperventilation — or maybe there was another logical explanation. But he definitely looked much larger, bloated, as though his body were ready to explode. The camera had captured him, covered in blood, staring upward, eyes almost rolling out of their sockets.

Chapter Twenty-One

She couldn't take much more. Waiting fifteen minutes on hold didn't help either. Still there was no one on the other end of the telephone. Her mind was racing. How long would it take? Jennifer had already spent an hour-and-a-half just to get this far. She tapped her fingers impatiently on Adrian's rolltop desk. When would Ricardo Sosa finally be on the other end of the line? This was getting ridiculous. To get the number for La Sorpresa had taken detective work. First with a travel agent, next with a tour wholesaler, then with the Cuban tourism ministry. The country's archaic telephone system had disconnected her twice. Finally after getting through to the resort, Jennifer had been put on hold while they tried to find Sosa. She didn't dare hang up, not after all this trouble.

Never before had she felt this much anxiety, as though she were in a room where all the walls were steadily closing in on her. Before Adrian had left for his recording session in New York the previous week, their relationship had deteriorated to new depths. He never mentioned the missing books — and neither did she. Whenever Jennifer attempted some kind of discourse, it was like he was in another world, only half-listening, never looking at her. She noticed his eyes twitching; sometimes his shoulders or arms would jerk slightly. Adrian's obsessiveness had reached a pinnacle too. Often at the oddest of hours — in the middle of the night even — she would hear him pumping iron in the gym, punishing endless workouts, the clanging of the weights yanking her out of sleep. Yet he never appeared tired; in fact, Adrian had energy to spare. Practicing his drums was the same story. Over the years Jennifer had watched him play hundreds of times but she'd never seen anything like this: his hands seemed faster than a hummingbird's wings, and he didn't just play the drums — he attacked them with intensity and precision that was frightening.

This wasn't the same man she'd known all these years, someone who, despite being driven, was considerate and idealistic, and had transformed himself from a hard-working musician into a wildly successful entertainer — and taken it in stride. No, this was someone else, and he was sick. As Jennifer sat there, telephone cradled on her shoulder and no one on the other end, she felt dizzy, as though the room were starting to whirl. An anxiety attack, she thought, complete with vertigo. Still, no matter what happened, she was determined to speak to Ricardo Sosa. Since their trip to Cuba, things had really taken a turn for the worst. It was now to the point where Jennifer was actually afraid sometimes being around Adrian. The day before, she'd overheard him talking to himself — more like an argument with himself. "No, I won't," he kept saying. "You can't make me. I won't." Then he rushed out the front door without even saying goodbye or where he was going.

Jennifer just couldn't stand any more — especially the lovemaking, if indeed it could be described as such. Lately she'd practically been fighting Adrian off her; occasionally when she did acquiesce he was all over her like an animal, so rough that she would scream at him to stop. Sex seemed to make him more aggressive, alien, dangerous even. Most shocking of all was how he could be aroused so quickly after they finished. Without even blinking he could begin again.

She was battling serious dizziness and claustrophobia. One more minute, she thought, and then she'd have to hang up the telephone and go outside for some air. Nothing was going right today.

Worst of all: how was she going to tell Adrian? Just thinking about it made her gut wrench.

"Hello." A voice on the line — finally.

"Ricardo Sosa?"

"Yes."

"It's Jennifer Lee. Remember…over Christmas?"

"How could I forget so soon?"

"I need to talk to you so badly."

His tone became serious instantly. "What's the matter?"

"It's Adrian. He's different now."

"What do you mean?"

"He's different, really different, not the same person at all."

"I do not understand. What makes him so different?"

Jennifer fought the dizziness that still caused the room to spin. "He's changed so much since we got back from Cuba," she said. "Quieter and quieter, keeping to himself. Reading all the time."

"Adrian told me he liked to read."

"No, not like this. I'd call it more like studying. Big reference texts on Santeria."

There was a pause. "I see. So he got those books that I recommended to him."

"You gave him a list of books!"

"Why not?" Sosa's voice sounded defensive. "He had been to the ritual with me and seemed very interested in Santeria."

"Well, something's going on. He's got those bongos you gave him attached to his drum set. There's some kind of…of altar, I think, too. And just the other day I stepped on one of those sacred stones. Remember? They were a present from you."

"Jennifer, Jennifer. Come now. Adrian doesn't know anything about Santeria. What do you think? He's practicing magic or something?"

"Don't patronize me, Ricardo." Jennifer's voice was like ice. "I'll tell you something: after the beating, Adrian was like the incredible shrinking man…insecure, complaining, bitter. Couldn't make love. Couldn't write songs. Couldn't do anything. I wanted him to see a psychologist but he wouldn't. Now he's completely opposite to what he was before our trip. Totally focused on himself but in a different way. It's weird…like he's not the same Adrian at all."

"How so?"

"It's hard to put my finger on. As if he's undergone a personality change, the way people do after breakdowns."

"Perhaps the trauma of the police beating and other stresses tipped the balance…and he did have a breakdown. It could be hypomania or even manic depression."

"I don't know," sighed Jennifer dejectedly. "He's like a madman, so obsessive and driven. His karate teacher raves about his progress. The other two in the band can't say enough about his songwriting and what he's like behind the drums. He just goes all the time. Hardly sleeping."

"What's he like with you?"

"A prick. Selfish. Self-centered. Won't even look at me unless he wants to make love. Sometimes I'd swear he's a different person."

"Could be some kind of emotional breakdown."

"Ricardo, I want a straight answer." Jennifer bit her lip and then went on. "I know I probably sound crazy too but…there's no way this Santeria stuff could…could affect him, is there?"

"Absolutely not. Even if Adrian is a believer, then he's tricking himself. It's all in his mind, I can assure you. He doesn't know anything; he's not a priest."

"Seems like there's more to it than that."

"You're just upset," said Sosa, switching to his doctor's tone. "And when we're upset we tend to bend reality somewhat. Forget about Santeria, and try to focus on helping Adrian get better."

"I'm afraid he's past that point."

"Really?"

"Yes." There was a pause. "I think my husband's gone over the deep end. But I don't know what to do about it."

"Listen — you must try to hang on. Get some professional help right away."

"Are you kidding? He won't see anybody, not when he's thinking things are going better than ever."

"That's too bad. I'm so sorry for you. I wish I could help more."

"But that's not the half of it. I've got to talk to him on another matter. An urgent one."

"What?"

Jennifer hesitated. Then changed her mind. "No, forget it. I don't want to go into it with you right now…not before I speak to Adrian."

"Suit yourself," said Sosa, "but please take down the name of the hotel where I'll be staying in Montreal next month. I'll be there for a conference. If you need me, perhaps we can get together."

***

Bolan finished at the photocopier and went back to Steve Polonski's desk.

"Here's the original back," he said, handing the other man a small sheet of paper.

Polonski flashed his usual silicone smile. "What are you up to, Chuck?"

"I just need to phone him, that's all."

"Why? Homicide's not your beat."

"I'll tell ya later. Gotta run." With that, Bolan sauntered back down the aisle to his own work station.

He procrastinated before dialing the long-distance telephone number. Rita was working outside the office this particular afternoon, leaving a vacant desk between him and other detectives — which was why he'd chosen this time to make the call. As it was he felt awkward enough. Finally he lifted the receiver and punched the numbers out on the keypad, expecting a long wait. Surprisingly, he didn't have any trouble getting through.

"Hello."

"Doctor Sosa?"

"Yes."

"This is Detective Bolan from Toronto."

"Yes, of course. Is there word on Maria?"

"No," replied Bolan, "that isn't why I'm calling. Actually it's…uh…to clarify something for me."

"Oh." The letdown was obvious in Sosa's voice. "What would you like clarified?"

"That ritual you mentioned, the one you took Adrian Lee to. Was it about magic?"

"I can't believe it."

194

"What?"

"Mister Bolan, this is such an amazing coincidence. I just got through talking to Adrian's wife, Jennifer. Just a few minutes ago. She was asking similar questions."

"Well, I'll be damned."

"Of course, there was no scientific basis to what she was implying."

"And what was that?"

"Oh…vague things. Adrian has become a different person, an unlikeable one. My view is that he had a breakdown, which has affected his personality and — "

" — What about the magic?" interrupted Bolan. "The ritual?"

Sosa became defensive. "Santeria is a primitive religion here in Cuba. Adrian became interested in it while he was at our resort. We attended a ceremony one night. I recommended some books he might read after he returned home. End of story."

"No, no, wait a minute…there's something goin' on."

"What makes you think such a thing?"

Bolan thought for a second, and then decided to give the Cuban some background. "I was on trial a couple of months ago, because of an altercation with Adrian Lee."

"Yes, I heard what you did."

"Anyway, I got off. He was really pissed at me and my lawyer, this guy Barry Brodsky. He threatened him. Went to see him even. Then Brodsky died."

"He was murdered?" asked Sosa incredulously.

"No…not quite. He got sick. This flesh-eating disease. Some kind of virus. Killed him real quick."

The Cuban laughed. "Come now, Mister Bolan. You're a detective. Don't you realize that what you're telling me sounds more than a little ridiculous?"

"Maybe. But what about this: the guy comes up to me in the parking lot here and starts asking me if I feel all right. Actin' real strange."

"He has read a few books on sympathetic magic. A little knowledge can be a dangerous thing, as we all know — especially if a person is emotionally sick. Certainly it does not mean he is casting spells like some witch doctor."

"Okay, Doctor." Bolan knew he wasn't going to get any further on this tack. "I'm barking up the wrong tree, I guess."

"Most definitely you are. How could Adrian Lee possess any special magic powers?"

"You tell me."

"Reading a book or two cannot turn you into a voodoo priest."

"There's more to it than that. I know it — especially with two deaths so far."

"Listen to me: I think Adrian is delusional, and his breakdown is manifesting itself in this manner — with him dropping hints that he possesses sympathetic magical powers. The result is that he has managed to frighten both you and his wife."

"Tell me something. Did you mention this Maria thing to his wife?"

"Of course not." Sosa's voice had an irritated lilt now. "It's not my place to interfere in their marriage. And as you and your associate told me, there is no case, nothing to go on. Why would I ever bring this up with Jennifer Lee?"

"Just asking," muttered Bolan. He was already planning to grab the police file on Adrian. In it he knew they had a home number, even though it was unlisted.

***

Jennifer was just on her way out to a meeting at CANFAR, throwing on a suede spring coat, when the phone rang. For a moment she couldn't decide whether or not to answer it. She ran the few steps down the hall to the nearest telephone.

Nothing could have prepared her for the voice on the other end. Her second shock of the day.

"Jennifer Lee."

She knew who it was immediately. "Yes?" she answered, voice faltering.

"This is Detective Charles Bolan."

"I know. What do you want?"

"Can we talk? I mean…are you alone?"

"Yes. Adrian's out of town."

"It isn't exactly a police matter." Bolan searched for the right words. "You might even think I'm some kind of nutbar but…" His voice faded.

"I've had a helluva day," said Jennifer coolly, "and the last person I expected to hear from was you. So get to the point."

"I don't know how to put this…but I think your husband is doing some kind of voodoo."

Suddenly Jennifer's mouth became desert dry. "What did you say?" she rasped.

"He's doin' something weird. I believe he was involved in the death of my lawyer — and now he's trying to get me."

It was hitting her again, another anxiety attack. The room started to whirl. Calm down! she told herself. Calm down! "Your…your lawyer had a virus, didn't he? It was in the papers."

196

"I think your husband wished it on him. I know he had something to do with it."

"That's crazy."

"Tell me — has he been acting strange lately? Anything out of the ordinary?"

Jennifer was trapped. Did she dare open up to the man who'd caused all the problems in the first place? But then again, Adrian wasn't himself anymore. Could he have really hurt someone — killed someone? Was he capable of it? This was too far-fetched though. She didn't know what to say. The walls were closing in on her again. "Yes," she blurted out, tears clouding her eyes, "he's changed — but it's none of your business! You — you started this whole mess. You hurt him so badly. Nothing's been right since then." Beginning to sob, she turned and slammed the receiver down.

There on the floor. A few feet away. The stone! It was the same one; she could tell by its size, ridges and sharp edge. A coat of ruddy brown muck still clung to it. Jennifer froze, unable to find her breath, to exhale even. Then she screamed out loud, an attempt to exorcise the demons from the worst day of her life. That same stone had been tossed in the garbage two weeks earlier. Bending down, she grabbed it and ran to the end of the hall, yanking open the front door and throwing it with all her might, across their lawn and onto the street.

She had to talk to Adrian. She must. She was going to tell him everything.

Chapter Twenty-Two

"Shit, I wish he'd get here." Bolan was growing extremely impatient. He glanced at his watch. Almost two. His eyes went back to the rearview mirror.

"He will be home within the hour," predicted Rita Barrett, stubbing out her cigarette in the ashtray. "That's the schedule he has been keeping the past three nights. And — if your informant is right — he will have the goods on him this time." She slouched down in the seat, collar up around her neck to fight the draft pouring in the open window. Otherwise, with the engine off and sitting for hours, the glass would fog up.

"I'll scare the piss out of him," said Bolan, "and then he'll cooperate, no problem."

"Just don't be too rough."

"Hey, this is the new, kinder, gentler me. Just like George Bush is saying about America. I'm a sensitive man now. Remember?"

Rita smiled. "I'll believe that when I see it."

"Don't worry, I'll keep it cool. But play along with me, no matter what I say I'm gonna do. Okay?"

"Uh-oh. I smell trouble."

"Honestly, it'll work out perfect."

"Do you really think he'll help us nab Richardson?" asked Rita.

"Positive. I've played this game before. We know our man Vinnie Colero supplies Richardson with porn…kids, maybe even snuff. That's the word on the street anyway. And we know from our friends in the drug squad who's been feeding him coke. Sounds like he puts a lot of money up his nose. Let's face it…Richardson's a multimillionaire, an icon in the local business community, overall good citizen who raises money for charities and sits with politicians at three-hundred-dollar-a-plate dinners." Bolan paused for a moment, scratched his stomach and then shook a Marlboro out of the pack. "We'll never get this guy by busting his gunrunners," he continued. "He's a kingpin; his underlings will take the rap. There's no connection. Then two weeks later, he'll be shipping more across the border. Business as usual again. Not to mention fencing parts and stolen vehicles from his dealerships. No, we've gotta ruin his reputation to bust his ass. It's common knowledge the guy's a pervert. So let's set him up — and after he's charged for drugs and kiddie porn, we'll take apart the arms-smuggling operation. If we play this right, Don Richardson might as well be a leper because nobody will go near him…not even his friends in the family. Who'd want to be seen with a sleaze-hole caught with kiddie porn?"

Rita nodded. "It sounds good in principle. I just hope everything works out the way we've planned, that's all."

"It better. I've called in all my markers. Anybody who owed me a favor had to ante up and give me some leads on this guy."

"Well, if tonight goes right, it will certainly be worth the trouble."

Bolan stared at the rearview mirror while he smoked. The odd time he glanced out the side windows, past the other cars in the parking lot, toward the deserted street. Few sounds — like a car's horn in the distance downtown — broke the stillness. It was an older neighborhood, middle class, with mature maples and two-storey, narrow brick homes stretching block after block, interrupted by a couple of low-rise apartment buildings such as this one. They were well maintained even now but sixty years ago must have been the picture of elegance.

The detective exhaled a drag of cigarette loudly and shook his head to himself. "I can't get over seeing the drummer boy last week. Really spooked me."

"So what," said Rita, shrugging her shoulders. "The guy's pissed off, that's all."

"No, there's more to it than that."

"Forget about him–and don't take the bait. If he starts bugging you, I'll haul in him for questioning on a public-nuisance violation."

"No, leave him alone. I don't want to see him again for the rest of my fuckin' life." Bolan moved about in his seat trying to get comfortable, cracked his knuckles loudly and scratched his stomach for a few seconds.

"Hey, you got fleas or something?"

Bolan kept scratching. "It's been itchy for a couple of days. But right now's the worst."

Rita looked over at her partner. "It's been at least three days because I noticed you scratching in the car the other night. What is it, a rash?"

"I dunno. When I checked I couldn't see anything. It just itches."

"You should have it looked at, Chuck."

"Naw, it's probably just a bug...a spring cold or something. I've been feeling a little off lately."

"Like how?"

"You know, a bit sweaty, tired — that's all."

Reaching across the front seat, Rita put her hand to Bolan's forehead. "Hmmm...it's cool and wet at the same time. You're sticky even though it's cold in here and your jacket's open." Her dark eyes showed concern. "I wonder if you should even be out tonight."

"You don't think…do you?"

"Think what?"

"That he's done it to me."

"Who — Adrian Lee?"

"Yeah. That the fucker has given me a disease or something?"

"Chuck, you're talking crazy. Adrian Lee did not do this to you. You're probably run down."

Bolan nodded. "Yeah, I guess so. If it keeps up I'll see a doctor. Anyway — " He stopped abruptly and moved down into his seat. "Keep still. Here he is, the man of the hour." His voice dropped to a whisper as a pair of headlights angled off the street and into the driveway.

Four parking spaces away a small man with shoulder-length black hair got out of an older-model red Alfa Romeo sportscar. He looked around for a moment and then opened the trunk, pulling out a small tan leather suitcase — the kind people used to carry on airplanes. He slammed the trunk shut and turned around, keys jangling noisily as he walked toward the apartment entrance.

Just when he reached the vestibule, Bolan jumped out of the car. "Come on, before he gets his key in." They both raced toward the entrance, slowing suddenly as they got close, and walked in nonchalantly behind the man just as he undid the lock and pushed open the front door.

"Thanks," said Bolan, following him, grabbing the top corner of the door and holding it open for Rita to enter first.

The man eyed them nervously as they all got onto a waiting elevator. He pressed the button for the fifth floor and glanced over to Bolan to see which one he wanted.

"We're going to the top too," Rita announced sweetly, smiling at the short man with the suitcase and noticing his bushy eyebrows and how greasy his long hair was. It looked as if he hadn't shaved in four days either.

The old elevator shuddered for a second then started noisily upward.

Bolan took a step closer to the man. "So how's it goin', Vinnie?" He grinned down at the man's startled expression.

"I figured you was cops," he shot back. "But unless you got a warrant, you're not comin' in…and I wanna speak to my lawyer."

"Let me see if I got this right," teased Bolan. "You want to see our warrant? Well, here it is." He reached into his jacket pocket and held out his hand palm up — with nothing on it. The next instant that same hand darted out and made contact with the side of Vinnie's face, a vicious slap that rocked the other man's head six inches. Bolan grabbed his shoulders and spun him around toward the elevator wall, ramming his face into it. The suitcase clattered as it hit the floor. Then with a jolt the elevator stopped and the doors slid open.

Bolan pushed him staggering into the hall and roughly frisked him, going through his leather biker jacket, and then retrieving a small switchblade knife from the front pocket of his black denim jeans with the zippered cuffs. Meanwhile Rita took the suitcase and flipped open the top for an instant. It was crammed to the brim with video cassettes. She snapped it shut and looked up at her partner.

"Sensitive man, eh?" she chuckled.

Bolan smiled back. "I'm workin' on it in stages. Last week I would've broken his arms."

Vinnie's apartment was like a TV studio, his living and dining rooms overflowing with equipment: a half-dozen monitors, at least that many video players and other sophisticated electronics for editing and making video dubs. A bookcase was stacked high with blank cassettes. Overall, the décor was sparse, only a few sticks of furniture and no paintings or shelves on the walls. The place could've used a good cleaning too.

"Whaddya want with me?" he whined, wiping blood from his nose.

Bolan took off his coat and tossed it onto an empty chair. "Plenty. We know you do business with Don Richardson — and we want him."

"I don't know this guy…never heard of him."

"Bullshit," snorted Rita.

"Whaddya mean?"

She glared at him. "We started at the bottom of the food chain and worked our way up."

"We didn't have to go far either," said Bolan as he scratched his stomach. "Once we got to leeches, we knew everybody who's been supplying Richardson — including you."

"So whaddya want me to do?"

"Meet with him, sell him something and we'll be there for the bust."

Vinnie laughed derisively. "No way. He always sends one of his dudes to make the purchase. Richardson don't come himself."

"That's crap," Rita barked. "A coke dealer's already said you've been at his place a few times when there was something…how do we say…special."

Bolan picked up the suitcase and walked over to the dining room table, where he dumped the contents all over it. "What do you say we watch some TV?" He turned on one of the sets and fiddled with the video player on top. He chose a cassette on the table, punched it in and pressed the fast forward button, stopping it at random.

On the screen was something more sordid than he'd bargained for: a boy of only seven or eight performing oral sex on some pot-bellied cretin whose face was hidden from the camera. Rita watched for a few seconds, then turned away, unable to stomach anymore. She stared contemptuously at Vinnie.

Bolan stopped the video and yanked it out. "We were told you recently got something really sick…you know…from that serial killer and his wife, the stuff he was selling before we got him. Is that true — or do I have to play every one of these fuckin' scummy tapes to find out?"

"Yeah, I got one."

"Amazing. I heard he sold those videos to some prick in Buffalo who does a million-dollar business in the Middle East. At least that's the story his sicko wife gave us in her confession."

"I managed to get one of them."

Rita shook her head. "Isn't it nice to know entrepreneurs are alive and well?"

"Okay, so there's your way in, Vinnie." Bolan walked over and stood in front of the other man, who cowered in his chair, dark eyes full of panic. "You get hold of Richardson and tell him about this once-in-a-lifetime smut."

"Listen, you don't understand; he's got connections…big ones. I can't fuck with him. They'd be all over me."

There was a moment of silence. Suddenly Bolan reached down and lifted Vinnie right out of his chair, slamming him up against the wall. With one oversized hand he held the other man under the chin, feet right up off the floor. In his right hand, Bolan flicked the spring on the switchblade and held it menacingly in front of Vinnie's face.

"Rita, will you cuff him, please?"

She pulled handcuffs out of her large black handbag and squeezed around the chair to where Bolan had pinned the other man. Without a struggle he submitted as Rita roughly grabbed his hands and locked the cuffs behind his back, which wasn't an easy task for her with Vinnie's body weight pressed right to the wall.

"Listen to me, you slimy piece of shit," growled Bolan in a low controlled voice, "I'd like to see you dead. Just looking at that filth you sell makes me want to waste you…and that's without even seeing two teenage boys being sexually abused and tortured." He moved the knife right up to the corner of Vinnie's left eye, until the point was virtually grazing the cornea itself. "Don't move. Don't even breathe. Because your eye will pop like a grape."

Rita watched the fear in Vinnie take over. A large wet spot stained the front of his Guess jeans. Some of it was dripping out of the zippered pant leg onto the worn wooden floor, seeping into the grain.

Bolan continued to hold him motionless against the wall, feet dangling in the air. "Here's how it works. You're gonna meet with Richardson — your place, his place, in the park, wherever. We'll be there. After that, you're free to run…and we won't press charges. Then I suggest you leave the city, get a haircut, a new name and a less stressful line of work. Okay?" The detective paused to let that sink in. "Now, there is another choice, Vinnie. I can shove a sock in your mouth, carve out your eyes and drive this fuckin' knife of yours right into your windpipe. Take you five or six minutes to die…blind and choking in your own blood. Even that's too good for you."

"He's not bluffing," cautioned Rita. "He'll do it. Then we'll go downstairs, ring for the building superintendent and tell him we want to talk to you on a police matter. He lets us in, all three of us discover your body — and the videos on the table. End of story, man."

Bolan eased the grip and let Vinnie slide down the wall until he was standing. His face was cherry red from the circulation being cut off. He coughed for a few seconds and then looked up at Bolan, trembling, about to cry.

"What's it going to be?" badgered Rita.

"Okay…okay…I'll do it."

Bolan folded up the knife and scratched his stomach. "Fine. Then I suggest we all sit down and wait. Maybe you'll want to call our friend Richardson at home during breakfast. It's up to you. But Detective Barrett and myself are going to be with you, no matter what time it is. Now…have you got his number?"

Vinnie nodded, wiping more blood from his nose.

"Good. So do we — his home, office and car phone. Maybe we should compare, just to make sure you dial the right one."

"I'll get my book," said the other man, who had regained a little of his composure.

"Hold on," ordered Bolan, "I'll come with you. And while you're at it, why don't you change your pants so we don't have to smell you?"

A broad smile spread across Rita's face. "We've done it, Chuck! It's only matter of time until Richardson is ruined."

"I have to admit," said the burly policeman, who was grinning now, "things are really starting to look up."

Chapter Twenty-Three

An engineer knelt in front of the drum kit, adjusting one of the microphones. Adrian used the break to remove his headset, get up off the drum throne and stretch for a moment. Their producer, Terry Kendall, sat in the control booth with Reg Howarth. Suddenly Kendall's voice came booming over the intercom into the studio.

"That last take was incredible," he said. "Wait'll we do it with the bass drum pumped up more. It'll drive the whole song."

The engineer finished and went back to join the others in the booth. Sitting back down, Adrian put on the headphones and grabbed his sticks. One or two more takes, he thought, and it would be over. For the past three weeks they'd been recording at The Power Station. Rhythm beds went down first, with all of them playing together. Then Denny's vocals were laid down over the course of a few days. Guitar overdubs came next, with Cam adding leads and breaks throughout all the songs, like sowing a field with seed. Now Adrian's drum fills were almost complete. Kendall couldn't believe it: nearly every take they'd done was perfect the first time. Adrian's performance was flawless. Any interruptions were due to Kendall's fidgeting in the studio until he got the sound he was after. That's why the three band members had to be back in the studio together tomorrow, to rework a song they'd already done but with a slightly different arrangement.

Through the headset, Adrian could hear Reg and the engineer talking in the booth as the tape was being cued up. Reg kept peering out at Adrian, as though he knew something were wrong. In the morning when they'd all arrived he'd made comments privately to Adrian, which the drummer had deflected. Small wonder he — and probably Cam and Denny — were concerned, thought Adrian, what with all the visible signs. Maybe it was the twitching or the way his limbs would sometimes jerk involuntarily. Or the dark circles under his eyes, which seemed to be getting larger each day, gradually giving him the visage of a raccoon.

Then there were those blackouts. He would zoom back from wherever the hell his consciousness had been — into the middle of a situation. A few days earlier he found himself in The Power Station recording with the other band members. Kendall complimented him on his drum parts. Adrian just nodded, shocked out of his brain that his body had been on cruise control without him even realizing. He wasn't even sure how he got to the studio because there was no recollection of going there. And that voice inside him too. Like he was sharing his body with someone else, and it would take the throttle every once in a while when he would vacate the premises for an extended leave.

"Adrian, all set?" It was Kendall's voice in the phones.

"Yeah, sure."

He heard his own count-off at the beginning, from one of the rhythm tracks previously recorded, and then he came in to start the song. On his headset the guitars, bass and vocals played, along with him just keeping a straight beat. Now he would add all of the drum parts he'd practiced by himself and tried out at rehearsal a couple of months before. For the final mix, the track with his basic timekeeping would be eliminated in favor of this performance.

The particular song they were recording now was about six minutes long with numerous time signatures, a difficult piece, yet Adrian's delivery was astonishing, absolutely faultless. Afterward, Kendall — ever the motivator — raved on about how excellent it was, and then asked for one more take on tape, just to be sure.

Years of recording had led Adrian to expect such a thing, and he waited in silence while the tape was readied. Through the headphones he heard the door to the control booth open; he glanced up and saw the studio receptionist leaning in. He couldn't pick up anything she said to Reg Howarth, except for the word "important."

"Let's take a short break," said Kendall into the headset. "It's your wife, Adrian. She needs to speak with you. Grab the phone in the small office."

Placing his sticks on a tom-tom, he got up and headed toward the exit door, making his way around the barrage of musical instruments, microphone stands, amplifiers, speaker boxes and a few miles of cable.

In the office he shut the door behind him and stood beside the desk — a relief because he'd been sitting all day. Lifting the receiver he said, "This better be good."

"Why did I expect that kind of greeting?" Jennifer's chilly sarcastic words caught him by surprise.

"Well...you know the rules about recording sessions."

"Fuck your rules," she spat at him. "I have something important you should know."

"What?"

"I'm pregnant."

"No."

"Yes."

"You know how I feel about having a kid," he started, voice rising.

"You're not Peter Pan. Okay? So grow up. Obviously it was an accident."

"An accident? But you use foam."

"Adrian, maybe you've haven't noticed lately but we don't make love — you just take me. Anytime, anywhere. Unless I really protest. It's practically rape."

"That's bullshit!" he yelled into the receiver.

Jennifer's rehearsed tough veneer started to crack. "What's wrong with you?" Her voice wavered. "Getting mad won't help."

"Who was it?"

"What do you mean?"

"Who made you pregnant?"

Silence for a moment. Then what sounded like Jennifer trying to swallow back some sobs. "How can you be such a prick!"

"I want to know whose it is."

"Yours. Yours. Yours." She was crying now. "I haven't been with anybody else."

"You're trying to replace me. I know it."

"Replace you?"

"You're using my genes to replace me with somebody else."

"Adrian," she began, incredulous, "you've got big problems. You need help."

"You need an abortion," he said in such a calm voice it was almost eerie.

"No, I have no intentions of aborting our child. Whether you want to be a father or not makes no difference."

"You listen to me — "

" — No, you listen…because there's more."

"What else?"

"When you come back I have a choice for you: get psychiatric help, or else we work out a separation. Soon too. I just can't take anymore. This is it."

"You're not serious, are you?"

"That's your only response?"

"You can't do this."

"I'm not your property…your possession."

A low guttural sound — a growl — spilled out of him. "You can't do this," he rasped.

Chapter Twenty-Four

In one dream he saw lakes of fire, molten orange and gold, swelling and heaving violently, the only light in an abyss of utter blackness. In another there were thousands of glinting, fiendish-looking swords lashing the air, swung by invisible hands. And in a third, syrupy crimson oozed from cracks in ancient stone walls, dark thick blood spilled over the brims of crystal goblets and entire landscapes turned cherry red. He heard sounds too, weeping and moaning, the most painful lament imaginable. Sometimes a snarl, low and menacing, jerked him partially out of his sleep with the realization that it actually came from his own body.

His eyes opened. Shaking off the dreams and letting the world in, he looked around. A park! He was in a park. On a green wooden bench. His garment bag and suitcase were leaning against it beside him. Nearby toddlers giggled and yelled as they ran wild. In this tiny emerald island in a sea of concrete and asphalt, dogs were everywhere, their masters in tow with plastic bags and poop scoops. Where was he? Still groggy, Adrian peered up at the skyline and saw the unmistakable outline of the Empire State Building. He was still in New York and should've known. That distinctive city smell was everywhere, the potent mixture of litter and people and bus exhaust, hanging low because of the extreme humidity this particular spring day. Over his right shoulder about thirty yards away was a fountain splashing loudly and behind it, a giant arch. He swung his head around to the left toward the intersection and saw the street signs: Washington Square Place and LaGuardia.

The last thing he remembered though was stepping out of the shower in his hotel room about seven o'clock and cutting his fingernails, getting ready for the recording session. Glancing down to his hands he could see the nails were getting long again already, and he could feel his toe nails touching the end of his shoes. He'd been trimming them twice a day lately yet they seemed to grow faster still. His eyes flashed to the Rolex on his right wrist: one in the afternoon.

Maybe this was the other side of the bargain, Adrian thought, as he sat up straight on the bench. It went with the territory. Be stronger, more creative, feel more alive, more powerful, take control — but there was a price. He'd always had vivid dreams, some prophetic and overflowing with déjà vu. But never like these, which were occurring with increasing regularity day and night. Despite what should've been sheer terror, they weren't really nightmares since he never felt frightened, the way he did with ordinary scary dreams. It was oddest thing because he was strangely aloof, almost psychopathically so, as the images paraded before his unconscious mind.

What did frighten him though was Ricardo Sosa's warning in Cuba about the Great Darkness, what it would be like to live without a conscience or soul after straying too close to the brink — and not realizing you'd fallen in. The nearer you got toward blackness, the more powerful you felt and stronger the attraction. Of course, coming down was hell, to put it mildly, an excruciating withdrawal that felt like an animal gnawing at an exposed bone. It was always with you, there in the back of your mind, along with that other voice, which planted thoughts in your head. Telling you how one more ritual would do the trick, put you back on top.

But Adrian had made up his mind before coming to New York. No matter how much he yearned for that orgasmic rush of power and strength, no matter what weakness or lack of confidence might await him, no matter how bitter the withdrawal symptoms, he would not give in to the yearning. He would resist. Enough was enough. Feeding the stones had been his last experiment with Santeria. Yet the other voice inside, an invader forcing thoughts on him, kept warning that time was running out. The jerks, spasms and blackouts would get worse. He must do something before it was too late. A simple chant to Ogun would save him from all this. It was that easy.

Suddenly something hit him — literally. Adrian bounced up off the bench as though a spring had been coiled under his seat. It was only a plastic ball. A little girl four or five years old stood in front of him looking up, smiling, eyes glued to his. "My baah," she said. He reached down and rolled it from under the bench. A few yards away her mother watched intently. "Say 'thank you' to the nice man," she instructed the girl.

Adrian watched her run back toward the others. A child. He thought of his phone call with Jennifer the day before. The voice inside his head insisted that she'd betrayed him. It planted horrible thoughts about her in his mind. She'd used him. Now she was replacing him and going to leave. "No," he said out loud, head jerking, "it's not true." People nearby turned to look at him, some edging away a little, unaccustomed to seeing a twitching well-dressed man talking to himself on a park bench. Usually they weren't dressed well. "No way, I won't do it. You can't make me. I won't." He was yelling now.

Leaving his luggage unattended Adrian got up and walked purposefully over to where the youngsters played. Every parent eyed him nervously and moved closer to their children. For a number of tense minutes Adrian stared intently at the boys and girls chasing each other and pushing their toys around.

Then he realized where he was, that he'd blacked out again. Panicking he swung around, searching for his suitcase and garment bag, and then calmed down as he caught sight of them. Walking back to the bench he was struck by a thought. It was his birthday today. He was forty now. That's what he'd been mulling over early in the morning before the blackout. The day before too he'd overheard Reg on the telephone with a caterer arranging for a chocolate cake and champagne to be delivered to The Power Station. So he'd missed his own birthday celebration.

"Fucked at forty," he mumbled to himself, grabbing his bags and heading toward the street to flag a taxi.

Chapter Twenty-Five

Sandra Bolan put down the telephone receiver and walked out of the kitchen down the hall to the living room. Usually her dark eyes were clear and alert but today they looked flat, dulled by weariness and worry. She sat down in an easy chair across from her husband, who was sprawled on the couch in a half-lying, half-sitting position.

"Was that the doctor?" he asked.

She nodded.

"So?"

"He needs more tests."

"What! This is gettin' ridiculous. I had all that shit done at the lab last week. Now I have to go back for — "

" — No, not there. St. Michael's Hospital. Tomorrow morning at eight."

Bolan exhaled loudly, exasperated. "I don't get it. Why doesn't he just tell me what's goin' on?"

"Because he doesn't know yet, that's why. He wants you to see a specialist — a Doctor Chow — and get more blood tests." There was a pause as she rubbed her forehead and swept a hand through a few locks of hair. "And…they have to put a tube up you or something. Shouldn't be a big deal, he said."

"A tube up me! Ah, great. What's next?"

"Chuck, it's for the best. Look at how things have changed since last week. Now your skin's kind of yellow; it wasn't like that before."

"Yeah," he sighed, "I suppose we gotta get to the bottom of it. This morning I noticed my piss is turning dark. Starting to look like tea. Maybe I should take a bottle in with me tomorrow."

Sandra's mouth dropped. "Why didn't you tell me!" she cried. "I would've told him on the phone. Oh, Christ, what can it be?"

"Take it easy. I figure it's hepatitis for sure. That itch is gone…and there's a bit of an ache from my gut to my back. Sounds just like hep to me."

She looked even more worried now. "You're not a doctor; you don't know. God, sometimes you make me so upset. You don't tell me anything."

He slid his bulk off the sofa and went to her, touching her shoulder gently, smiling at her. "Don't worry, Sandy. I don't feel that bad."

She stood up and hugged him, squeezing him, noticing how cool he felt.

He shook his head. "If only I knew how he did it."

The words were muffled by the embrace but she heard enough of them to make her recoil instantly. "Oh, please don't start that again," she pleaded, tears welling up in her eyes.

"He put some kind of spell on me."

"Stop it!" ordered his wife, starting to sob. "I've heard enough. You're talking crazy, Chuck. He didn't do this to you."

"How do you know? Maybe he had some hepatitis virus or something and put it into the air where I was. I dunno, but he did it."

Sandra was crying hard now. "No...no more. I can't take anymore. Don't you see?"

He pulled her back to him and kissed her forehead lightly. "I know you think I'm nuts. So does Rita. And I don't blame either of you for not believing me. But it's true. He did it to me in the parking lot...same as he did it to Brodsky at his office."

That night he lay in bed, sleepless, not tossing and turning with his brain kicking double-time but on his back, motionless, almost meditative, thinking about his life, wondering if it were about to be cut short. The big fear. The great equalizer. Because everyone bites the bullet sooner or later. At least the past few months had been the happiest for him in years. He wasn't stumbling around in an alcoholic haze. His outlook was positive, family life gratifying, work going well. Even coaching minor hockey had given him a strong sense of purpose and released a flood of enjoyable memories, of his children when they were young — and his own boyhood. He'd come back from games feeling completely refreshed, as invigorated and energized as the ten-year-olds on the team.

His father had that kind of spirit until the day he died. Fred Bolan had been a cop too for his whole career, making the rank of sergeant before he retired. He always told his son there was no finer calling. For two decades Chuck believed that. Then somewhere along the way his spirit broke, cynicism clouded his vision and he lost touch with everything that was meaningful in his life. Maybe it was having to deal with society's underbelly day after day, year in, year out — so there got to be a buildup, like a thick ring of grime around the bathtub. The court case had been a warning for him, sounding the alarms, giving him a second chance that he wasn't going to blow. But now there was another obstacle in his path, perhaps the final one. He rolled over onto his side, facing Sandra's back. She stirred in her sleep as he as placed his arm over her shoulder and nudged up against her. If this were to be the last battle, Bolan thought, then he would definitely go out fighting.

The next morning the entire family squeezed into the Oldsmobile for the drive to the hospital. Their son and two daughters sat in the back; they were missing school to come along, something Bolan felt was totally unnecessary. But they'd insisted. Trying to downplay the gravity of the situation, he made small talk all the way downtown. Derek, the eldest, looked very serious, completely lost for words, probably because he comprehended more than the others. The youngest, Melissa, toyed with her barrette, seemingly oblivious to the world and engrossed in her twelve-year-old thoughts. Nancy just stared at her father. Bolan could see her eyes on him every time he glanced into the rearview mirror.

Surprisingly admission into the hospital had been speedy, although afterward their crowded elevator stopped at every floor as patients were wheeled on and off and visitors piled out. Down one nondescript aqua hall that smelled of disinfectant was number twenty-nine. Spring sunlight beamed into the large window of an austere room, bringing warmth to its cold grey walls and steel bed. Nobody noticed the sun though. Sandra Bolan did up the two ties on the back of the stiff light blue gown that her husband had just put on in the bathroom. The kids sat silently in a row on the bed.

Bolan's street clothes were in a heap on the only chair in the room. Sandra picked them up and hung them in the small closet near the door.

Just then a smiling Asian man walked in, clipboard under his arm. "Mr. Bolan," he said in heavily accented English, "I'm Doctor Chow."

The detective nodded and forced a weak smile. Then he turned toward the bed. "Hey, kids, how about taking a stroll down the hall while we talk?"

Without a word they all got up and left the room quickly. Sandra closed the door behind them.

"Any news?" asked Bolan.

"Well," replied the doctor, adjusting his thick glasses with the square black frames, "we don't know exactly. Your sympathico-adrenal system is constricting arterioles in parts of your body and — "

" — Wait a minute. Do you wanna talk so I can understand?"

"It means your blood volume is reduced, which accounts for the low blood pressure. This makes your skin cool and wet. But what we don't know is why you have this rush of adrenaline that speeds up your heartbeat and constricts the arterioles. That's what we are going to find out."

Sandra looked perplexed. "What about his color — and those pains around his stomach and right into his back?"

Doctor Chow put his small hand to his chin and shrugged. "That is something else entirely. It could be many things. Which is why you are here for more tests. Not to worry though, because we will discover the answer very shortly. So try to relax until the nurse comes for you. The first test will be done downstairs. It may take a couple of hours. And, if there are no more questions…" His words trailed off. With a perfunctory smile, he turned, opened the door and was gone.

A moment passed without a word being spoken.

Bolan sat on the edge of the bed, staring vacantly around the room. "You might as well go home now, Sandy."

She came over and sat down beside him, grasping one of his hands and squeezing tightly. "Yes, I suppose so. We'll come back later — about five."

Out in the hall collecting the children, Sandra saw Chow speaking to a nurse. She waited until they were finished and the nurse brushed by before calling after him; he stopped and turned.

"Don't you know anything more at this point?" she asked, rushing to his side. "Our own doctor…Doctor Stein…well, he's asked so many questions and taken so many blood tests the past week or so. Don't you have any ideas? Has he talked to you at all?"

Chow took off his glasses and began cleaning them with a tissue he pulled from his pocket. His face looked much friendlier and less officious without the oversized spectacles. "Yes, we've spoken about your husband. And I have his report and all the test results so far, Mrs. Bolan."

"Is there anything you can tell me?"

"I don't like to make assumptions," he answered, squinting at her, "because sometimes it needlessly upsets people."

She persisted. "You must have some clue."

"From what I've seen so far, it could be the high adrenaline and low blood pressure are caused by severe emotional stress. Doctor Stein told me your husband has been through a terrible period, almost losing his job and being on trial. Perhaps he was very close to a breakdown. Of course, none of this I know for sure. But things seem to point in that direction."

"What's funny is that he's been feeling great lately."

"Perhaps he bottles the stress up inside."

Sandra nodded. "But what else? Why is he yellow, even around his eyes? And what's the matter with his stomach?"

"I'm sorry but we haven't ascertained that yet. It could be — in the worst case — cirrhosis of the liver, for instance. Or something else related to the liver. Doctor Stein says your husband used to be a heavy drinker. Maybe it's hepatitis. That's a real possibility too. The point is, jaundice could be one of many things. We'll know soon enough."

She strained for a polite smile, unable to think of any other questions, but feeling just as confused and in the dark as before. "Thank you, doctor."

"No trouble at all," he said, starting toward the elevator. "As soon as we find out anything, you will be informed."

She motioned to her children across the hall.

***

All of a sudden there was a blinding light, ripping her out of sleep. Jennifer sat up in bed with a start. Adrian turned to face her, about fifteen feet away, his trim body framed in the doorway to their dressing room, where he'd just flicked on a lamp.

"My God, what are you doing back!"

"I live here, remember?"

She shook her head in disbelief. "Everybody's been calling — Reg, Cam, Denny. Nobody knew where you were. I phoned to wish you happy birthday, and there was no answer. Then FedEx called with your birthday present I'd sent. They couldn't deliver it because the hotel said you'd checked out."

"So?" Adrian looked at her, emotionless.

"That's all you can say?" Jennifer's eyes were growing accustomed to the light behind him now. He was more than a silhouette. She could make out his features — and was in for a shock. Blackness around his eyes had spread down onto his cheeks and back toward his ears. Reaching over to the bedside table she turned on a light. "Adrian, what's going on! Look at you. Your eyes…your face! What's happening?"

"Cut the shit," he said forcefully, his chest and stomach muscles tensing. "I want to know the real story."

Jennifer glared at him. "You don't talk to me like that. And I haven't got a clue what you mean."

"Whose baby is it?"

"You bastard. You know damn well whose baby it is."

"No, I don't. Whose is it?"

She eyed him nervously. "Go fuck yourself," she said quietly, almost under her breath.

"What did you say?"

"Go fuck yourself." Louder this time.

Turning back into the dressing room, Adrian slid his hand across the tie rack and pulled out a silk Armani, one with purple geometrics on a taupe background — a favorite of his. Without a word he stood there pulling at it with both hands, like a tug of war with himself. Then he walked out in the direction of the bed.

Her eyes followed him, uncomprehending what he was up to, until suddenly he yanked the covers down, exposing her nude body, and pressed his weight onto her, roughly grabbing her wrists and winding the tie around them.

"Let go of me, you prick!" she screamed out.

"Shut up." He pulled the knot tightly on her wrists, took the remainder of the tie and began to hitch it to the brass bedpost.

"You're crazy — you can't do this!"

"Now I want some answers from you."

"Piss right off. I'm not going to talk to you when you're doing this to me. Who do you think you are anyway?"

"Your husband."

"Untie me this second before I call the police — "

" — Shut up." He grabbed Jennifer's shoulders and flopped her over onto her stomach. Then he sat on the back of her knees, rendering her immobile, arms outstretched in front, straining at the tie. He forced her thighs apart with his hands and knees.

She screamed. "Get off me!"

"I want to know it all…every detail of what happened."

"You're sick, Adrian."

He glanced down at the button-sized rose, the skin shiny and taut, and moved his hand up and put two fingers on it. "Start talking."

"What — while you play proctologist?"

He roughly forced the middle finger in a little. She was so dry it felt like sandpaper.

"Stop it — you're hurting me."

"What happened?" He jammed the forefinger up too.

His fingers dug in more deeply, all the way to his knuckles. She was so tight it seemed his circulation was being cut off.

"Stop it!" she cried out.

"Tell me."

"How many times do I have to say it: there's nothing to tell. Nothing."

He slid his fingers back and forth. "You're lying!" he screamed. Right after that, they both heard it: a strange animal-like growl. In spite of his rage, it shocked Adrian; he hadn't even noticed himself making the sound.

On her stomach Jennifer squirmed, turning her head around as far as possible to look at his face. Her usually cool grey eyes were round and wide now, fear evident after hearing that sound.

"I want the truth," continued Adrian, his voice calmer now. "When did you plot it all out?"

"No plot. Nothing. I'm pregnant, that's all. You're the father. What more is there?"

Adrian pulled back and then shoved in his remaining fingers. She whimpered into the pillow. "You tell me."

"I don't know anything more," she said, starting to cry.

He couldn't stand it, like his every emotion was on a roller coaster, dipping and careening. One instant he was so angry he couldn't contain it; the next he was overflowing with revulsion; and now he was disgusted with himself too, filled with shame — because he was so aroused. He glanced down to where the seam on his briefs was straining with the bulge, where his pulsing hardness protruded out the top.

"You're wet right now, aren't you?"

"You're twisted, Adrian. So fucked up. You've got to see a doctor right away."

He removed his fingers and grasped her by the hips, keeping her buttocks spread. "You're turned on."

"No, no," she answered, starting to sob. "You're sick."

Tugging his underwear down to his knees, Adrian mounted her and plunged inside, thrusting as though he were wielding a weapon, his hands squeezing her small breasts until they hurt. Jennifer's head was turned sideways, eyes open and fixed upon the window across the room. Tears streamed down her face. He was like an animal on top of her, without a trace of tenderness or love, without even a single kiss, just ramming her. It seemed to take forever. He moaned out loud as he peaked inside.

"Untie me now," she said, hoping to interrupt his pleasure.

There was a pause while he finished. Silence. Then he looked around, bewildered, as though he couldn't comprehend the situation. "Oh God, what am I doing?" he whispered.

"Untie me."

"I'm sorry." He reached out to touch her head. She craned her neck to avoid his fingers.

"Untie me."

Adrian sat up and leaned across the bed, reaching for the post. The necktie had been stretched and the knot tightened, so it took a minute to undo. Then he freed each of her wrists. "I don't know what's happening," he said. "Honestly."

Jennifer didn't say anything. She turned over, sat up and spat in his face. He didn't utter a word either, no response, just sat there motionless, not even bothering to brush away the bubbly white saliva that was trickling down his nose.

***

Even right downtown there was so much greenery, little parkettes and expanses of trees, alive with new spring growth. Ricardo Sosa marveled at the view of Montreal from the window in his suite at the Hotel Méridien. This island in the St. Lawrence River was breathtakingly beautiful to him, so different from Havana. All the buildings, old and new, were immaculate and fresh looking, as were the streets. It made him realize with a measure of objectivity, followed by envy and then sadness that, despite Havana's rich character and tropical flavor, the city — and the country, for that matter — were crumbling, dying a slow death through attrition and neglect.

Sosa was pleased the World Psychiatric Association was meeting in Montreal this year, and that the conference was being held in the Méridien, which was a hotel where most of the staff and visitors alike conversed in French. This afforded him the opportunity to bone up on his command of the language. His only other practice came from banter with French Canadians visiting La Sorpresa, whose patois was markedly different from Parisian French.

Still gazing out the window, Sosa knew he was procrastinating and that work beckoned him. Although he'd just finished breakfast and it was only eight o'clock, his keynote speech was scheduled for four that afternoon — and he hadn't done any preparation yet. All the material he needed was in a paper he was presenting, Psychiatry At The Edge: After The Revolution. Still, there was considerable work in just pulling out information and writing it in a conversational style. Sosa wasn't worried, having spoken in public many times; anyway he never followed what was written down, preferring instead the extemporaneous approach. He pulled out a Monte Cristo, squeezed it lightly to test the moisture content and ran the chocolate-brown cigar back and forth under his nose a few times, taking in the overwhelming scent of the tobacco before he lit it. Surveying a foreign city from atop an elegant perch and smoking one of the world's finest cigars seemed the most pleasurable way to spend a few minutes that he could imagine.

But not for long. His bedside telephone rang. Probably someone from the conference, he thought, as he ambled over slowly and picked up the receiver.

"Is this Ricardo Sosa?"

He could sense incredible stress in the voice. "Yes. To whom am I speaking?"

"It's me, Jennifer."

"Yes, of course. I didn't recognize you at first."

"I called the resort; they told me you were here. I'd forgotten. You gave me the hotel name, remember? I don't want to bother you…but…"

"Certainly it is no bother. You sound like there's trouble."

"I need you here…to help me. Please. You must come. You must." She sounded on the verge of a breakdown.

"Tell me, what's happened?"

"He's crazy — Adrian is. Last night he raped me. He's insane because I'm pregnant. Insane. Doesn't even seem like him. Like it's somebody else."

"He's exhibiting multiple personalities?"

"How do I know!" she screamed through the telephone. "You tell me. Maybe it's something to do with those rituals…and those stones you gave him."

Sosa was starting to wonder. "Please, Jennifer, try to calm down."

"You wouldn't even recognize him — he's not the same person. You've got to come right away."

"Don't worry, I will, as soon as possible. This afternoon I have to give a talk. Right after that, I'll catch the first plane."

"Oh, God, thank you. I'm so afraid of what he might do to me…or himself. If you could talk to him."

"I will see him when I get there."

"I'm not living in our house. This morning I took some things and moved in with a friend. You can meet me here."

"All right. About the flight: I'm told it's quite short from Montreal to Toronto."

"Yes. About forty-five minutes. I'll give you my credit card number and expiry date. Charge it to me."

"I have an idea," said Sosa as he rummaged through the night table drawer, sifting through a room-service menu, city directory, entertainment listings and other papers, searching for one sheet in particular. "In a moment I'll give you the fax number here at the hotel…once I locate it. Send me detailed instructions of how to find you when I arrive in Toronto, what I should tell the taxi driver and so on. Make sure you give me the telephone number where you are."

The voice on the other end sounded a little calmer now. "Of course. I'll do it right away."

"So I'll see you tonight then. Do you have a pen? Because I have the fax number here."

Chapter Twenty-Six

Outside, six floors down, it was cloudy with a nasty wind — unusual for May — that bowed the faces of passersby. Traffic clogged the streets; many vehicles, mainly trucks, were lined up at the four-way stop sign. Bolan noticed the trucks most of all because he could hear them sometimes, sputtering, gears grinding as the drivers roared into motion, causing the windows of the hospital room to vibrate slightly. No other exterior sounds penetrated his environment. Hundreds of people trod on the sidewalk below with noiseless footsteps, and cars sped by soundlessly. Cabbies waiting by the hospital entrance yelled to each other inaudibly.

A few feet away in the next bed was an elderly Korean man who spoke next to no English, so he wasn't much company. Right now one of the rental televisions with the pivoting arm was placed right over his chest, and he seemed to be engrossed in a soap opera even though the volume was turned down all the way — not that he would've understood what the actors were saying.

Bolan continued to sit on the edge of his bed staring out the window. Viewing life's silent movie helped time slide by more quickly. As he watched everyday dramas unfolding from above, only a few interior sounds pierced the dead air around him: the occasional flurry of footsteps in the hall; the shrill ring of a telephone at the nurses' station; the flush of a toilet in an adjoining room; and three times a day, the clatter of food trays arriving on the sixth floor.

Leaning forward until his nose was almost pressed against the glass, he surveyed the length of the old mud-colored brick building, trying to count the windows on each floor. He thought about the number of patients in this hospital, let alone how many there would be throughout the city. There was never a shortage of sick people. Or dead people. He'd seen enough of both during his tenure on the force. Hospitals were no stranger to a cop like him, who over the years had escorted dozens of miscreants for first aid — usually drugged or badly beaten. Of course, he'd been in more than a few times himself to be patched up after a scuffle. And then there was the time he'd been shot through the shoulder and thigh by an escaped convict. But that wasn't like being ill. Until now Chuck Bolan had never been sick enough to require a hospital stay.

He lay back on the bed, feet hanging over the end unless he bent his knees, head propped up on three pillows. At least whatever they'd given him made the ache in his stomach go away — or dulled it so it seemed to disappear. He felt a little groggy but not sleepy at all. It was as if he were dreaming on his feet, wide awake. The main thing was he didn't hurt anymore.

Footsteps click-clacked on the linoleum floor in the hall. Doctor Stein, their family physician for twenty years, stepped in and held the door for Sandra and the specialist, Doctor Chow. His wife's face was long and ashen. Even through his sedated gaze Bolan knew something was wrong — terribly wrong. He noticed her wet brown eyes, stiff body with both hands clenched tightly onto her purse and the way she drew each breath heavily.

"We didn't wake you, did we, Chuck?" asked Stein, a tall sloping man with a full head of muddy hair and eyes so light blue they were almost translucent.

Taking in the situation, Bolan didn't respond for a moment. He shook his head.

Stein dug his hands deep into the pockets of his grey suit pants and stood over the bed looking down, shuffling uncomfortably. "So...how are we doing today?"

Bolan sat up. "Okay, cut the crap, George," he said, with the interrogating tone of a cop. "What's up?"

"Well, the X-rays are in..."

"And?"

Chow spoke up. "We now know there is a large tumor in the middle of your pancreas, Mr. Bolan."

"Is it cancer?"

"We can't be certain until we operate tomorrow but — "

" — Wait a minute," broke in Bolan, his voice louder. "George, what do you really think?"

Swallowing hard, Stein looked right into the eyes of the other man. "Probably it is cancer."

"Oh, shit. How far is it?"

Chow's turn again. "Judging by the discoloration of your urine and feces, it's fairly advanced."

"Chuck, I don't know what to say," said Stein.

Sandra was crying now, her sobs like coughs. She moved over to the bedside and draped her arms around Bolan's shoulders. One of his large hands stroked her hair while he stared impassively out the window.

Chow cleared his throat. "We should tell you too that there are dark areas on other organs in the X-rays, and we suspect they may be cancerous also."

"Wow, I'm really batting a thousand, aren't I?" Bolan sighed.

"We'll know better tomorrow," added Stein, "after Doctor Chow has a look inside."

A few minutes later the physicians left. Bolan was still hugging his wife. Her crying had subsided.

"That bastard Lee," he said quietly. "I can't believe it."

"No," implored Sandra, "please don't say that." She hugged more tightly, fingers digging into his broad shoulders.

He cupped her face gently in his hands and moved her away from his chest slightly. "You know more, don't you?" he asked, looking deep into her eyes. Tears rolled down her cheeks onto his fingers. He leaned over and kissed her forehead many times, soft quiet kisses. "I gotta know," he said, voice cracking a little. "Tell me, Sandy." She began sobbing loudly again. He squeezed her to him again.

After a few moments they both sat in silence, looking at each other, like two people who've just met for the first time. He reached over, grabbed a tissue and handed it to her. After wiping her nose and eyes she started to speak, haltingly.

"A month…or less," she said in a faint voice. "That's what Doctor Chow told me." She covered her mouth now, face stippled with disbelief. "He told me they've never seen symptoms spread so quickly before. Ever. He can't believe it."

That's when Bolan erupted. Maybe the drugs were wearing off; maybe realization had replaced shock and denial. Whatever it was, he eased away from her and slammed his fist into the mattress. "No!" he yelled, more like an order than a plea. "That guy Lee did this to me! It was him. I know it." His voice bounced off the walls.

The old man in the next bed turned with a startled look on his face. Just then a nurse burst in. "Everything all right?" she asked.

"No!" bellowed the cop. "Everything's fucked up good."

Sandra tried to restrain him as he stood up. "Honey, calm down," she pleaded.

The nurse rushed out and returned with Doctor Stein. He glanced at Bolan nervously and turned to the nurse. "Bring me two milligrams of Demerol, please."

"Somebody did this to me, George," said Bolan. "It's true. That rock star — y'know, the one from my court case — was out to get me. He made it happen, I swear."

Stein grasped his patient's arm and began to edge him back to the bed. "C'mon, Chuck, nobody can give you a tumor." He looked over at Sandra, who was standing now too, and beckoned her with a nod of his head. "Why don't you come here and sit with him?"

She walked over and helped the doctor get him on the bed.

"It was Lee; he did this to me." Bolan sat hunched over, like a player in the dressing room after a losing game. Sandra's arms were around him again.

The nurse returned with the needle. Stein took it and approached cautiously. "This will make you feel better," he said, lightly lifting the detective's arm.

"I know you don't believe me, but it's true. Lee practically told me it would happen. I just wish I knew how the hell he did it."

The doctor nodded, not in agreement, just to placate him until the drug kicked in. He didn't want any trouble, not with a patient whose arms were like ceiling beams. He removed the needle, then exhaled loudly, mopping his brow.

***

Rain pounded the roof in sheets. Along with the thunder, there was enough noise to drown out the television. Trevor Barrett, a slim black man with a shaved head and trim moustache, got up off the sofa and turned the volume knob on the set. Then he rejoined his wife, Rita, who was stretched out comfortably, feet up on the coffee table in front of her. She wasn't paying attention to the video they'd rented though. And despite her husband's comments about the storm, she was barely aware of it.

Tonight her thoughts were with her partner, Chuck Bolan. When Sandra had telephoned with the news, Rita had been dumbstruck. It couldn't happen to Chuck; he'd always cleared the hurdles, somehow, even in the tight squeezes. Over and over she flashed back to when the two of them had started working together, and how much he'd taught her. Now at fifty his life was slipping away rapidly. She imagined what Sandra must be going through and wondered whether she'd broken the complete story to the kids. That was the trouble with death, the way it clung to the living, spreading its blackness over them as well.

She reached over to the side table for her cup of tea and sipped a little. Even with the volume up she couldn't concentrate on the film.

"Sounds like a flood out there," said Trevor.

"Pardon."

"Just talkin' about the rain…since neither of us is takin' in much of this movie."

"Sorry, Trevor. I know I'm not good company tonight." She put down her cup and reached over to him, nuzzling his cheek.

He smiled sympathetically at her. "I know what you're goin' through too, baby." He stopped the video and started it rewinding.

Just then the telephone rang.

Rita was about to get up but Trevor waved her back and ran to the kitchen to answer it. Often police business roused her from bed, interrupted meals or spoiled her free time. Tonight she dreaded the thought of having to go in.

"It's for you," Trevor called from the other room. "Sandra Bolan's on the line."

She leapt off the sofa and ran to the kitchen, a barrage of terrible thoughts coming to mind. Snatching the receiver from her husband's hand, she closed her eyes, mentally preparing herself for the worst. "Hello," she said anxiously.

"Sorry to bother you, Rita." A wavering voice.

"Sandra, tell me, what is it?"

"He's gone," she wailed. "He's gone."

"What! He died?"

"No — he disappeared."

"What do you mean?"

On the other end Sandra took a deep breath and sniffled loudly, trying to compose herself. "A nurse just called from the hospital, asking if he was here."

The words were like a slap in the face to Rita, stirring her into clear thinking. "Shit," she muttered.

"My God, what's happening? What next?" sputtered Sandra.

"How long ago did they notice him missing?"

"They said it's been about an hour since someone last looked in on him."

"Shit," said Rita again, only this time louder. "He's gone to that drummer's place, I'll bet. It's been an obsession with him these last few days."

"Oh, no, please, not that."

"Don't worry, Sandra, I'll get him. I'm on my way now." She slammed down the receiver without even saying goodbye and immediately dialed Fifty-Two Division to get Adrian Lee's phone number and address, knowing he wouldn't be listed in the white pages. "Quick," she barked to Trevor, "get my coat and purse!"

Chapter Twenty-Seven

The taxi inched along Queen Street with an occasional spurt of speed, dodging parked cars and weaving around the deep puddles. Visibility was severely limited because the car's windshield wipers couldn't keep up with the torrent. Pedestrians ran, their umbrellas twisting inside out, offering no protection against the wind and downpour.

Inside, the taxi driver — a bald man with a bulbous, veiny nose and red face — glanced at his passenger for a second in the rearview mirror, giving him a once-over as only a cabbie can, and then looked back at the traffic-snarled road. "You call this spring?" he asked rhetorically. "I don't call this spring. Cold and wet after a long winter. We must all be crazy to live in this kind of climate."

Bolan grunted and turned to the window. He didn't feel like talking — in fact, that was the last thing he wanted to do right now. Then his eyes, as dull as the rain clouds, darted back to the driver. He looked like a smoker. Bolan leaned forward, sniffing the car. Even though it had been sprayed with air freshener, he could still detect a whiff of tobacco on the driver.

"Can I bum a butt off you?" he asked. His were at home, forgotten in the rush to the hospital, and now more than ever a smoke might help put him on the right track because the sedatives and painkillers were affecting his speech and vision.

Not even attempting to conceal his displeasure, the cabbie shuffled around in his jacket, fished a cigarette out of the pack with one hand and reached back, never taking his eyes off the traffic for an instant.

Bolan reached forward for the cigarette, his hand unsteady as he grasped it.

Figuring he was owed one now, the driver started talking again, expecting a friendly, even thankful, response. "I knew you were a cop," he said, proud of his little deduction. "Nobody asks to go to Fifty-Two Division unless it's a cop…'cause the only people there besides cops have been run in, and they don't wanna stay, that's for sure." He laughed, and his squinty eyes moved to the mirror again, waiting to see the reaction from the big man in the back seat. There wasn't even a grunt of acknowledgement this time.

As the car crawled up to a busy intersection, Bolan watched a family of three rushing across the street under a single umbrella, laughing as they ran, the father in the middle, arms around both his wife and daughter. He thought about his own children and Sandra, how they'd go on without him, how their lives would change, how he would become just a memory, fading a little every year. A tear tumbled down the flattened bridge of his nose; he mopped it quickly. He sniffed.

His head was whirling from the medication and the heat inside the cab. He opened the window a crack, which was enough to allow in some spray from the driving rain. A sudden thunder crash caught him by surprise. The anguish Bolan felt changed quickly to anger as he turned his thoughts to the musician. He took a lengthy drag on the cigarette and straightened up in the seat.

"If you don't mind me askin', was something big goin' on at the hospital?" queried the driver as they approached the police station.

"Lookit, give me a break — I don't feel like gabbing," Bolan snapped, sliding out of the seat into the teeming rainstorm. "Wait here. I'll be back in five minutes."

The cold wet air cleared his head somewhat but he was still groggy as he walked. He tried his best to pull himself together before opening the wide glass door. Inside, harsh white fluorescent light bathed him, almost nauseating, as it had been in the hospital. Everywhere there were sounds — laughing and talking and yelling and the shuffling of chairs and the stale ring of telephones — that Bolan had heard a million times but right now they grated on him like steel scraping steel. Despite the medicine he'd been given, there was a churning in his abdomen; as he walked it felt as though he might just keel over at any second. He propped himself up against the staff sergeant's desk.

"Evening, Chuck. How're you doin'?" Barry Saxon was peering above his bifocals at him. "What's this I heard about you being in the hospital or something?"

Bolan tried his damnedest to look offhand, normal even. "Turns out it was just a touch of the flu. Nothin' to worry about."

"Well, you don't look good at all...worse than some of those skid row assholes, if you ask me."

"Christ, no wonder you're the easiest desk sergeant in the city. Like having your own mother in the station." Bolan cracked a tight-lipped smile, pain spreading to his back now. He was trying desperately to appear casual. "Anyway, I've got something on and I won't be in tomorrow...so I thought I'd pick up my gun. Who's the station duty man tonight?"

Saxon leaned back, brushing a shag of silver hair from his brow. "That young kid — I think you know him — Glen Conklin. I'll get him to take your pistol out of the gun locker."

"Thanks. It's twenty-nine. I'll be at my desk." He was relieved to be going down the hall out of Saxon's sight. Even as he walked it felt like the staff sergeant's eyes were drilling holes in his back. He'd looked at Bolan quizzically, and that kind of nerve-racking experience was something the detective didn't need at the moment, when his head was spinning and his insides were rolling around like a bowling ball.

While he sat alone flipping through a stuffed file folder — records of the incident involving Adrian Lee — a rookie constable with a smooth milky face and short-cropped fair hair marched over with the .38 Police Special and holster. Bolan finished scribbling down the address he'd been looking for and snapped the folder shut. He nodded his thanks to the other man and took the weapon, checking the magazine and strapping on the black leather shoulder holster.

After the constable was out of sight he rummaged through a couple of drawers in the old desk until he found his old hangover Aspirins, popped four into his mouth and stood up, leaning on his chair until some of the cloudiness left his vision.

He turned around suddenly but nobody was there. He could've sworn someone called his name. His senses were beginning to play tricks on him. And the pain was getting worse too, but the Aspirins would soon help that. He had to leave right away in case any of the other cops got suspicious talking to him — or even worse, answered a call from the hospital, where they must've noticed him missing by now.

His eyes were focused on the hallway, which would take him from the offices back to the main desk and reception area. Along the way he glanced at a clock — almost nine. When he got to reception the first shift in a continual nighttime parade of gritty soiled souls was waiting to be booked: overweight whores chewing gum, shabby winos with phlegm-filled coughs, open-mouthed smack freaks with lolling heads — all refugees from straight life, who cops stopped feeling sorry for after their first day on the force. No one could hack the job if they became emotionally involved, letting exposure to society's other side get to them. Police officers always ended up choosing sanity over compassion — or else they quit the force.

Bolan tramped out, nodding to casual acquaintances, refusing a coffee and saying goodnight to Saxon, who still eyed him rather warily.

"Chuck," he said with a concerned tone, "take care of yourself — I mean it."

"You bet."

The rain pelted him as soon as he stepped outside but the fresh air actually felt good and cleared his senses somewhat. He galloped a little, hurrying because his spring jacket was soaking through. The taxi was still standing illegally in front of the station.

"Up to Forest Hill," he said curtly to the driver after slamming the door. "I'll tell you where to go from there."

"That sure was a long five minutes," griped the cabbie as he turned down the radio, tuned to one of those classic rock stations, which was playing the Dire Straits song, "I Want My MTV." But the irony was lost on Bolan.

***

It was the last night of his Montreal conference, and how appealing the thought of cocktails and a banquet seemed. He'd be in the limelight, accepting accolades from his peers for his insightful and moving speech. Enthusiastic applause a few hours earlier from the six hundred conference attendees still echoed in his mind. But instead of professional discussions over an icy extra-dry martini, Ricardo Sosa had chosen to excuse himself and rush to the airport, catch a plane to another city and now ride endlessly through rain-drenched suburbs in an airport limousine. Jennifer had arranged for the car to be waiting when he arrived at Pearson International Airport in Toronto.

By now he'd spent more time on the road than he had in the air. The driver — a thick-bearded Sikh who wore a turban with his blue uniform — told him they were almost there. Sosa was jittery, wondering what would happen when he and Jennifer confronted Adrian. What kind of approach would he use? Could he actually help? Among the mish-mash of thoughts colliding in his brain at this moment was a strong sense of guilt. By introducing Adrian to Santeria, was he at least partly responsible for the musician's personality disorder and ugly behavior — including the possible murder of Maria Cuevas? Could the Cuban religion, in combination with the beating by police and subsequent stresses, have been the detonator that set off Adrian's schizophrenic behavior?

"Here is the house, sir."

The driver's voice brought Sosa out of his thoughts and back to reality — in this case, driving winds and pounding rain. He pulled his wallet out of his suit jacket. "How much do I owe you?" he asked.

"Nothing, sir. Everything, including the gratuity, is prepaid." The driver turned the Lincoln slowly into the driveway, edging up as near as possible to the front walk and stopping behind a big BMW. "This music group Tangent, they are very good customers of ours."

Before opening the car door, Sosa glanced up and down the street, noticing in the dimness outside how all of the narrow two-storey townhouses looked alike. He thanked the driver and jumped out, slamming the door, cold rain pelting him instantly and soaking into his light-colored clothing as large dark blotches. Sounds were everywhere, and made him feel even wetter: splashes down eaves troughs, droplets pounding asphalt and a stream of run-off pouring through a grate into the storm sewer on the street.

227

Sosa ran alongside the black German sedan, bounded up the porch steps two at a time and stood at the front entrance to the house, where there wasn't much of an overhang, so he was afforded little protection. His finger was glued to the doorbell; for good measure he knocked hard and loudly too. Finally — although it couldn't have been more than thirty seconds — the porch light above him came on. Then a face peeked out of the small oval window in the front door, scrutinizing him.

"Jennifer told me to come," he yelled, aware that a single woman wouldn't open the door to a stranger. By now he could feel the rain seeping right through his jacket and into the white linen shirt he wore.

The door slid open. "Come in," said a slim woman with dark hair and eyes to match, backing away from the door to allow the Cuban some room in the narrow hallway.

He was only too glad to step in. "You don't know me, do you?" he asked.

"No," she replied. "I assume you're a friend of Jennifer's."

"I'm Ricardo Sosa." He offered her his hand, which she took in a quick but firm shake. "Jennifer asked me to help her deal with Adrian. I'm a psychiatrist."

"Katherine Bontempo. Glad to meet you. Jenny and I are old friends. She's crashing at my place for a while."

"Yes, she told me this morning. I was in Montreal and came as soon as I could."

"Jenny's been so upset."

"Can I speak to her then?"

"She's not here. To tell you the truth, I'm worried. I didn't get home till late this evening — half an hour ago — and there was no sign of her. Except her car is still in the driveway. That's unusual, especially out here in the boonies…and on a night like this."

Suddenly Sosa look worried. "She's not here?"

"No. She didn't call me either. And she didn't tell me about you."

"Did you telephone her?"

"I've called her house five times since I got home. No answer." She motioned for him to follow her down the hall into the brightly lit kitchen.

"May I use your telephone, please? I'll try one more time." Sosa fished soggy papers out of his jacket pocket, looking for the one with Jennifer and Adrian's number on it. He dialed and let it ring thirty times.

She fidgeted with her fingernails. "No luck, eh?"

He nodded. "Can you get me the number for a taxi?"

"You're going over there?"

"Well, I can't think of anywhere else she might be. Possibly Adrian will be there…even if Jennifer isn't." Sosa pulled one of the bow-back chairs from the small wooden table and sat down. "I suppose you are a non-smoker."

"That's right," Katherine replied. "In fact, my house is a smoke-free environment."

"Yes, of course," said the Cuban wistfully, hands on the breast pocket of his shirt, lightly fingering the leather cigar case. "A smoke-free environment."

"Here we go." She handed him a rumpled piece of paper with a number scrawled on it.

Her handwriting indicated that she was an impatient person, thought Sosa. "One more thing, if it's not too much trouble. Will you please write down directions that I can read to the driver? The last thing we need is for me to get lost."

"Would you like a coffee while you wait? Taxis will be at a premium in this storm." Katherine hovered over him, ready to jump as soon as he answered.

"Yes, thank you. That would be nice."

She opened a cupboard and took out some filters, then grabbed the beans from her freezer. "Tell me something," she said, turning her head in his direction as she started grinding the beans, "what are you going to do when you get there?"

"God knows," he answered, lifting the receiver to call the cab. A chill glided up and down his body, probably from being soaked to the bone.

Chapter Twenty-Eight

A tremendous thunder crash seemed to rattle the car as it stood on the street outside the imposing 1920s home. Ricardo Sosa practically threw money at the driver and then jumped out. The rain had abated for about twenty minutes but was beginning again, with the addition now of a full-fledged electrical storm, just to make things even more difficult for him. Wind in his face, Sosa walked up the driveway, unperturbed about getting wet anymore; he was still soaked from the last downpour. It had been his idea to have the taxi stop on the street, though he wasn't quite sure why. Perhaps there should be some element of surprise, he thought.

Even in the darkness he could tell that this was a grand house, as were all of them lining both sides of the street. Only a flicker of amber light came from the front, probably in the living room. Sosa looked around — not that anybody could see him on this ugly night even if they happened to be staring out a window — and dashed across the spongy lawn, stopping for a moment behind a huge old maple. The smell of old wood and wet leaves filled his nostrils. From there he rushed up to the grey stone fascia of the house and leaned against it, edging toward the window with the light.

Suddenly the memory of a similar night more than forty years before came to mind, in his hometown of Santa Clara, when as an adolescent he snuck out of his bedroom and raced over to his neighbor's home, hugging the wall as he strained to catch a glimpse in a window. What he witnessed that night had had a profound effect upon him. His heart pounded as he moved closer to this window, in another city, another country, another part of the world and in another time. Sosa was now under it and had to practically do a chin-up on the window ledge to raise himself into a viewing position. The drapes were closed — except for a crack. Behind them were lace sheers, but the more he stared, the more he picked up what was going on inside that room.

It was beyond anything he could've ever imagined.

Trembling like one of the tree branches in the storm, he dropped from the window and sprinted toward the front porch. He leapt for the door, crashing into it, pounding it with his fists as hard as he could.

"Adrian!" he screamed. "It's Ricardo Sosa. Open this door! Open this door!" He clicked the door handle over and over. Nothing happened. Flying down the stairs and splashing along the driveway, he headed toward the garage, his surroundings illuminated by lightning for an instant. The side door was ajar. Sosa stopped just inside, groping in the blackness for a light switch. He flicked on an overhead fluorescent. Two automobiles — a Jaguar and a Porsche — were parked near the front, and on the wall were garden tools. He reached up and grabbed a large spade, and in his panic fumbled it, watching helplessly as it came crashing down on the muscular curves of the black 911S, scratching paint on the hood. Ricardo dragged it across the car and ran out with it, staring into the ever-increasing rain, trying to find a way into the house.

A sunroom with white French doors stood out, even in the darkness of night. He galloped straight at it, swinging the shovel like a baseball bat, eyes shut tightly and head turned as glass exploded in every direction. Dropping the shovel, he reached inside through the empty pane and turned the deadbolt latch.

There were no lights on. Inside, it was as hot as a blistery summer day, as though the furnace had been set to maximum. Ricardo stumbled over furniture — white wicker, he could make out — and ran his fingers along walls until he passed into a very large room. There could be no mistaking the kitchen. LEDs from the refrigerator, coffee maker, microwave, oven and digital shelf clock provided enough illumination for him to get his bearings. He switched on some track lights and ran clattering across the terra cotta tile through a doorway and onto hardwood, down a seemingly endless black hall, the light from the kitchen receding behind him as he headed toward the flickering glow up ahead. After passing half a dozen rooms along the way, he finally approached the brightness.

It was as if he'd entered a dream, a very nasty one. Jennifer was strapped on her back to the marble coffee table, her arms, legs and midsection tethered with chains, locks and knotted yellow nylon rope. A large scarf was tied roughly about her neck and chin as a gag. At least, Sosa assumed it was Jennifer. She appeared so different, nude, with her head and body hair shaved, looking somewhat like an alien, complete with large eyes because hers were wide with fear. Right now she turned to stare up at Ricardo and was screaming incomprehensibly into the scarf. Everywhere on the floor was dirt, wheelbarrows full of it, spread over the rug and hardwood. In the fireplace a huge four-log blaze crackled and spit. An easy chair and two floor lamps had been tipped over. A couple of table lamps were on, just naked bulbs, their shades removed. All around the room were candles — maybe a dozen of them — which cast a soft fluttery halo, in sharp contrast to the goings-on.

He stood there brandishing a knife in his left hand, with a foot-long blade directly over top of Jennifer. Behind Adrian, Sosa saw the pine altar with the sacred drums beside it. As he glanced there, what caught his eye was the old bowl — a gourd fashioned from a coconut — with a concoction inside it that included the stones he'd given Adrian in Cuba.

Sosa tried with all his might to stifle the terror ripping strips off him and spoke in a relatively calm voice. "Adrian," he said, "it's me, Ricardo."

The musician stood there, shirtless and barefoot, his jeans partially unzipped. He held the knife just a couple of inches above the exposed flesh of Jennifer's waist. "I'm sorry, but Adrian's indisposed right now." His voice was unnaturally serene.

"Well…the person I'm talking to looks like Adrian and sounds like Adrian."

"But I'm not him."

Sosa moved a little closer. He noticed the house lights waver and go off for a moment, then come back on — probably a brownout because of the storm. "If you're not Adrian, why do you speak in English and sound just like him?"

"I inhabit his mind — put thoughts into it. Of course I'm bound by his physical being, his vocal chords, the language he uses, the way he communicates."

"Who are you then?"

"I was a warrior. Ogun sent me. Do you know who Ogun is?"

"Of course — the god of war, vengeance, hatred."

"Doctor Sosa knows everything, doesn't he?"

"How do you know I'm a doctor?"

"I know all about you."

"Adrian, you must listen. Just put down the knife, will you? Adrian — "

" — How many times must I tell you, I'm not Adrian."

"You have to realize something: you're very sick, Adrian. You're suffering from schizophrenia and a dual personality. These are delusions you are experiencing, nothing more. That other personality is subjugating yours sometimes. Don't let it take over, Adrian. Fight it. Come to your senses. You can be in control."

An ugly smile crept over Adrian's face; then he tilted his head back, laughing loudly, roaring as though he'd just been told the world's funniest joke. He didn't move the knife though, not an inch. "You're really quite humorous, Doctor, especially when you play psychiatrist."

"Adrian, listen — "

" — Stop it now!" The mirth of a moment before had been instantly replaced by a hideous look and a twitching body. "What will it take for you to understand? How do you think Adrian could have arranged for all this?" He raised his head, surveying the room around him.

Sosa's eyes darted furtively down to Jennifer, who was still looking up at both of them. "I gave you many titles of reference books. Anybody can read." It was almost as though he were trying to convince himself. He paused to wipe away sweat from his brow. With wet clothes it felt like a sauna. "In your mental state at the time, you came to believe that these Santeria rituals were actually working, that a spirit had invaded your body."

The telephone rang.

"Answer it."

Ricardo looked at Adrian incredulously. "Me?"

"I don't see anyone else here who's capable of picking it up, do you?"

The ringing continued. Sosa looked around and spotted a cordless phone atop an antique French desk just outside the doorway, in the hall. "Why do you want me to answer it?"

"Because, as you can see, I'm occupied with the ritual that you rudely interrupted. So go and get it — now!"

Probably Katherine Bontempo, thought Sosa. His mind raced. Could he give her some sort of signal without endangering Jennifer even more? He walked into the hall and picked up the receiver on the eighth ring. "Hello."

"Mr. Adrian Lee?" It was a male voice.

"Yes," he lied, hoping to stall for time.

"Sir, this is Sergeant Saxon at Metro Police Fifty-Two Division. We have reason to believe that Detective Bo — "

— Deafening thunder and off went the lights. A hydro blackout. And suddenly just static on the telephone. "Hello, hello," Ricardo repeated, heart sinking. Just a dial tone. He looked at the receiver and realized that being cordless it required electricity, unlike the standard issue phone they used in Cuba. Now it was dark.

"Who was it?" asked Adrian.

"I have no idea; the phone went dead."

"Get back in here," he ordered.

With reduced visibility and the shambles of the living room, Sosa stepped carefully back in. It had taken on a dim orange hue, lit only by candles and the crackling fireplace. Slowly he approached Adrian, glancing down at Jennifer now and then, creating eye contact. He came to the altar and stood beside it.

"Mind if I smoke?" he asked.

"Hah!" laughed Adrian. "You want to know if it's all right to smoke. In the midst of all you see around you, do you think anyone would care if you indulge in your filthy little habit?"

Sosa pulled his Dunhill English cigar case out of his shirt pocket. Although it had space for four cigars, only one remained. He took out the cigar, squeezed it and sniffed the tobacco for a second before striking a match. Just then thunder shook the house as though a rocket had exploded there. Ricardo barely flinched as he puffed and inhaled a waft of smoke. No one else in the room made a sound either. Then a barrage of rain followed, driven by the wind, sounding like pellets penetrating the walls and roof.

"So what kind of ritual did I interrupt?"

"That doesn't concern you."

"Adrian — or personality number two, whatever your name is — this is sheer madness. What do you hope to accomplish?"

"You are the expert on Santeria, Doctor. You figure it out."

"This is your wife...the woman who loves you," began Sosa, pausing to let the words sink in. He had to draw Adrian's real personality back out. "You can't commit such an act of violence against her."

"Listen to me, you sister-fucking piece of Cuban excrement, I am not Adrian. Call me that again and you risk having your heart cut out."

"Pardon me," said Sosa, guts churning but still maintaining a relatively placid exterior. Could it be possible that a spirit had entered Adrian's body? "Tell me more about this ceremony...please." He stole glimpses about the room, memorizing the obstacles around him and what could be used as a weapon if necessary.

"Fuck the ceremony."

"Then tell me — why Adrian?"

"He has the knack, the ability to open himself, like a freshly cleaned fish. He has always had this remarkable ability but never put it to use."

"What do you mean by ability?"

"Adrian is a seer. Sometimes his dreams enter my world. And, of course, he is a leader."

Sosa looked puzzled. "A leader?"

"He has power. Millions of people listen to the words he writes in songs."

"That's why you chose him?"

"Oh, there's more to it than that. Do you think Caligula, Genghis Khan, Hitler — and thousands of others lesser known — just happened to turn out the way they did? Or were they given a nudge?"

"You are the catalyst for Adrian then."

"His state of mind at the beginning made it very easy — full of unresolved anger, a venom that wouldn't go away. So he was receptive, thankful even, by my presence. Little by little, with each ritual, he let more of me in. It was an acquired taste...but one he couldn't be without. He was unable to resist. Until now; now that he's lost within himself and has no choice."

Sosa swallowed hard. He didn't want to believe it. "If you are not Adrian, then what are you doing to his wife?"

"Making the strongest magic my people have made in a thousand years."

"Take me," said Sosa, sucking in cigar smoke, wondering where in God's name he found the courage to make such an offer. "Let her go. Put me in her place. Use me for your magic." In this sweltering hell he felt sweat dripping annoyingly from his nose onto his moustache but made no motion to remove it.

Adrian laughed yet still remained poised over Jennifer's belly, the knife blade pointing straight down. "I don't want you!" he shouted. "You're like the swine from my village. And just like them you'll be slaughtered. Your end is drawing near, Doctor."

"But what is it you want with her?" Even as he spoke, Sosa was thinking of what he'd say next, and after that, and after that, like a master working out moves in some devil's chess game.

"You must have guessed by now." Adrian pointed his free hand, fingernails like claws, directly down at Jennifer. "I'm going to take the baby. Some of me is in there. I need it — to become the most powerful being…the most feared warrior…in yours or any other world. She and the baby must be sacrificed."

Time was running out, Sosa knew. "Adrian, is that what you did to Maria?" he asked, steadying himself for the repercussions, should they come.

"You provoke me on purpose, biting like a flea. Your last breath is ever closer. So listen well: Adrian did nothing to Maria that she didn't like, didn't want, didn't want to stop. He made love to her over and over again."

Jennifer's already wide eyes seemed to open still farther. She began to shout something through her gag but again it was too muffled to be understood. Sosa looked down at her, nodding his head slightly, trying to silence her, to deflect all attention to himself. "How did she come to die then?" he asked.

"Our friend Adrian disappeared for a short time, just as he has now. I had my own designs on the girl…for other purposes. She struggled and managed to free herself from my grip — but fell backward, down, down, nearly all of the way to the bottom. Adrian joined up with his own self again, only to find his lover gone. He thought she'd left for home while he'd been sleeping. The last thing he remembered was rolling off her after their third bout of sex."

"Then he found me on the road looking for him," Ricardo commented.

"How nice of you to use the word 'he' instead of 'you.' I think you are finally coming around, Doctor."

A trail of smoke, looking almost bright white in the dimly lit room, left Sosa's mouth as he exhaled slowly. "On the contrary, Adrian. It was a mere slip of the tongue."

All of a sudden the knife was directed away from Jennifer and up toward the Cuban. "You stinking rotted bile!" Adrian screamed out. "How close you come to being carved up like a chicken."

Ricardo dropped his cigar butt into the dirt and stepped on it. "Listen to me, Adrian, you must fight, fight to come back. Bring yourself to the surface. You can do it. Can you hear me?"

"You still don't believe it, do you?" His voice was calmer again.

"If what you say is true, then let Adrian return. Prove it to me."

"All right."

Sosa watched intently. Only half a minute passed before a transformation occurred. Adrian's eyes closed for an instant. His shoulders slumped. It was as though he were coming out of a hypnotic trance.

"Whaa, what, where…where…what?" His eyes opened. "Ricardo — what, what's going on?" He looked around, disbelieving, horror evident in his features. Then he saw her down below. "Jennifer!" he shrieked. "What the — " The knife caught his eye. He threw it down.

At that second Ricardo leapt forward, yanking the gourd bowl from the altar, and smashed it into Adrian's head as hard as he could, knocking the other man off his feet. The altar went down too, along with the sacred drums, everything crashing so loudly it drowned out a thunder clap and the teeming rain.

"No! No!" cried out Adrian from the floor. "I won't let you. Get away from me." Then his voice — but with a ghastly tone: "Get back, I say. Get back!" Adrian returned. "I won't let you," he shouted painfully.

Sosa couldn't believe his ears. Adrian was having a violent argument with himself. He'd never witnessed such an astounding case of dual personality and delusion before.

But the Cuban stood there a few seconds too long and let the bowl drop a little, his grip loosening. Up out of the dirt Adrian sprang, flying almost, diving straight at Sosa and screaming, gripping him by the shoulders and hurling him backward with a savage strength. Ricardo felt his feet leave the ground and then a painful thud, agony as his shoulders and back made contact with the wall. But he was still standing — just. He raised his hands to defend himself.

Adrian glared at him, eyes jumping out of the dimness. Then a roar like a big jungle cat, a raging beast. In one gliding motion he reached down as he ran, grasped the knife and swung it up.

And in that tenth of a second, Ricardo saw it in those eyes. He knew two things were certain: it wasn't Adrian inside that body, and that he was about to die.

The knife ripped past Sosa's outstretched hands and was driven straight into his throat, severing his windpipe. He gasped for air but choked up blood instead, falling slowly.

Watching, Jennifer struggled with the ropes, her body shaking violently as she screamed through the scarf.

Adrian knelt over Sosa, who was slumped partially against the wall. There was a foul odor as his bowel and bladder lost their contents. His brain began to shut down. Meanwhile something strange was happening inside Adrian. He started to swoon, looking intoxicated. Then the next instant his face looked tortured. "No!" he screamed. "Get the fuck out of me!" Then back to a glazed-over look. It was as though the thing inside him were growing stronger at the sight of fresh blood, the smell of death. He thrust his long fingernails at the dead man's throat, smearing them until they were the color of black cherry. Next he scooped from the wound, where the blood was warmer, as if this were a ritual sacrifice.

He was oblivious to everything around him for a moment. Jennifer craned her neck toward Adrian, and noticed something on Ricardo's body. Even in the faint candlelight she could make it out clearly in the Cuban's hand: a broken string of small dark beads. The resguardo or protective charm. Sosa had ripped them off Adrian's neck just before he died.

Chapter Twenty-Nine

The cab stopped a few doors down. He got out and walked toward the house, unfazed by the driving wind and rain. Without streetlights there was almost total darkness except for the faint flicker of candlelight visible in some living rooms. Lightning lit up the street for an instant, turning the big brick homes an ominous grey. Bolan walked part way down the driveway and stared up at the imposing house, unsteady on his feet and feeling sicker than ever.

"Chuck!"

He swung around in the direction of the voice. "Rita?" She came out from behind a large old maple tree, her hair, coat and jeans soaked through. "What the hell are you doing here?"

"I was going to ask you the same thing," she replied.

"I gotta see Lee — it's my only hope."

"No, you can't go in there, especially in the state you're in." Even in the darkness, Rita could make out how terrible he looked.

"How long have you been waiting for me?"

"About half an hour. A few minutes after I got here, a taxi pulled up. I thought it was you. A man got out, looked like the guy in the white suit from that TV show…you know…Fantasy Island. He banged at the front door, yelled something and then took off down the driveway. I was going to tail him but thought I'd better wait for you."

"I think I know who it was," said Bolan, starting toward the house. "Come on."

"Chuck, we just can't burst in there. Remember the court order?"

"Fuck the court order."

"But we don't have a search warrant."

"Fuck the warrant. Are you with me or not?" Lightning illuminated his features as he looked back at her.

Rita started to speak when thunder crashed, drowning out her voice. "Years of hard work to get where I am today — and now I risk blowing it all."

"Are you coming or not?" yelled Bolan.

"Yes, I'm coming, I'm coming," she grumbled and ran to his side, and then up the stairs onto the porch.

He grabbed the door handle. Locked. "No way I can break that down," he said, eyeing the thick oak door. "Let's head to the back."

Splashing through puddles, they ran past the garage and into the garden. Both of them noticed at once the sunroom door with the broken window and let themselves in. It was as though they were blind in the house, feeling their way along, bouncing off furniture and walls, until they spotted a faint bit of orange light at the opposite end of a hall and headed for it. Bolan arrived first and swung into the living room, with Rita following up the rear.

"Don't move!" he shouted, trying to see in the dim light from the fireplace and candles. His body swayed slightly, the pistol in his unsteady right hand, face pasty with glassy sunken eyes, but he was finally there — two hundred and forty pounds of him — in pain but determined. Wind had lifted strands of his drenched wispy hair, making him look like a mad professor.

Nothing could've prepared him for what he saw at that moment. Horror and revulsion swept over him like a blanket of cockroaches. "You filthy scum sack," he spat out. "Stand up and face me — now."

Hands and mouth glistening red, Adrian started to get up slowly. His long hair was greasy and matted, hanging in clumps, and the upper half of his face was black, as though he'd been pummeled around the eyes. Another shock. There was no mistaking it. Through his partly unzipped jeans, an erection was visible. Sosa's body was crumpled against the wall.

Bolan felt his stomach turning. Rita covered her mouth in shock. "Back up," Bolan ordered Adrian. He gestured toward Jennifer while keeping his gun trained on the other man. "Rita, think you can free her?"

She started to undo the gag but the scarf had been knotted over and over, so a couple of endless minutes passed. Finally it was loose enough to yank down. Jennifer panted for air and looked up at Rita. "Thank you," she whispered between breaths.

"We'll get you untied now," said Rita, beginning what appeared to be an arduous task, since there were dozens and dozens of knots on each rope. She wondered how crazed the musician must've been to tie them this way. Then there were the chains.

Adrian's eyes rolled in his head, until just the whites were visible for a moment. When the pupils returned, he took a glimpse of his blood-covered hands and screamed. "What happened?" he shouted. "Oh, God, no!"

"You tell me," said Bolan tersely.

Jennifer broke in. "He doesn't know what he's doing. Something inside is making him."

Bolan stepped over and grabbed him by the shoulder, slamming him back to the wall. "Stay there, you fuckin' ghoul."

"You don't understand," said Jennifer.

"We'll talk about it when you're untied."

Adrian looked down at Sosa's body. He began to whimper. "No, no. Not that."

"I wanna know something," said Bolan. The gun he held was wobbling. "What did you do to me?"

Suddenly a wave came over Adrian and then it started: the other voice. He's sick and weak. You have the strength. You have the chance. So take advantage of it. The voice sounded calm and confident. The fear he'd felt initially was spurting out of him like liquid from a broken blister. In fact, he was quickly beginning to feel in control, despite the tenuous situation. "Get out of me," he screamed at the voice in his head.

Bolan looked confused. "What is this crap? Speak up! What did you do to me?"

"He doesn't know," said Jennifer.

Adrian's face was contorted. The voice was getting stronger, taking over. Get ready for your move. He's weak. You are strong. "Leave me alone...please," he pleaded.

"Listen!" shouted Bolan. "I want to know what you did to me."

"Nothing." Adrian appeared completely calm now.

"That's shit. I know you did it — but how."

"Santeria."

Gone was the sallow look on Bolan's face; now he had a scorching glare. "What the fuck are you talking about!"

"A religion...a Cuban religion called Santeria."

"What's that got to do with me?"

The thing inside Adrian laughed. "Everything. I put a taboo spirit into your body."

Bolan gave him a quizzical look and moved a little closer. "How'd you do it?"

"That day outside the station...remember? Adrian and I wanted you to know. That's part of it. Of course, I don't know exactly what the end result will be."

"You don't know!" bellowed the detective. "You don't know — and now I got cancer."

"Take it easy, Chuck," said Rita, looking up at him from where she was kneeling and loosening knots.

Adrian's breathing was getting heavier. The thing inside was growing explosively, the way it had during the rituals, with a rush of overwhelming power.

Jennifer spoke up. "It's not Adrian — he didn't do this to you."

Bolan ignored her. "I'm gonna die. And I don't deserve this, you hear? Do you understand? I don't deserve this." His roar was turning to a wail, and a tear fell down his clammy cheek, visible even in the candlelight, glistening like an icicle. "When I thumped you, it was an accident. Everything had been messed up for me...nothing was goin' right. My life was a bag of shit. And I was so sorry about what I did to you." His words were broken as he tried to choke back the crying.

Rita stopped untying ropes for a moment and stood up. "Oh, Chuck."

"He's not in control," explained Jennifer, trying to reason with the detective. "It's not his fault."

"What about Brodsky — my lawyer?"

"What do you think?" hissed the thing inside Adrian. "You're a detective, so figure it out. But here's a clue because you're such a stupid ass. We paid a visit to Mr. Brodsky too, at his office. Funny how things turned out, isn't it?"

A battle raged within the deepest reaches of the musician. He was fighting to be heard, to make decisions. But instead something else was in charge now, and he could hear his own voice speaking words and giving answers that weren't his. He was powerless to interfere but was trying with all his might. One part of him felt guilt and pity, while the other — which was untamed, malignant and growing stronger by the second — thirsted for savagery. Looking at the cop now brought out a sense of shame, at how much anger and hatred he'd pent up against what was in essence a pathetic individual, someone he should've felt sorry for. But the other side of him, which had taken over his body, remained unmoved, full of rancor, plotting a warrior's revenge.

Adrian moved one leg to his rear slightly, his weight on it, and lifted his front foot off the floor about an inch, dropping slowly and unnoticeably into a karate cat stance. Under his clothes every muscle flexed and tightened; his breathing, while expertly controlled, continued to gain in intensity. "I don't think I'm responsible for your condition," he said cruelly, voice lower-pitched and raspier than usual. "You were well on your way without me."

"No way, you prick. You knew — you told me, for Chrissakes — and you gave me cancer."

"Maybe you deserved it." His words were a snarl more than speech.

"You bastard," snapped the detective, scowling. He straightened his arm, leveling the gun at Adrian's chest. His finger tensed on the trigger. "If I have to die, then maybe you will too."

"Stop it!" shouted Jennifer. "Don't let him do this to you."

"Chuck," said Rita, jumping up and moving toward him, "give me your gun. I'll watch him. You try to get her loose."

Bolan glanced at her for an instant and eased his finger back on the trigger. Thwack!

It was the fastest hardest snap kick; a lightning blow that connected the ball of Adrian's left foot with Bolan's hand and sent the gun clattering across the floor into darkness. He landed on the same foot in the middle of a spin and completed the half-circle move, using his hip as a lever to send a straight-legged kick with the other foot into the side of the cop's face.

Rita started for the gun but Adrian leapt beside her, yanking her by the hair and her shoulder, lifting her off the ground with almost superhuman strength and throwing her into the air. She flew a dozen feet right into the fireplace, headfirst, smashing into the mantle, and slumping into a heap.

Adrian jumped back in the ready stance, arms up and knees bent, expecting Bolan to be off balance or stunned from the blow. But the detective didn't reel long — years of surprises had taught him better — and his left hook was powerful and swift, with a cantaloupe-sized fist, and full sturdy knuckles that easily drove past Adrian's attempted block and crashed into his cheek, cracking the bone and heaving him off his feet as though he were a mannequin. He was propelled backward and bounced off an easy chair onto the floor. The side of his face felt like it had caved in, crushed by an avalanche instead of a man. But he didn't stop moving, rolling with the blow and bouncing back up just as Bolan was at him again, this time with his size thirteen foot poised for a field goal. But the kick never made contact, as Adrian danced to one side and then hopped in close, landing four back fists to Bolan's face in two seconds. They were just glancing blows, an element of surprise. Then he leapt backward into a crouch, coiled for release. The detective jumped at him and threw a roundhouse punch, which Adrian blocked easily, driving his forearm into the other man's elbow. Immediately he followed with straight fingers to the eyes. Bolan avoided blindness by jerking his head a fraction of an inch just in time, taking the fingertip stab on his eyebrows instead. Surprisingly fast considering his sickly condition, he managed to seize Adrian's bicep for an instant and then wrap his other arm around the neck, forcing the musician into a headlock. Adrian lashed out with a vicious punch to the ribs but Bolan didn't relent, still squeezing the other man's head like a professional wrestler, dragging him forward off balance and using the free arm to hammer his face.

Blood blossomed like a crimson carnation on Adrian's cheek but he didn't notice the blows, wasn't aware of any pain. He began to growl, the sound of a vicious caged animal. Suddenly an infusion of brute force spread through him and flooded every sinew of every muscle in his body. Still bent over and trapped in the headlock, he reached up swiftly and circled Bolan's neck with one arm, and then proceeded with extraordinary strength to stand up straight, throwing the cop off balance and tossing them both onto a side table — which collapsed under their weight with a crack, scattering mosaic pieces all over the floor and extinguishing two candles that had been there.

In a second Adrian was on his feet. Then it happened.

A demon scream so piercing and unearthly that Bolan did a double take in the dim firelight, to see if it really had come from the musician's lips. What happened next made him doubt his eyesight. Adrian seemed to be getting bigger, inflating like a beach ball, his chest expanding rapidly, looking three sizes too large for the rest of his body. Confusion and fear gripping him now, the cop rose and stood there, fists shoulder-height and ready for whatever might be coming.

Jennifer screamed at Adrian, implored him to stop.

It was like a flash, as if he had wings, Adrian bounding almost six feet into the air, body sideways, arms up, one leg outstretched in perfect form for a flying kick, so fast the cop couldn't prevent it from slamming his collar bone and knocking him back a few steps. But the big man managed to keep his balance anyway and stay on his feet. Adrian landed on the floor in a roll, doing two somersaults and vaulting up again instantly. He rushed in with one kick after another and a flurry of punches that were faster than in any karate movie's sped-up filming, his feet, fists, open hands and fingers now serious weapons.

During those nine or ten seconds the stinging blows buffeted Bolan in every vulnerable place: groin, knees, kidneys, heart, eyes, temple. He couldn't match the speed or power of his opponent, who seemed otherworldly at the moment. The floor and walls began to tilt; his tear-filled eyes saw four of everything. The pain was excruciating. He sank to his knees.

Adrian stepped back and waited. He was shaking his head violently, as if that would exorcise the invader who'd taken over his mind and body. Stop fighting! Leave him alone now. Arguing with whatever dwelled inside him. Trying to let the real him come to the surface again. He'd blacked out for the fight, although some of it had appeared to him, dream-like, as he stared into that same dark vortex he'd seen during the rituals. He tried to control his breathing, slow the hyperventilating.

Light flooded the room. The power came back on.

Bolan was shakily trying to stand up. One of his eyes had swelled shut from a blow and his nose and mouth trickled blood. Slowly and painfully he managed to get to his feet.

"No, don't!" screamed Adrian at the fiendish thing occupying his soul, as his body lunged forward against his will and directed a kick straight into Bolan's gut. The detective crumpled. Three more vicious kicks into his midsection, and he was down.

"Please, Adrian, don't," begged Jennifer.

But the kicks came furiously, one after another, dozens and dozens of them as a scarlet puddle formed around Bolan's head.

Then a pause. Adrian turned around toward Jennifer. "I'm not finished with you yet," said the thing inside. "We'll take up where we left off." He bent down, running his fingers through the blood. "Stop it," shouted Adrian. "Get the fuck out of me! Give me my body back."

"Freeze!"

Rita Barrett stood in the doorway holding Bolan's revolver, which she'd just picked up, legs apart, slightly crouching, gun hand steadied by the other hand, thumb cocking the trigger. Blood was streaming from her forehead, the contact point where she'd hit the fireplace. Beyond her wildest, ugliest dreams she never could have imagined the scene spread before her at this moment.

The musician stood up and started to move very slowly. He was hardly recognizable, covered in blood and dirt, his good looks contorted into manic ugliness. A throaty noise, like a wolf's snarl, came from his direction. It was getting louder and changing, ceasing to be at all like an animal because nothing on earth could make that kind of sound.

Rita didn't know what to make of it. "Shut up!" she barked, trying to be heard, her finger twitching on the trigger, wondering what to do next.

Slowly and methodically the musician pulled aside the fire screen and reached in among the coals, grasping a burning piece of log in his left hand, one that was at least three inches in diameter and entirely in flames. Then he rose and turned in her direction.

Her mouth dropped. She glanced at his hand — no visible burn marks. He didn't seem to feel any pain. Rita was in for another shock. She blinked a few times in disbelief. He was growing, definitely becoming larger, his upper body blowing up like a dinghy. She took a deep breath and squeezed the trigger.

The shot was earsplitting in the house and reverberated off the walls, more like dynamite than a handgun. Rita placed it exactly where she'd aimed — just inches above Adrian's head as a warning.

The weirdest thing happened next. Fear evident in his eyes, he shriveled up like a burst balloon, and his attention immediately focused on the burning wood he was holding. The most unimaginable searing pain overtook him; he was literally being branded. He shrieked from the bottom of his lungs and flung the orange-hot ember sideways.

"Hold it right there, man" she yelled. "Now don't move or the next bullet will be lower, I guarantee you." She looked down behind her at Jennifer. "Are you all right?"

"So far," came the reply, along with a weak smile. "God, please get these chains off me. They're hurting."

"As soon as I can." Rita turned her attention to Bolan, whose inert body lay in the dirt and debris. She raced to him and knelt over him, using her free hand to feel for a pulse in his neck. Satisfied he was alive she focused her gaze back up at the musician, who was whimpering in agony, pressing a charred and quickly blistering hand against his body.

"Okay, where's a phone? We need some help here."

But the musician didn't answer; he seemed comatose, a completely changed person now instead of the aggressor of a few seconds ago.

"Look!" screamed Jennifer.

Smoke. Rita smelled it too — and then saw where it was coming from. The torch Adrian threw had landed under the floor-length drapes and ignited them very quickly. They were burning like newspapers. "Oh, my God! Quick — there's a fire. We have to get some water and wet towels." Glancing down at Jennifer, she realized there was no time to finish untying her, start on the chains and keep watch on Adrian at the same time. She ran up to him, waving her gun in his face. But he was slow to react, lost in his pain. Nothing seemed to faze him. "Into the kitchen — now!" She shoved him, and he started to stumble forward. But a precious few seconds had been lost.

Rita turned back for another look. The fire was spreading to Adrian and Jennifer's most prized possession: a large painting, over a century old, by the impressionist Georges Seurat. Its subject — a lighthouse in rural France — was turning black and starting to smoke. As they rushed toward the kitchen the entire oiled canvas exploded into flames. On the floor the edges of the Persian wool rug were beginning to burn too, which would surely carry the fire to the furniture. And just past another window with long flowing drapes there was an entire wall of masks — thirty demonic wooden faces from India, Nepal, Burma and China. Rita knew they'd be excellent kindling. The fire would have a life of its own shortly, devouring everything in its path.

Running through the dining room, she realized that water and wet towels would be a waste of time. There was nothing they could do to extinguish the fire or even slow its pace; the best thing would be to use the telephone and go back for Bolan and Jennifer. As a young cop Rita had been at the scene of several burning buildings and talked to firefighters, who let her in on a simple fact: once the room temperature reaches a certain point — which wouldn't take long because this house had already been extremely warm — the fire will travel in high gear and be completely out of control.

She spotted a telephone as soon as they reached the kitchen. "Hold it," she ordered Adrian, gun still trained on him as she dialed 911. Considering what she'd just seen, Rita was surprisingly calm while speaking, providing details about the fire and the address. She'd get a kitchen knife to cut Jennifer free and drag Bolan outside. What she hadn't counted on was the musician suddenly bolting like a colt out of the kitchen and back into the dining room. She dropped the receiver in mid-sentence and rushed in after him. He lurched left through a doorway into the hall. She followed. He was taking the spiral staircase three steps at a time to the second floor. No way she was going to give chase — not when it was a life-or-death situation in the living room. She contemplated another warning shot but thought better of it, in case the bullet hit him. It was getting difficult to see anyway because there were no lights on at the top of the stairs. She must get back to the others immediately before the fire got much worse.

An unholy head-splitting scream came from above. Her eyes darted back up the winding stairs but she couldn't make out anything.

"You stinking whore! Take a look at yourself."

Only at the last second did she see it but by then it was too late. The most she could do was put her head down. There was an explosion of glass as a large heavy mirror with an ornate gilded frame came down squarely on her head and shoulders, driving her face-first to the floor. Everything went black — for the second time.

Somewhere in the distance she heard noises. Getting louder now. Cough, cough. Cough, cough. Then a realization through the haze. She was coughing. Opening her eyes slowly it all came back to her — where she was and what was happening. Smoke was filling the rooms, wafting thick grey plumes that hugged the ceiling first and replaced breathable air with choking carbon. She felt wet, and her head really hurt. She touched it gingerly. Blood was pouring out of the first wound — probably opened up more from the mirror. All around her were broken pieces. Trying to shake off the grogginess, Rita sat up, choking, and swept razor-like mirror fragments off her coat, then pulled it up over her mouth to help her breath. She wondered how long she'd been out — probably not long. But the fire had gotten so much worse. Thinking about Bolan made her panic. She jumped to her feet. It was impossible to see anything, with columns of smoke rising up the stairs. A few feet away flames were licking out of the doorway to the dining room. The heat was overpowering and her eyes felt scorched. She glanced around. Synthetic foam from inside the two hall chairs was smoldering and ready to feed the flames. If it were like this here, she wondered, then what about the living room?

She stuck to the hall, knowing that the front foyer and door were probably fifty or sixty feet ahead, with the inferno that had been the living room along the way to her right. Without hesitating any longer she dashed past the staircase and down the hall, just inches from the flames. Only a few more feet to the living room entrance, and then she could look in, to see if Bolan and Jennifer were still there. Then —

— A scream as she tripped over something, a wooden desk that was sizzling to the touch. She sprawled onto the floor, hands and knees searing as soon as they made contact.

It was like the worst nightmare she'd ever had: alone, blinded, wounded, choking, burning.

She jumped to her feet, cursing out loud, smoke filling her lungs, tears pouring from her eyes, and tried to orient herself. The living room was very close, just ahead, because billows of smoke and unbelievable heat were pouring from it combined with ever-spreading flames. There was no way she could even get near the doorway. In fact, it was going to be very difficult just getting by there on the way to the front door.

So she sprinted. Twenty steps later she smacked right into the door. Ripping off her coat, she wrapped some of it around her hand before trying the brass doorknob. It was like touching a frying pan on the stove. Heat shot right through the material but she didn't care; her hands were burned anyway. She yanked at the door but the fire had sucked up so much oxygen there was almost a vacuum. Again and again she strained at it without success. Panicking now Rita heaved with all her might, her whole body leaning into it, like she was pulling on a rope in a tug of war, while the blaze moved hungrily down the hall toward her. A tremendous crash came from the living room, as if a ceiling beam or part of the floor had caved in.

Finally the door gave way. Just as she frantically tore it open there was a deafening explosion — the back draft — as an onrush of smoke and glowing orange flame shot right for her, funneled toward the door by the colossal exchange of air, like the draw up a fireplace but about a thousand times stronger. Rita felt it at her back, the hot breath of a charging animal, when she leapt through the doorway and went rolling onto the concrete floor of the porch. She dragged herself down the stairs on her stomach and then crawled on hands and knees into the sopping wet grass, which soothed her burns. Though the rain had abated, moisture still seeped from the ground through her denim jeans and cotton shirt. Without moving her prostrate body she raised her head and turned it in all directions to see if they were outside. No sign of them. In the cold damp air her heavy breath was visible, pouring out of her like the vapor trail from a jet.

"Chuck," she cried out, "Chuck. Chuck, where are you?"

But there was no reply.

Just then the big bay window blew out with a bang, sending shards of glass all over the lawn — and her. But she'd been quick enough to cover her head with her hands at the sound. Now she didn't dare move until help came, which would be soon. The shrillness of sirens filled the air, close enough to be heard over the roar of the fire. There were voices too — the neighbors, perhaps — coming out of the darkness toward her.

***

"But my partner's still in there," Rita told the fire captain as paramedics bandaged up her head and hands. "So are the guy and his wife."

"I keep tellin' you, it's too dangerous," said the lanky grey-haired fellow with the platinum jaw that jutted out past the high collar of his raincoat. "I don't take chances with the lives of my men."

"Then give me a helmet and coat — and I'll go," she yelled, throwing her hands up in the air in despair, much to the chagrin of the ambulance paramedic who was attempting to finish bandaging her head, to hold until she went to the hospital for stitches.

"You'll do nothing of the sort," the fire captain said sternly. Then a pause. "Look, we're almost done hosin' down the front. I'll send in a couple of men any time now…when it's safe enough."

A few minutes before, the wooden garage door had caught fire; now one hose was aimed directly at the Porsche and Jaguar inside to prevent their gasoline tanks from exploding. The rest of the house was going quickly because once the ceiling and floor joists gave, the blaze traveled down to the basement and up into the second floor. Even the roof was ready to tumble down in places where the two-by-fours and plywood underneath were being eaten away by red-hot fire. Melting asphalt from the shingles blanketed the air with acrid black smoke and, in places, burst into flames.

It was a first-alarm fire, warranting full response: two pumpers, an aerial truck and rescue van. If it weren't under control soon, the district chief would arrive with another team and more pumpers.

"We'll go in now, cap'n," offered one burly firefighter in a Scottish burr. He motioned to another near one of the trucks, who dropped what he was doing and started toward them.

"Are you sure?"

"Yeah, we're ready." They both grabbed axes and began to strap on oxygen masks. Over on the aerial truck, a firefighter sixty feet up the ladder turned his hose heavenward, spraying the air above the house in an attempt to cool it so the fire would slow inside where the men were going.

Extensions were attached to the pumper hose and handed to one of the two men on their way in. This charged line — a lighter hose with high-pressure spray — would be their only defense once they were inside the house. As they galloped toward the gaping smoldering hole that was once the front entrance, the sheer daredevilry of the situation suddenly occurred to Rita. Imagine running into a burning building, straight at the flames and smoke and heat, like stepping into a blast furnace.

But they stopped short and aimed the hose upward above the doorway. Rita caught a glimpse: silhouettes against a wall of smoke in what had once been the foyer of the house. One was carrying the other. Her eyes widened. "Chuck," she called out at the top of her lungs. One firefighter dropped his axe and rushed to help. The figure doing the carrying stumbled and almost fell. Rita broke into a run, as the fire captain yelled at her to wait. She could see through the smoke, just barely enough to make out Bolan with his shirt up over his head hugging the coffee table, and Jennifer — still chained to it — the top of her body covered by his coat and her bare arms around his shoulders. As the firefighter took Jennifer and the table from him, the detective collapsed. Other firefighters ran over. Rita slowed down at the sound of voices behind her. She could hear the fire captain and some of the men shouting.

"Get out now!" one voice could be heard above the din. "The roof's coming down."

There was a startlingly loud choking and heaving, a death knell if there ever were one, followed by a sickening crack and then a crash like a sonic boom.

Chapter Thirty

The fresh scent of freesias filled the room; over every available space were spread dozens of arrangements bursting with color — red tulips, pink carnations, yellow daffodils, white narcissuses. "When the hell am I gonna get these bandages off?" grumbled Bolan. "I itch like crazy."

Sitting across from his bed, Rita broke into a smile. "You must be feelin' good, Chuck, because you're starting to bitch again. I've gotta tell you: I've missed it for the past three months."

Even lying propped up on pillows with half of his body wrapped in gauze didn't prevent him from grinning. "Hey, here I am in the hospital like some barbequed burger…but I feel great." Only his mouth and his eyes — where the brows and lashes were growing back — escaped being bandaged.

Bolan's light mood was enough to bring Sandra out of her usual worried state. "It's true," she said. "Yesterday and the day before, you told me the same thing — how good you feel. Finally you're over the hump. I don't know how many times we thought we'd lost you in the burn unit. Without skin, you pick up any infection."

Ten weeks he'd spent in the hydrotherapy room, laid out on a stainless steel table, washed continually with hoses, pricked with an intravenous line, an internal monitor and a catheter. They'd given him two hundred units of blood. Fluids poured out of every part of his body — but Bolan didn't notice because, for the first three weeks, he was fed paralyzing narcotics that slipped him into a coma-like state. His horribly foul-smelling dressings had to be changed on each nurse's shift. Now, with surgical grafts and the appearance of new skin, he was on the way to recovery.

"I'll tell ya," he said, "if you could see through the bandages and scabs on my face, I betcha it wouldn't be yellow anymore."

Sandra facial expression tightened a little, and she became serious again.

Rita caught on. "What's it like living in a flower shop?" she asked, changing the subject. "You must have more in this room than the florist has downstairs."

He glanced around at them all: from the mayor, the guys on the force, the chief, from people he didn't know who'd read the story in their newspapers or caught it on radio and TV and were touched. Week after week the bouquets arrived, dozens of them, and showed no hint of slowing down. "I figure I'll give 'em out to everybody on this floor when I leave. One for each nurse too." After speaking he began to cough hoarsely, his lungs still weakened from smoke inhalation.

"That's pretty ugly, isn't it?" Rita looked concerned.

"Nah," replied Bolan, clearing his throat. "It's ten times better than it was last month."

Sandra nodded in agreement. "Oh, you should've heard him. He was coughing every five minutes."

He smiled. "Anyway…it's the first time I can remember not wanting a cigarette."

"Tell ya what," said Rita, "when you're back at work we'll both quit."

"You're on. First one who lights up owes the other a month of lunches…in a good joint too."

The door to the private room swung open, and in walked Doctor Chow, white coat and clipboard, effectively silencing all of them.

"Good day," he said, eyes wide through his thick eyeglasses.

"Since when do you work the burn unit?" asked Bolan.

"Well, I don't," replied Chow, taking the detective's sarcasm seriously. "I have to speak to you."

Sandra's back stiffened and she sat bolt upright in her chair. "What is it?"

Chow looked uncomfortably at Rita. "May I have a few words with you, Mister Bolan…just you and your wife?"

"Listen," Bolan said, "go ahead. Whatever you've got to tell me, you can say in front of my guest here. This is Rita. She's my partner at work."

Rita rose to leave. "I've got to be going anyway," she mumbled, barely audible.

"No," barked Bolan from his bed. "Doctor Chow, meet Rita Barrett. Now sit down, Rita — please." She shrugged and obliged.

Chow approached, looking down at his clipboard. "I had your blood checked while you were in hydrotherapy a couple of months ago. And re-member those X-rays and blood tests I had done while they were changing your dressing yesterday?"

Bolan nodded.

"Well, something absolutely astounding has happened. We can't quite believe it — and I'm ordering more tests."

"C'mon, doc," said Bolan, "cut to the chase. What's up?"

"Nothing. Nothing at all. There's no trace of your cancer anywhere. No dark spots on the X-rays. Your blood is perfect. All your vital signs. It's the…the strangest thing I've ever seen."

Sandra leapt out of her chair and approached the bedside, careful not to touch her husband anywhere except his scabbed lips as she gave him a light kiss. "I can't believe it," she gasped. "Oh, Chuck, my prayers have been answered. It's a miracle."

Rita just sat there, her mouth open, so relieved she seemed to be in shock.

Bolan wasn't entirely surprised. Grateful maybe, but not surprised. In fact, he was about to say something, put forth his own theory, but decided against it. Some things were better left unsaid, he thought.

"First of all," began Chow, who was beaming himself now, "we had never seen cancer of the pancreas take over so quickly. None of my associates had ever treated anything like it. I had to operate. Terribly urgent situation. Then, of course, you were gone and everything else happened. You were so badly burned that this cancer seemed the least of your worries. But even though you were quite seriously injured, I was afraid you were going to die from the cancer before the burns would heal. But now this…" He let the sentence dangle.

Jumping up, Rita went over and threw her arms around the doctor, who was completely taken aback. "Hey, man," she shouted, "you've just made our day. This is the best damned news there could ever be. Thank you." She hugged him, almost knocking the clipboard from his hands.

"Please," he began, blushing and searching for words, "don't thank me. I had nothing to do with this. In fact, when you're up and about, Mister Bolan, I would like to have your permission to use this case in a paper I'm preparing for a medical journal."

"Be my guest," said the detective. "I'd sign the consent form now but — " he held up his bandaged hands, " — I'm kinda like the Invisible Man or the Mummy or something."

"There's no hurry." Chow smiled. "Anyway, tomorrow I would like to do some further tests to confirm these findings. I'll see you then." He said his goodbyes and made his way around the flowers out the door, forgetting to close it behind him.

Sandra got up and was about to shut it when she froze for an instant.

"May I come in?" A voice in the hall.

"Certainly," replied Sandra.

Jennifer Lee walked in slowly. Overall she looked quite good, although her arms and hands were still bandaged and her face had some peeling skin. She approached the bed.

"Here, sit down," said Rita, leaving her own chair and gesturing to it.

"No, thank you. I'd prefer to stand."

"How are you doing?" asked Sandra cautiously.

"Quite good," came the reply. "I've been living at my friend's place for the past few weeks." She laughed nervously.

Bolan looked into her face. "I'm glad you pulled through this so well, kid."

"That's why I came. I just wanted to…to thank you again for what you did. Putting your coat on me and hugging me so close probably saved my life — at least, spared me what you've had to go through."

"I think the table helped too. After I found the knife under that guy Sosa's body — or maybe inside — it was hotter than hell. Slicing those ropes with the smoke so thick was no treat either. Then I couldn't unwind the chains — and they were locked to boot. So I carried the table out with you attached to it." He cracked a slight smile.

"You could've left without me — and probably saved yourself a lot of burns. But you stayed. I'll never forget that…ever."

"Balls!" said Bolan, awkwardly trying to avoid an emotional scene. "Anybody would've done the same thing."

Rita decided to change the subject. "You look great, considering…"

"Thanks," replied Jennifer. She ran one bandaged hand across her head, where the hair was less than an inch long. "I am going to have to change my look though."

"Ah, it's fine," said Bolan. "Just like one of those radical lesbians."

Sandra and Rita both chided him at the same time.

"We were just celebrating when you walked in," explained Sandra.

"What happened?" asked Jennifer.

"It's a miracle, a true miracle. Chuck's sickness — his cancer — has disappeared. The doctor just told us."

"My God," said Jennifer in a hushed voice, "that's incredible."

"I'm with you there," piped up Bolan.

Rita turned to Jennifer. "What about you?" she asked. "How are you holding up?"

"I guess I'm still in shock. It's not easy losing your husband — even after everything…"

Rita nodded. "What about the…the…?"

"My pregnancy?"

"Yeah. I hope…"

"Don't worry," Jennifer said, smiling. "I didn't miscarry. Everything's fine. In fact, it's kind of a miracle too."

"No kidding," said Sandra, "considering what you went through."

"Well, it's not just that." Jennifer paused for a moment, as though she were thinking about how to phrase it. "Right after the fire the ultrasound showed something just amazing."

Bolan's eyes narrowed just a little. "What?" he asked. He could see the anticipation on Rita and Sandra's faces too.

Jennifer grinned. "The baby was just fine. Now it's growing faster and stronger than ever. Nobody can believe it. It's like nothing even happened to me."

"Isn't that great!" exclaimed Sandra, shaking her head.

"Good for you," chimed in Rita.

Underneath all the bandages, Bolan's face was anything but smiling. His mind started racing. But he kept his thoughts to himself.

Epilogue

Canada, 2002

Two months into his retirement and Chuck Bolan hadn't adjusted yet. With the kids grown up and moved out and Sandra away for a week visiting her sister in Vancouver, the house seemed almost funereal. He'd never cultivated any friends outside of the force. And, for most of his career he'd lived to work — instead of the other way around. Now he didn't know what to do with himself.

Closing his book and glancing up at the kitchen clock, he decided a walk on a sunny fall day would work off the lunch he'd just eaten and perhaps lift his spirits. Just as he started clearing away dishes the phone rang.

"Hello."

"Chuck, it's me."

"Hey, Rita, how are ya?"

"Busy as usual. But that isn't why I called." In her mid-forties now, Rita Barrett had been promoted to detective-sergeant a couple of years before.

"What's up then?"

"Turn on your TV to CNN. You'll be interested, I'm sure."

"What's this all about?"

"Check it out while they're covering it live. Then call me back, okay?"

"Sure."

Mystified, Bolan rushed into the living room, grabbing the remote and flicking on the television. On CNN there was a talking head, with "Live from Los Angeles" supered on the bottom right of the screen. He cranked up the volume.

"So far, eleven students and three teachers are known dead. Dozens of other people have been wounded — some critically. Police have confirmed that Jason Lee, the fourteen-year-old who went on a murderous rampage at the high school, is also dead. He was shot by police marksmen when he rushed them with a machete and spears after refusing to put down his weapons. We know that Jason was a precocious child who had actually skipped three grades. He was the youngest student in the twelfth grade, and his marks were near perfect. Most surprising of all are the witnesses' accounts. They say that Jason was painted like a tribal warrior of some kind. According to witnesses, he arrived just before the nine o'clock bell and began throwing spears and slashing those around him with a machete. It would appear that his victims were chosen at random. Perhaps it was the chaos and horror at the scene, but some witnesses claim that Jason seemed to possess almost superhuman strength. Supposedly he tossed one teacher right up into the air and down a corridor. It's also being reported that the spears he flung would sometimes pass right through his victim's body. This tragedy is the second for Jason's mother, Jennifer Feldman. Some of you might remember that her first husband, Adrian Lee, was a member of the rock band Tangent and died in a terrible fire at their home after assaulting her. She moved here to Los Angeles almost a decade ago, after marrying studio boss Jeff Feldman. But what's happened here today is a stranger tale than in any of the movies he's ever produced — "

Bolan hit the power button and stood there watching the screen grow dark. All of a sudden, that walk to the park seemed more inviting than ever. He'd call Rita back another day.

Iguana Books
iguanabooks.com

If you enjoyed *DarkBeat*...
You can learn more about James Solo and his upcoming work on his blog.

jamessolo.iguanabooks.com/blog/

If you're a writer...
Iguana Books is always looking for great new writers, in every genre. We produce primarily ebooks but, as you can see, we do the occasional print book as well. Visit us at iguanabooks.com to see what Iguana Books has to offer both emerging and established authors.

iguanabooks.com/publishing-with-iguana/

If you're looking for another good book...
All Iguana Books books are available on our website. We pride ourselves on making sure that every Iguana book is a great read.

iguanabooks.com/bookstore/

Visit our bookstore today and support your favourite author.

IGUANA

CPSIA information can be obtained at www.ICGtesting.com
Printed in the USA
LVOW071920130712

290015LV00004B/10/P